Journal of Prisoners on Prisons

I0122136

... allowing our experiences and analysis to be added to the forum that will constitute public opinion could help halt the disastrous trend toward building more fortresses of fear which will become in the 21ˢᵗ century this generation's monuments to failure.

Jo-Ann Mayhew (1988)

Volume 31
Number 1
2022

JOURNAL OF PRISONERS ON PRISONS

EDITORIAL STAFF:

Editors: Justin Piché
Kevin Walby
Associate Editors: Susan Nagelsen
Charles Huckelbury
Issue Editors: Katharina Maier
Rosemary Ricciardelli
Shadd Maruna

Dialogue Editor: Sarah Speight
Prisoners' Struggles Editor: Vicki Chartrand
Book Review Editor: Melissa Munn
Editorial Assistants: Jaai Kuncher, Xuyang Li
and Nicole Necsefor

The *Journal of Prisoners on Prisons* publishes two issues a year. Its purpose is to encourage research on a wide range of issues related to crime, justice, and punishment by current and former prisoners. Donations to the *JPP* are welcomed.

SUBMISSIONS: Current and former prisoners are encouraged to submit original papers, collaborative essays, discussions transcribed from tape, book reviews, and photo or graphic essays that have not been published elsewhere. The *Journal* does not usually publish fiction or poetry. The *Journal* will publish articles in either French or English. Articles should be no longer than 20 pages typed and double-spaced or legibly handwritten. Electronic submissions are gratefully received. Writers may elect to write anonymously or under a pseudonym. For references cited in an article, the writer should attempt to provide the necessary bibliographic information. Refer to the references cited in this issue for examples. Submissions are reviewed by members of the Editorial Board. Selected articles are corrected for composition and returned to the authors for their approval before publication. Papers not selected are returned with editor's comments. Revised papers may be resubmitted. Please submit bibliographical and contact information, to be published alongside articles unless otherwise indicated.

SUBSCRIPTIONS, SUBMISSIONS AND ALL OTHER CORRESPONDENCE:
Journal of Prisoners on Prisons
c/o Justin Piché, PhD
Department of Criminology, University of Ottawa
Ottawa, Ontario, Canada K1N 6N5

e-mail: jpp@uottawa.ca
website: www.jpp.org

SUBCRIPTIONS:	**One Year**	**Two Years**	**Three Years**
Incarcerated Subscribers	$20.00	$35.00	$50.00
Non-incarcerated Subscribers	$35.00	$60.00	$90.00
Prison Libraries & Schools, Libraries & Institutions	$65.00	$120.00	$175.00

Subscriptions by mail are payable in Canadian or American dollars. In Canada, 5% HST must be added to all orders. We encourage subscription purchases online at http://www.press.uottawa.ca/JPP_subscription

BACK ISSUES:
Each back issue is $20 and each back double-issue is $30 (Canadian dollars) + shipping costs. In Canada, 5% HST must be added to all orders. Back issues can be purchased from the University of Ottawa Press at www.press.uottawa. ca/subject/criminology. If interested in obtaining issues that are out of print, please contact the JPP directly. Further information regarding course orders and distribution can be obtained from the University of Ottawa Press at:

University of Ottawa Press
542 King Edward Avenue
Ottawa, Ontario, Canada K1N 6N5

phone: 1-613-562-5246
fax: 1-613-562-5247

email: puo-uop@uottawa.ca
website: www.press.uottawa.ca

Co-published by the University of Ottawa Press and the Journal of Prisoners on Prisons.

ISSN 0838-164X
ISBN 978-2-7603-3741-1 (print)
ISBN 978-2-7603-3742-8 (PDF)

IN THIS ISSUE

INTRODUCTION FROM THE ISSUE EDITORS
Desistance, Social Justice and Lived Experience
Katharina Maier, Rosemary Ricciardelli and Shadd Maruna..................1

ARTICLES
Desistance, Anomalies and Rabbit Holes:
A Transformative Experience from Inside Out
Christopher Havens and Marta Cerruti................................10

Desistance and Prisoner Re-entry:
A Real-time Perspective
Kris MacPherson..20

Co-producing Desistance Opportunities with Women in Prison:
Reflections of a Sports Coach Developer
Christopher Kay, Carolynne Mason and Tom Hartley...........40

Desistance and Prison Culture:
A Trifurcated Prisoner Classification Theory
Ruth Utnage..65

Twenty Years of Incarceration in the Garden State:
Reflecting on the Barriers and Facilitators in the Desistance Process
Stephon Whitley with a forward by Nathan W. Link................77

Captor Story and Captive Story
Francis X. Kroncke..94

What Can the Legal Profession Do For Us?
Formerly Incarcerated Attorneys and the Practice of Law
as a Strengths-Based Endeavour
James Binnall 110

The Contradictions of Prisoner Life and Rehabilitation:
An Auto-ethnographic Life Sentence Experience
Daniel Micklethwaite..132

RESPONSE
On Desistance and Resistance
Justin Piché 167

PRISONERS' STRUGGLES
A Call for Memorials, Writing and Artwork
by Imprisoned People and their Loved Ones
Mourning Our Losses 170

COVID-19 Pandemic Struggles of Prisoners' Families
Joanne Fry 172

BOOK REVIEWS
Available Titles and
Call for Book Reviews
Journal of Prisoners on Prisons 176

UPCOMING SPECIAL ISSUES – CALLS FOR PAPERS
Homelessness and Incarceration
Erin Dej and Dale Spencer 179

Emotions and Carceral Spaces
Jennifer Kilty, Rachel Fayter and Justin Piché 182

COVER ART
"Transition" (front cover)
Steel Door Studios
2022 186

"Turbulent Tenacity" (back cover)
Steel Door Studios
2022 186

INTRODUCTION FROM THE ISSUE EDITORS

Desistance, Social Justice and Lived Experience
Katharina Maier, Rosemary Ricciardelli and Shadd Maruna

A central aim of the *Journal of Prisoners on Prisons (JPP)* is to (re-) centre criminalized and marginalized people's voices as essential to our understanding of punishment, law, and justice, as well as on-the-groundwork by people toward change and reform. *JPP* positions actors in justice as experts and highlights their identities as much more than their legal status of 'offender'. The journal seeks to situate the essence of incarceration and reentry (as well as of being criminalized and striving to remove the label of 'criminal') within lived experiences. In this *Special Issue*, we engage with an area of criminological research that has sought to endorse precisely these principles almost from its origins: *desistance from crime.*

First emerging as a field of study around the turn of the last century (see Farrall, 2002; Giordano, Cernkovich & Rudolph, 2002; Maruna, 2001; Laub & Sampson, 2001), desistance from crime has in recent years become an almost ubiquitous concept in academic criminology and criminal justice (see Sered, 2021; Bersani & Doherty, 2018). Conceptually, desistance theory has served to expand, refine, and challenge the more traditional concepts of reintegration, rehabilitation, and recidivism (see McNeill, 2012; Ward & Maruna, 2007), inspiring rich and varied empirical studies on how criminalized people manage to re-build their lives in the face of structural marginalization, socio-economic disadvantage, and stigma (see Abrams & Terry, 2017; Richardson & Vil, 2016). Yet, beyond providing a conceptual and empirical hook to those interested in punishment, crime, and justice, desistance theory has a wider and also deeper significance – desistance signals a broader shift in how societies ought to think about crime, criminalized people, and recovery. To this extent, desistance pushes academics to re-think their representation of criminalized people's voices in academia, while encouraging scholarly work and grassroots reforms aimed at (re-)building a criminal legal system that emphasizes compassion, humanity, and well-being over exclusion, stigma, and distrust (see Hart & Van Ginneken, 2017; Maruna, 2017). Like the *JPP* itself, the engine driving so much desistance theory and research is the concept of lived experience and the wisdom that can only be gained from listening to those who have themselves escaped the cycle of crime and justice (Bernard, 2015; Hart & Healy, 2013; Maruna, 2001; Weaver & Weaver, 2013).

In light of the above, the goal of this edited collection is to provide a conversational space for the theoretical and empirical advancement of the study of desistance, social justice, and lived experience. The journal issue aims to highlight the voices and experiences of those impacted by the criminal legal system inside and outside the prison, as integral and essential to our collective understanding of what desistance is, how it works, and the changes necessary to establish systems and structures to facilitate desistance and inclusion.

Desistance scholars are interested in *how* people manage to forge and sustain a path away from criminal engagement – or, simply, how people 'make good' or 'go straight' (Maruna, 2001). Desistance research examines the events, processes, and social institutions that shape people's agentic ability to re-build their life and develop a positive narrative of self (e.g., Giordano et al., 2002; Laub & Sampson, 2001; Vaughan, 2007). Desistance may encompass different phases or aspects. For instance, Maruna and Farrall (2004) initially differentiated between *primary desistance* (i.e., a change in behaviour away from offending) and *secondary desistance* (i.e., a subjective change or identity transformation as a non-offender). McNeill (2015) later added another facet or phase, *tertiary desistance*, which refers to the shift in people's sense of belonging to a community. Importantly, however, desistance does not describe a temporally linear process. For instance, *secondary desistance* may precede *primary desistance* (see King, 2013) and tertiary desistance may be necessary before achieving secondary desistance (see Maruna et al., 2004). Nor is desistance always a smooth, positive, or neatly bounded episode in people's lives. As Nugent and Schinkel (2016) have shown, desistance can be painful, lonely, and isolating, at the same time as desistance can be hopeful, positive, and rewarding. Seeing desistance as a highly subjective experience laced with different emotions and feelings requires scholars to pay attention to the events and processes that can facilitate change, and to take a deep look at "what these events and changes *mean* to the people involved" (McNeill, 2006, p. 47). Such meaning is best understood by listening to and learning from the personal narratives of desisters themselves, which we do in the collection of articles in this special issue.

The importance of studying and understanding people's stories of desistance cannot be overstated. Each year in Canada, around 100,000 people reenter the community after a period of confinement (Maier & Ricciardelli, 2020). In the United States, around 600,000 people are released back into the community after being incarcerated. Returning prisoners face a range of socio-economic challenges (e.g. finding employment and housing), in addition to being confronted with a range of rules, expectations, and norms that govern their movements, conduct, and ways of being in the community (see Miller, 2021). Desisting from crime is no easy journey, and desisting individuals have to face and overcome many personal and structural barriers on their 'road' to desistance. We asked authors to provide theoretical and empirical accounts of desistance, as well as reflect on established conceptions of desistance based on their own experience within the penal system. Many of the authors of this special issue talk about the harms they dealt with at the hands of the prison system, but they also describe positive experiences and sources of support that helped or even 'saved' them when working toward re-establishing their lives.

Our goal for this project is to add theoretical and empirical insight to the existing literature on desistance, which is rich and varied, by covering diverse topics. These topics include the emotional dimensions of desistance (e.g. Farrall & Crawley, 2005; LeBel et al., 2008), the role of relationships in desistance (e.g. Weaver, 2021), the interplay between structure and agency in such processes (e.g. Bottoms et al., 2004; Giordano et al., 2002), and how desistance may happen even within the harmful environment of the prison (e.g. Ugelvik, 2021). Contributions in this edited collection extend the empirical realm of desistance research, exploring a range of issues, from desistance and prison culture (see Utnage, 2022), to prisoner reentry (see MacPherson & Whitley, 2022), sports and desistance in prison settings (see Kay et al., 2022), and law and desistance (see Binnall, 2022).

Desistance is a topic central to criminological inquiry and practice, not least because one of its underlying goals is to advance a 'desistance-focused' legal system guided by humanity, compassion, and a genuine belief in people's willingness to 'make good'. Maruna (2017, p. 6) very succinctly said: "At the heart of desistance research is a very simple idea: people can change". Desistance challenges the objectification of criminalized people as 'offenders' that need to be treated or 'cured' (Bottoms & McWilliams, 1979), highlights the importance of meaningful relationships and support over a narrow focus on 'treatment', and directs attention toward criminalized people's futures, rather than their 'criminal' past. In short, desistance is forward-thinking and hopeful, based on future aspirations and leaving the past behind.

Also informing this special issue is our desire to push understandings of desistance beyond the individual actor. Maruna (2017, p, 11) suggested scholars conceive of desistance not just as an individual process, but also as a "social movement", which entails a focus on rights, advocacy, collective action, and moving the concept of desistance "back to the communities where desistance takes place". Community is a central place for desistance to be discussed, practiced, and enacted, and desistance in the community requires academics to listen to and learn from those directly impacted by the criminal legal system in their day-to-day lives. Required here, as Maruna (2017) emphasized, is for academic research to become more inclusive, to forge new collaborations with community organizations, and create more sustainable structures that enable criminalized people to be involved in research and other creative endeavors tied to desistance. Recent collaborative projects, such as *Distant Voices*,[1] an arts-based project between songwriters, academics, and (ex-)prisoners in Scotland, are creative and promising examples of the positive outcomes tied to community efforts and engagement. Our hope is that this collection of writing will further engage diverse audiences in the study of and interest in supportive desistance.

In this special issue of the *JPP*, we include nine articles that each examine various theoretical, empirical, and experiential facets of desistance. Christopher Havens and Marta Cerruti's (2022) piece offers readers a conversation between the two authors from their respective vantage points as an incarcerated independent researcher in mathematics and advocate for prison education. Their contribution provides insight into Christopher's conception of desistance, defined by the author as "a pattern in which one chooses to live a life where their decisions are followed by actions that do not involve breaking the law". The conversation offers deep reflection on how and why people use the label of "desister" drawing on Christopher's experiences in prison and the way math "saved" him, while challenging the dominant conceptions of what is considered the "norm" versus an "anomaly". The content and format of their contribution highlights the value of relationships and stories in understanding desistance from crime.

Kris MacPherson (2022), drawing on the literature of 'convict criminology', provides a critical reflection on his emotions and experiences when transitioning from prison to community living. Kris explains the significance of prisoner re-entry for desistance theory and research, and highlights the importance of roles and routine activities, such as being a father and academic, in the context of his own desistance journey. He also tells us about some of the challenges tied to prison release, including experiences of stigma, which can frustrate and impede the desistance process. He ends with an important question: "How can one expect people to desist if they are still struggling with the same issues they experienced prior to custody?"

Christopher Kay and colleagues (2022) examine a sport coach developer's reflective narrative account of their experience of delivering a football-based program within a women's prison. The authors argue their contribution offers "an account of the 'up-front' work that takes place with individuals who may be taking their first steps towards change, and how this change is supported externally". They highlight how desistance is a co-produced effort between clients and service providers, and call for further research on experiences of facilitating early desistance transitions. In their article, the authors emphasize the role and weight of relationship building in facilitating desistance, whether in prison and beyond.

Ruth Utnage (2022) draws on years of experience in prison to explore the connections between desistance and prison culture. She proposes a trifurcated classification theory of people in prison: active persisters, passive desisters, and dedicated desisters. Ruth underlines the importance of researching desistance with reference to institutional prison culture and norms. Relationships within prison and with "non-offenders", such as visitors and community members, are explored in the context of Utnage's own experience. The author highlights that for prisoners, interactions with "non-offenders" in prison play a meaningful role in shaping one's sense of self and belonging to the community, even while they are incarcerated.

Stephon Whitley (2022), with a forward by Nathan Link, reflects on the barriers and facilitators in the context of Whitley's own desistance story. Their piece starts with a summary of how the two contributors met, and then explores Stephon's own experiences of the dehumanizing and degrading treatment of people in prison, and the stressors and barriers of transitioning from prison to the community. Stephon provides deep insight into the realities of prison living, specifically in the realms of employment, abuse and violence, and other struggles and harms, reflecting on these experiences in the context of their story of desistance.

Francis Kroncke (2022) tells their "captive story" which includes a deep account of the experience of what taking the first step *"inside"* and the last step in the "*outside* world" felt like. Francis argues that telling stories of confinement and captivity require introspection and reflection. Through an honest, deep account, Francis tells the story of how imprisonment "effectively re-embodied me as a subhuman", referring to the subjugation and degradation they experienced at the hands of prison officials and the system as a whole. The author shows how they navigated and resisted this "subhuman" position, creating alternative accounts of self and their past.

James Binnall, drawing on their own journey from prison to becoming a practicing attorney, draws readers into the nuances of the legal profession. Binnall argues criminalized people bring unique skills to the legal profession, such as empathy and an understanding of structural barriers, which actors can positively use in providing legal support and advocacy for marginalized populations. Positioning the legal profession as a viable option for formerly incarcerated people, James proposes several recommendations related to how legal education and the profession more broadly could be made more inclusive.

The final article in the special issue is an autoethnographic account by Daniel Micklethwaite, who is serving a life sentence, detailing prison life and rehabilitation. The author problematizes the interaction between risk-based prison rehabilitation interventions and prison culture and masculinities. Daniel shows how risk-based programs enable and reinforce "toxic masculinities" in prison settings. Based on his own experience, he proposes various recommendations for how prison programs could be more rehabilitative and attentive to gendered dynamics but without creating toxic prison cultures.

Overall, our hope is that this thematic collection moves interdisciplinary scholarship on desistance and social justice forward in new and creative ways. Together, the contributions by authors discuss and advance established ideas in existing desistance scholarship. More importantly, they feature the voices of desisters impacted by the criminal justice system, providing deep, personal narratives of what desistance is, what facilitates and frustrates desistance, and the meaning of relationships in the desistance process. The articles embody a diversity of perspectives and disciplinary positions that promise to open up new insights into desistance and social and legal justice. We hope that the special issue provides a challenging yet rewarding read into the personal struggles and harms of actors and experiencers of systems of justice, while highlighting the resiliency (however defined) and hope of desisters. As guest editors we recognize how privileged we are to have worked with authors, and we thank each for sharing their perspectives and contributing to the collection.

ENDNOTES

[1]　For more information, see: http://www.sccjr.ac.uk/wp-content/uploads/2017/02/Distant-Voices-Information-Pack-1.pdf

REFERENCES

Abrams, Laura S. and Diane J. Terry (2017) *Everyday Desistance: The Transition to Adulthood Among Formerly Incarcerated Youth*, New Brunswick (NJ): Rutgers University Press.

Bernard, April (2015) *Transforming Justice, Transforming Lives: Women's Pathways to Desistance from Crime*, Lanham (MD): Lexington Books.

Bersani, Bianca E. and Elaine E. Doherty (2018) "Desistance from Offending in the Twenty-First Century", *Annual Review of Criminology*, 1: 311-334.

Binnall, James (2022) "What Can the Legal Profession Do For Us? Formerly Incarcerated Attorneys and the Practice of Law as a Strengths-Based Endeavourt", *Journal of Prisoners on Prisons*, 31(1): 110-131.

Bottoms, Anthony and William McWilliams (1979) "A Non-Treatment Paradigm for Probation Practice", *British Journal of Social Work*, 9(2): 160–201.

Farrall, Stephen (2002) *Rethinking What Works with Offenders*, Cullompton (UK): Willan Publishing.

Giordano, Peggy C., Stephen A. Cernkovich and Jennifer L. Rudolph (2002) "Gender, Crime and Desistance: Toward a Theory of Cognitive Transformation", *American Journal of Sociology*, 107: 990-1064.

Hart, Emily L. and Esther F.J.C. van Ginneken (eds.) (2017) *New Perspectives on Desistance: Theoretical and Empirical Developments,* London: Palgrave Macmillan

Hart, Wayne and Deirdre Healy (2018) "'An inside job': An Autobiographical Account of Desistance", *European Journal of Probation*, 10(2): 103-119.

Havens, Christopher and Marta Cerruti (2022) "Desistance, Anomalies and Rabbit Holes: A Transformative Experience from Inside Out", *Journal of Prisoners on Prisons*, 31(1): 10-19.

Kay, Christopher, Carolynne Mason and Tom Hartley (2022) "Co-producing Desistance Opportunities with Women in Prison: Reflections of a Sports Coach Developer", *Journal of Prisoners on Prisons*, 31(1): 40-64.

King, Sam (2013) "Early Desistance Narratives: A Qualitative Analysis of Probationers' Transitions Toward Desistance", *Punishment & Society*, 15(2): 147-165.

Kroncke, Francis X. (2022) "Captor Story and Captive Story", *Journal of Prisoners on Prisons*, 31(1): 94-109.

Laub, John H. and Robert J. Sampson (2001) "Understanding Desistance from Crime", *Crime and Justice: A Review of Research*, 23: 1-69.

MacPherson, Kris (2022) "Desistance and Prisoner Re-entry: A Real-time Perspective", *Journal of Prisoners on Prisons*, 31(1): 20-39.

Maruna, Shadd (2017) "Desistance as a Social Movement", *Irish Probation Journal*, 14: 5-19.

Maruna, Shadd and Stephen Farrall (2004) "Desistance from Crime: A Theoretical Reformulation", *Kolner Zeitschrift f¨ur Soziologie und Sozialpsychologie*, 43: 171–94.

Maruna, Shadd, Thomas P. Lebel, Nick Mitchell and M.ichelleNaples (2004) "Pygmalion in the Reintegration Process: Desistance from Crime through the Looking Glass", *Psychology, Crime & Law*, 10(3): 271-281.

McNeill, Fergus (2015) "Desistance and Criminal Justice in Scotland", in Hazel Croall, Gerry Mooney and Mary Munro (eds.), *Crime, Justice and Society in Scotland*, London: Routledge.

McNeill, Fergus (2012) "Four Forms of 'Offender' Rehabilitation: Towards an Interdisciplinary Perspective", *Legal and Criminological Psychology*, 17(1): 18-36.

McNeill, Fergus (2006) "A Desistance Paradigm for Offender Management", *Criminology & Criminal Justice*, 6(1): 39-62.

Micklethwaite, Daniel (2022) "The Contradictions of Prisoner Life and Rehabilitation: An Auto-ethnographic Life Sentence Experiencet", *Journal of Prisoners on Prisons*, 31(1): 132-166.

Miller, Reuben J. (2021) *Halfway Home: Race, Punishment, and the Afterlife of Mass Incarceration*, New York: Little, Brown and Co.

Nugent, Briege and Marguerite Schinkel (2016) "The Pains of Desistance", *Criminology & Criminal Justice*, 16(5): 568-584.

O'Sullivan, Kevin, Rochelle Williams, Xiang Yan Hong, David Bright and Richard Kemp (2018) "Measuring Offenders' Belief in the Possibility of Desistance", *International Journal of Offender Therapy and Comparative Criminology*, 62(5): 1317-1330.

Richardson Jr, Joseph B. and Christopher St. Vil (2016) "'Rolling dolo': Desistance from Delinquency and Negative Peer Relationships Over the Early Adolescent Life-course", *Ethnography*, 17(1): 47-71.

Ugelvik, Thomas (2021) "The Transformative Power of Trust: Exploring Tertiary Desistance in Reinventive Prisons", *The British Journal of Criminology*, 62(3): 1-16.

Utnage, Ruth (2022) "Desistance and Prison Culture: A Trifurcated Prisoner Classification Theory", *Journal of Prisoners on Prisons*, 31(1): 65-76.

Vaughan, Barry (2007) "The Internal Narratives of Desistance", *British Journal of Criminology*, 47(3): 390-404.

Ward, Tony and Shadd Maruna (2007) *Rehabilitation*, Abingdon, Oxon: Routledge.

Weaver, Beth (2012) "The Relational Context of Desistance: Some Implications and Opportunities for Social Policy", *Social Policy & Administration*, 46(4): 395-412.

Weaver, Allan and Beth Weaver (2013) "Autobiography, Empirical Research and Critical Theory in Desistance: A View from the Inside Out", *Probation Journal*, 60(3): 259-277.

Whitley, Stephon (2022) "Twenty Years of Incarceration in the Garden State: Reflecting on the Barriers and Facilitators in the Desistance Process ", *Journal of Prisoners on Prisons*, 31(1): 77-93.

ACKNOWLEDGMENTS

We would like to thank Jaai Kunchur for their help in preparing this journal issue.

ABOUT THE SPECIAL ISSUE EDITORS

Dr. Katharina Maier is Assistant Professor in the Department of Criminal Justice at the University of Winnipeg. Her research focuses on the experiential dimensions of punishment in prison and the community, as well as on issues surrounding drug use, public health, poverty and social marginality. Her work has been published in *Theoretical Criminology*, *Punishment & Society*, and *Criminology & Criminal Justice*, among other venues.

Dr. Rosemary Ricciardelli is Professor (Sociology) and Research Chair in Safety, Security, and Wellness at Memorial University's Fisheries and Marine Institute. Elected to the Royal Society of Canada, her research centres on evolving understandings of gender, vulnerabilities, risk, and experiences and issues within different facets of the criminal justice system and among mariners. She has published in the areas of PSP, criminalized persons, and wellness – broadly defined. As a sex and gender researcher, her interests lay in the social health, identity construction, and lived experiences of individuals.

Dr. Shadd Maruna is Professor of Criminology at Queen's University Belfast and President-Elect of the American Society of Criminology. His book *Making Good: How Ex-Convicts Rebuild Their Lives* was named the "Outstanding Contribution to Criminology" by the American Society of Criminology in 2001. His other books include *Rehabilitation: Beyond the Risk Paradigm*, *After Crime and Punishment*, and *The Effects of Imprisonment*. His work has been recognized with awards by the Howard League for Penal Reform and the Economic and Social Research Council of the UK.

ARTICLES

Desistance, Anomalies and Rabbit Holes:
A Transformative Experience from Inside Out
Christopher Havens and Marta Cerruti

ABSTRACT

Desistance, plainly stated, is the discontinuance of criminal behaviour. This article presents an informative conversation on the topic of desistance through the lived experience of a currently incarcerated individual. The conversation that took place over the span of several months includes the factors that led to the desistance of one of the authors, Christopher Havens, as well as his story from a behavioural perspective, which in the process suggests the idea that prisoners can be categorized by their readiness for positive change and personal growth. While this article can be viewed as a single empirical data point by sociologists and criminologists, the authors hope to present one particular case of desistance which can serve as an inspirational tool for the readers, including other incarcerated people so as to make this very same step.

Marta and Christopher's stories intersected in December 2012, when Christopher sent an email to the editor of Mathematical Science Publishers, where Marta's partner Matt was working as technical editor at the time. Christopher was asking for information on how to subscribe to *Annals of Mathematics*, a very high-level academic mathematics journal, as well as for help from any mathematician willing to guide him in his mathematical explorations. Marta asked her mom, Luisella Caire, a mathematician working in Torino, Italy, if she was interested. Luisella and Christopher started corresponding, which continued with the involvement of Marta's dad Umberto Cerruti. Christopher joined Umberto's research group and after about four years of back-and-forth letters flying across the ocean, they came up with a new contribution to the field of continued fractions, a big topic in number theory. Their results have been published on "Research in Number Theory" in January 2020 (Havens et al., 2020).

Marta has followed these developments from a distance until she decided to write an article about Christopher's story for *The Conversation*, a news website dedicated to evidence-based journalism with articles written by academics with the help of journalists (Cerruti, 2020). The article was a huge success. It has been translated into German, Chinese, and Spanish, and was re-published by countless news websites, leading to about 140,000 views in the first month of its publication. About ten mathematicians got in touch with Christopher to further help him in his mathematical endeavors. Marta and Christopher have been interviewed by multiple news channels including the *Global News* and *CBC*. The story has been re-written by *Inside Time*, the United Kingdom's national prisoners' newspaper, which circulates 60,000 copies monthly in every UK prison. This tremendous success showed the inspirational power that Christopher's story can have on people.

Since writing the two publications noted above, Marta and Christopher have exchanged countless emails. This article is an edited transcription of their three-month long email conversation on the topic of desistance.

M: What does desistance mean for you?

C: I believe that desistance is a pattern in which one chooses to live a life where their decisions are followed by actions that do not involve breaking the law. You can think of as an accessorial attribute to an already healthy lifestyle. To me, desistance is only part of the rehabilitation process that should begin before being released from incarceration. It is a necessary part of justice.

M: Why would you call yourself a desister?

C: Well, I suppose I call myself a desister because I have made the choice to live a life that does not include breaking the laws. My state of incarceration does not change this. Contrary to popular belief, it is not necessary that "When in prison, do as the other prisoners do". I do not consider being in prison a reason to break the law, nor do I consider it a means to become a better criminal. I reject the viewpoint that incarceration is a reason to put our goals and dreams on hold. Imagine serving a 25-year sentence waiting for the gate to open. That is the common practice by most prisoners, for the length of their sentence. What people fail to see is that we can still contribute to society, we can make beautiful memories... If we get creative and work hard enough, we can even become members of research groups and make advancements in science... if we simply work for it. This is my life. I am an amateur mathematician, a prisoner, and an individual who does not commit crimes. I believe it's my responsibility to make sure that justice is served to the victims of my crimes by rehabilitating myself in such a way that I am no longer a risk to society. This is why I consider myself a desister.

Desistance is actually a hot topic for me, and I often think of how we could make it easier for others who want to desist... because there is so much recidivism! And why is the rate of recidivism so high? When I consider situations similar to my own, part of the adversity we face as prisoners attempting to redefine our role in society is in the public's perception of incarcerated individuals. It seems, from the inside, that most of society does not distinguish from different types of prisoners unless one is making a distinction with respect to the severity of our crimes. For example, I have experienced a very inclusive mathematical community. Do you think that recidivism would decrease if society were more inclusive? The amount of interaction I've had in the community was a huge factor in my successes. I wonder, if other prisoners had experienced similar inclusion in the community, would they have pursued different lifestyles as well?

M: That would be my guess, too. Being treated as marked cannot help anyone change their lifestyle. I read some articles that discussed how hard it can be to try to go back into society if you have a criminal record. As you write in your own story, most people don't really spend much time thinking about prison other than what they see on TV. They have little idea of what happens in prisons to help people change, and of their own role and responsibility in helping that change once people are released, and even before. I was appalled when I heard that there were several negative reactions to the program "Walls to Bridges", which strives to create a connection between prisoners and community members by allowing professors to teach courses inside prisons, and students to take the courses along with prisoners. Apparently, several community members have been critical of the idea that students would go inside prisons, and that prisoners could take courses for credit without paying! So yes, I agree. A more inclusive community could definitely help decrease recidivism, and obviously this would help back the community, by making it safer and more functional. How can we create such a change? Have more information about what goes on inside prisons, which is different from what people see inside movies? I think this is why we are writing this article, as one of the many steps in this direction.

C: One of my goals is to show the world that prisons do not only consist of their stereotypical convict. In prisons, there are three different types of prisoners. The ones that we see in the movies and on the media... the stereotypical dangerous drains on society are called convicts. The arbiters of the convict mentality proudly wearing the badge of the convict code. Next, are the common prisoners. They generally wish only to serve their sentence while making as little waves as possible. Some prisoners practice the convict mentality, and some choose to better themselves along the way. Finally, on the other end of the spectrum, there are people who do amazing things with their time... anomalies among the prison population.

M: Can you tell me more about the 'anomalies'?

C: Sure. Of course, this is a made-up classification. I hear about the societal viewpoints on prisoners and it's sad that most people seem to think that we are what we are portrayed to be by the media. A single category where all of us are lumped together. I think that most of the anomalies have had this same thought. The societal view taken towards prisoners affects us and so most of the other anomalies I've met have worked to change this in their own way. The way the public perceives us is important. Not because we strive for recognition. It's not about that. It's important because the anomalies move things and make changes in the prison. Without some support from the community, our hands are tied. For example, much of the community frowns on college education for prisoners. And why not? If all I knew about prison was that it was full of the convict variety, I would be a little bitter as well. But anomalies are active inside the prison and the community because to some of us, the prison walls serve primarily as a metaphor. We live in a gated community... maybe a bit of a ghetto, sure. But the prison is in our minds. Let me ask you... if all of the sudden, all modes of transportation were cut off to you, what would you do with your life? Would you wait until the problem solved itself or would you find a way to be productive despite the adversity? That's at the heart of the question. Most anomalies have spent their time in self rehabilitation, and so our minds are no longer stuck inside our own prisons. Of course, we continue to make positive changes, but we must also carry on with life... except we can't leave. Our transportation to and from our previous circumstances has been cut off. And so we find ways to be productive and work through the adversity.

M: Can you tell me about some of the anomalies you've met?

C: Absolutely! Here's a good one. Ruth Utnage is a transgender person who previously committed with a sex offense. She has been very active as a model for other prisoners while incarcerated. I have lived around her for quite a while and one specific story sticks out. Ruth was denied eligibility for SOPT (Sex Offender Treatment Program) because she didn't present enough risk to reoffend. She then proceeded to write the treatment coordinator every two weeks. The treatment coordinator got tired of this and told her to stop. Instead of stopping, she wrote to the review board, and continued writing this treatment coordinator. The reply was usually that there were higher risks that needed the treatment. So Ruth began accumulating the materials that they provided in treatment, like worksheets and exercises. Then, once the work was finished, she made copies and sent it to the review board, the treatment coordinator, and other staff. This went on for a year. Finally, and begrudgingly, she was accepted for treatment.

During the writing of this article, the COVID-19 outbreak was at its peak. As masks have been vital to the prevention of the spread of COVID-19, Ruth has contributed by making several thousand masks for the Community Aid Coalition. At the same time, she owns and maintains a website (HumanMe.org) aimed at highlighting the shared humanity of prisoners and un-incarcerated people. It seems like this true engagement in the better aspects of the human experience that make a prisoner anomalist.

It's a shame that there is such a contrast between certain types of prisoners. Really, why should the stories of these anomalies in prisons be so special? When the deeds of a prisoner begin to transcend the walls of confinement it speaks to the fact that this is not expected of us. It takes people by surprise. But here is what I hope is the reality. These things we do, our walk, and our role in prisons... we are setting the stage for future prisoners desist. They are seeing things done that most would say is not possible from inside prison. We want these impossible things to become common. There should be no anomalies.

M: Is this really possible? Even in 'the outside world', anomalies, meaning maybe people who actively try to improve the world around them, are not the norm. I can make some easy parallels in my mind. There are some people that truly bring positive change around them or try to. Would there be the anomalies? Can we say that everyone could be an anomaly? True, everyone could do wonderful things in their life. Yet many people choose not to; sometimes they just don't think about it as they are too busy with something that they enjoy doing or who knows, looking for power or money. Nothing necessarily bad in this but nothing that brings positive change in the world necessarily. Or sometimes people don't do wonderful things that bring positive change because of the situations they live in; they are really hard. We don't all have the same possibilities at birth. Or sometimes just a few wrong steps bring to disasters.

C: I never thought about how my metaphor can apply to the outside world. I like what you had to say on this... I tend to agree with you about your view on this, except for one part. I think adversity is common for most anomalies. I suppose it's all in how we deal with it. I think that anyone can be an anomaly. Especially for the people whose circumstances cage them. Imagine a person who fits the circumstantial limits you described. Imagine that every time they tried, they failed. Every attempt to succeed, they fell. Every chance to advance, they failed... but imagine that in each of those failures, they still tried. What if nobody had ever been impacted by that person because they spent their whole lives trying to live their dreams, after endlessly failing. Trying and failing, trying and failing... For whatever the reason, however circumstantial, they always failed, but always picked themselves up and tried. Is that person an anomaly? :) Some of the most beautiful aspects of the human condition go unnoticed by others... As far as prison, adversity is one of the most common ingredients to an anomaly. Not a necessary ingredient, but a sufficient one.

M: Thanks for a really good point you made. I love your point that it is not crucial that things are noticed by others and that trying and failing, and keep trying again can be seen as 'anomaly'. Back to the point of this conversation, 'desistance'. In that sense, it's true. We all have that capability inside us. We can see it in our kids when they're really small. Think about a child learning to walk or trying to climb on something. If you allow them to keep trying instead of solving the problem for them, they will find their own solution and won't be afraid of the repeated failures.

Now let's get back to your way of being an anomaly. You just published a first author paper on the academic journal "Research in Number Theory".

That's clearly an 'anomalous' achievement for someone who's in prison. Tell me something more about this. How did your passion for math started?

C: Let's begin the story right after being sentenced for making the worst decision in my life.

As soon as I arrived in prison, I was scouted by the gangs. I was fully in the convict mentality at that time and so it wasn't long until I was involved in a hit, landing me in solitary confinement for a year.

Our name for solitary confinement is 'the hole'. A prison within prison. It's 24 hours a day of people banging on the walls and yelling out their cell doors. The bed is a concrete slab and the large fluorescent light directly above your head never shuts off. Most people don't handle it too well. When the main form of entertainment comes from watching the guards pepper spray an angry prisoner, it's not surprising that people begin losing parts of their minds. Indeed, some of them snap. Myself… I played Sudoku.

I've spent so much time on the streets that isolation was already familiar. I'm very comfortable being alone with myself. And so, I filled my time involved in puzzles, which were quickly losing their challenge. It wasn't long until I noticed an older gentleman making rounds to some of the cells. He was passing around manilla envelopes full of… something. I had no idea. By this time, I was ready for any different type of stimulation, and so I was compelled to ask, "Can I have an envelope too?" This, I suppose, is where it all began for me. The man's name was simply "Mr. G". He worked in education and the contents of the envelope was enough math homework to keep you busy for a week or two. When you finished, you'd give him your envelope and, shortly after, he'd replace the envelope with graded papers, comments, and more work. My mind was like a sponge. I believe the old man took to a caffeine habit because of me. Suddenly everything seemed less important. The sounds of the yelling and banging faded into nothing. I had tons of books sent in and lesson after lesson… But before long I received a kite (message) from Mr. G saying: "Mr. Havens. At this time, you have surpassed my mathematical abilities and I wish you luck on your journey". That was the spark. A proper invitation to a life of mathematics.

From that moment on, I studied and learned about different maths that went beyond the basic curriculum. I studied different mathematical histories and philosophies. My journey into mathematics began having transformative powers. Things were coming together in my mind that I'd have never previously thought about. This was right about the first time I remember ever having planned a long-term goal. The memory is still clear in my mind... I was becoming enamoured with mathematics and I had these image in my mind of mathematical movies... I had always viewed mathematicians to have an almost legendary status. I viewed cryptographers to be the intellectual equivalent of a fifth degree wizard... slinging symbols like Gandalf the Grey. And as I pictured these images, I decided that in 25 years, I had enough time to work towards becoming a mathematician.

After some time, I was transported from Walla Walla to Clallam Bay Prison, where I was released back into general population. My studies continued the entire time, and I was immersed to such an extent that I began changing more and more. I was finding myself having less and less in common with the old gang. I realized it and they realized it. There were two things going on at that time. First, I was changing so much that I found myself becoming a little lost in the turmoil. My thoughts weren't the same types of thoughts that I was used to having and my actions were based on decisions that followed this type of thought. Second, the gang felt that I should be focusing on the ins and outs of their politics and philosophical ideals, and not wasting my time studying mathematics. I found myself standing at a crossroads.

... I can't explain this appropriately, because so much happened in my mind rather quickly. I think I had seen my entire past flash before me... in comparison with how I felt while doing mathematics, it took me only fraction of a heartbeat to decide that I needed to leave that life behind... and as I made this decision, I knew that what I was doing was going to decide the rest of my life. And so I decided to enter into the Intensive Transition Program (ITP). The ITP is a one-year program for prisoners want to make positive changes in their life, but perhaps lack some of the tools that might help them in their journey. For me, I had been experiencing so many personal changes that I needed a safe place where I would completely open-up and allow the floodgate to open... because I wanted more of this change. Even today, I think this personal growth resulted from my mathematical focus. Something pure and positive came into my life and I fell in love. I let my love grow because it felt so good and for the first time, I knew it was right. The resulting changes slapped me in the face... and I suppose it's as simple as saying that I finally woke up, after all those years.

Let me say that when your life isn't focused on plotting, scheming, and getting high, you have much more time to reflect on things that matter. That seems like an obvious statement, but don't take that simple fact for granted. Please take the time to read that sentence again. For somebody who has wasted their entire life and then – at the pinnacle of their mediocrity – they kill a man, think of what this might mean. I'll tell you. I began thinking on all the things that had gone so wrong in my life. Then I'd think of how I can repair some of those things. I thought of how it felt being the unfortunate person who stood downwind from my actions... all of the people I hurt and affected from either trying to fit in or simply not thinking. Empathy began. I wondered how I would feel in similar scenarios. Then, I let the thought of myself go... Be those people I hurt. Now. How does it feel? ... What the hell am I doing? I realized that my actions were beginning to initiate actual justice. I was finally working to correct the behaviours that led to my past decisions.

Here's when my ITP treatment began, right in the middle of some of the most important realizations in my life. Imagine going through so many changes and then continuing at a much faster pace. Then imagine being in the best possible place to truly grasp those changes. Imagine having a team of professionals to help you when you need it. This was a pivotal part of my life. I had finally grown up... at 32 years old. Here's something interesting that I had never thought of before now. I was in prison now for three years. My old friends had long abandoned me. Some of my family had even become very distant. I left the gang and the convict mentality behind me. Truly, I had only two people actively in my life: my Mom and my daughter, Hope. This was precisely the time when I met my first member of the mathematical community. Luisella Caire, your mom. She's changed my perspective on mathematics. She introduced me to number theory and gave me different ways of learning. My interactions with her were so impactful for me that I actually devoted the rest of my life to the study of mathematics. She then introduced me to your dad, Umberto Cerruti, and gave me an opportunity at research. Hence, I had responsibilities doing something that I love, while interacting with real mathematicians.

REFERENCES

Cerruti, Marta (2020) "An inmate's love for math leads to new discoveries", *The Conversation* – May 14. Retrieved from https://theconversation.com/an-inmates-love-for-math-leads-to-new-discoveries-130123

Havens, Christopher, Stefano Barbero, Umberto Cerruti and Nadir Murru (2020) "Linear Fractional Transformations and Nonlinear Leaping Convergents of Some Continued Fractions", *Research in Number Theory*, 6, 11.

ABOUT THE AUTHORS

Christopher Havens is the Executive Director and a founder of the Prison Mathematics Project organization. Aside from an interest in understanding the role of mathematics in self-identity and desistance, he spends his time researching mathematics in the realm of number theory. The area he is most passionate about is the study of various types of convergents of continued fractions, specifically naturally leaping and leaping convergents of both linear and quadratic convergents. Christopher one day hopes to show the world that the service of Justice can be a meaningful and beautiful pursuit, and that it should not stop when one leaves the gates of prison. He can be reached by email at chavens28@gmail.com and christopher@pmathp.org.

Marta Cerruti is a professor in the Department of Mining and Materials Engineering and Co-director of the Institute for Advanced Materials at McGill University (Montreal, Quebec, Canada). She is also an emerging watercolour artist. Her research interests lay at the interface between materials science, chemistry, biology, and medicine. With her students, she published more than 100 papers on journals such as the *Journal of the American Chemical Society, Advanced Materials*, and *Chemistry of Materials*. She is a member of the College of New Artists, Scholars and Scientists of the Royal Society of Canada, and was a Canada Research Chair and a Young Scientist invited at the World Economic Forum. Her research is often featured on *CBC Radio, Global News*, and *The Conversation*. She can be reached by email at marta.cerruti@mcgill.ca.

Desistance and Prisoner Re-entry:
A Real-time Perspective
Kris MacPherson

ABSTRACT

In the current paper, I explore the state of desistance from crime and prisoner re-entry, primarily in Scotland. As a criminology graduate recently released from a long prison sentence, I gather and analyse the thoughts, emotions, and experiences of the prison to community living transition to contrast and compare my experience with relevant academic literature through the lens of convict criminology. Furthermore, I draw upon relevant first-hand knowledge of desistance and re-entry as each occurs to assess the current rehabilitative climate in Scotland. I discuss the notion of "judicial rehabilitation" and the effects of a criminal record in modern society, questioning the impact of these subtle forms of punishment upon those leaving custody. In doing so, I question whether more could be done to catalyse and sustain these transitions in the hope that society can better enable people to desist and eventually lead fulfilling crime-free lives upon their re-entry.

INTRODUCTION

In the current paper, I compare my own desistance and re-entry journeys with relevant literature interwoven with my own lived experiences. Succinctly, desistance is referred to as abstinence from criminal behaviour for those persistently engaged in offending (Maruna, 2001). On the other hand, prisoner re-entry could be described as the study of "reintegrating returning prisoners", to borrow a phrase from Travis and Petersilia (2001, p. 308). Since my own release from an extended custodial term in September 2019, it could be said that I am in the unusual position (for me at least) of trying to cogently weave these experiences with relevant literature through the lens of convict criminology. Briefly, convict criminology is composed of people with first-hand experiences of the criminal justice/penal system who subsequently go on to pursue academic work to contest mainstream notions of criminology advanced by conventional academics (Drake & Gunn, 2013).

While many studies have alluded to individual experiences of desistance as well as its aspects and complications (Maruna, 2001; Giordano et al., 2002; Kazemian, 2007; Nugent and Schinkel, 2016), first-hand experiences of criminological phenomena arguably provide an important way to explore these issues. In this sense, my thoughts analyse and interrogate the literature while, in turn, the literature questions my own thinking and experiences. My process arguably reflects Macedo's (2000, p. 19) assertion that "If students are not able to transform their lived experiences into knowledge and to use that already acquired as a process to unveil new knowledge, they will never be able to participate rigorously in a dialogue as a process of learning and knowing". In this way, it could be argued that I can utilise a negative historical narrative of criminal behaviour and incarceration to my advantage by filtering such experiences through an academic lens to contribute to a cause greater than oneself (Maruna, 2001).

The fact that most people who enter prison will, at some point, return home (Travis, 2005, cited in Boppre & Hart-Johnson, 2019) arguably highlights the importance of creating socio-economic opportunities that not only catalyse desistance but also help to sustain it, thereby reducing recidivism. Crucially, one could say that the *raison d'être* of prison is the rehabilitation of the convicted person (not to mention punishment and public protection). But how does society expect people leaving prison to live law-abiding lives when they come home? From this perspective, the potential reduction of reoffending (and the harm catalysed by crime) arguably reinforces the significance of the desistance/re-entry nexus.

For example, how can people returning from prison initiate and maintain desistance without developing links to employment agencies or academic institutions prior to or post re-entry? As Aresti and colleagues (2010, p. 169) point out, "Understanding the factors that lead to criminal desistance […] is vital to the development of interventions that reduce reoffending. Such a reduction has several implications for society, in terms of economic gains and issues of public welfare". In other words, there is more to consider than the person simply 'going straight'. In fact, the positive impact of a successful re-entry/desistance model not only benefits the person leaving incarceration, but also strengthens society as a whole.

Nevertheless, can society help people with convictions bridge the gap between the barriers of the individual's past and their prospective future? Can successful re-entry and desistance be considered the sole responsibility of the 'offender'? One could postulate that communities and wider society have roles to play. For instance, how can we expect people with criminal lifestyles to 'go straight' if they are marginalized and stigmatised in the very communities to which they return? That being said, how do we understand the factors that lead to desistance so we can develop ways and means of creating an environment conducive to reducing recidivism? In my own experience, it seems essential that the desister should comprehend their journey and its root causes just as much as those who study these issues. At the time of writing (November 2020), I have been free for a period of fourteen months and have embarked on the next chapter of my desistance odyssey.

Coincidentally, my own brush with desistance theory occurred while studying for a criminology degree in prison. In the final year before my graduation, I inadvertently discovered the literature whilst trying to decide what criminological topic to use in my independent research project (see McNeill & Weaver, 2010; McNeill, 2014). Initially, my heart was set on composing a piece on Middle Eastern terrorist groups or serial offending. In preparation, the manager of the prison's learning centre downloaded a variety of academic papers that I could choose from in my forthcoming assignment. Tellingly, I opted to write about desistance and rehabilitation in Scottish prisons because it seemed to be a perfect fit. In other words, I felt that the fact I was 'living the literature' gave me a head start and a unique perspective from which to question the processes and policies that impacted my daily life. However, I did not know I had already embarked on the desistance journey until the point I had discovered the literature during my studies in custody.

Succinctly, there are three notable aspects of the desistance journey. The first two, as described by Maruna and Farrall (2004), are "primary desistance" (cessation of criminal behaviour) and "secondary desistance" (identity shift from seeing oneself as an 'offender' to a more pro-social role). The third, "tertiary desistance" (McNeill & Schinkel, 2015), is especially intriguing because it implies that society has a role to play in absorbing the returning individual within a moral, social and political society. In other words, if the individual stops committing crime (primary desistance), they will eventually move away from identifying with pro-criminal identities and attitudes and shift to a more socially acceptable role (secondary desistance). Once these have been achieved and maintained, the individual should be accorded the same socio-economic opportunities as would be extended to others in society and not be penalised or marginalized due to a criminal past. Society has an obligation to help people leaving incarceration if such individuals have demonstrated a willingness to refrain from resuming a criminal lifestyle.

Regardless of whether or not an individual can be classified as a desister whilst still in custody (MacPherson, 2017), the real test of one's commitment to desistance will be seen upon re-entering society. For example, people in prison are unlikely to be viewed as desisters without demonstrating a sustained crime-free lifestyle in the community. Arguably, the 'probationary period' can make-or-break one's potential to 'go straight'. Brickman and colleagues (1982) assertion that those who first help themselves are subsequently helped by others may reinforce this point (cited in Maruna, 2001). In my opinion, I have a significant chance of desisting thanks to my responsibilities as a father and my academic studies, both of which functioned as a 'hook-for-change' (Giordano et al., 2002), as well as my deep immersion in the desistance literature during my incarceration. Briefly, a hook-for-change describes a catalyst for transformation which subsequently initiates the desistance journey.

I could feel the pressure in the back of my mind as I walked out of the prison gates. I carried in my hand a copy of *Making Good: How Ex-Convicts Reform and Rebuild their Lives* (Maruna, 2001), which I thought would act as a good luck charm on the first day of re-entry. My incarceration had been put to good use by learning and reflecting on my past and the kind of future I wanted. The pervasive pessimism of prison provided me with a moment of clarity where I realised that the end result of my life would either be premature death of life imprisonment. As one can imagine, this was not something I wanted for myself (or my son's future). Perhaps not wanting said life enforces the notion of the 'desired self' and the 'feared self' alluded to by Paternoster and Bushway (2009) to describe who the desister wants to be and the malaise they feel they could become if they continue to offend. This, in turn, seemingly reinforces Maruna's (2001) argument that people must formulate a semblance of pro-social identity if they are to enable desistance from offending.

Although I had received a 16-year prison term in 2003 and was released in 2010, I was recalled to custody fourteen months later for a minor charge of breach of the peace (or 'disturbing the peace' as it is referred to in the United States). Two weeks after I returned to prison, my ex-partner gave birth to our son and I was determined that I would do my best to turn my life around for his sake when I was eventually released. Ironically, discovering desistance projected me on to a path where I was best placed to achieve my objective. Re-entering society from prison has placed me in a position where I can put desistance theory into practice by demonstrating a pro-active willingness to disengage from offending behaviour. Personally, desistance and re-entry are two sides of the same coin, especially in cases of more serious offending. I now turn to examine the literature on desistance and prisoner re-entry.

REVIEW OF THE LITERATURE

The vast scholarly work on desistance alludes to multiple aspects associated with the desistance journey, such as cognitive change (Giordano et al., 2002), acquisition of social capital (McNeill & Weaver, 2010; Kay, 2020), the significance of family bonds (Cid & Marti, 2012), as well as shifts in behaviour and self-identity (Shapland & Bottoms, 2017). The academic literature on re-entry, while overlapping with some elements of desistance, references obstacles that are activated when the individual leaves custody (see Wacquant, 2010; Pinard, 2010; Logan, 2013; Durnescu, 2019). These barriers are threefold: personal, social, and structural (Durnescu, 2019). Some of these features include restricted employment prospects, voter disenfranchisement, no access to public housing and welfare, especially in the United States (Wacquant, 2010; Pinard, 2010), as well as stigma and marginalization of a criminal record (Lammy, 2017; Weaver, 2018; Piacentini et al., 2018). Certain aspects associated with re-entry may feature in one particular culture, while not being present in another. For example, there is no universal ban on voting, applying for social welfare or attaining public housing extended to people leaving prison in Scotland as opposed to the United States, as described by Wacquant (2010).

One aspect of the re-entry process impacting the individual's potential for success across cultures is the marginalization and stigma of a criminal record. For example, rather than protecting the British public, Lammy (2017, p. 64) argues that criminal records have the opposite effect by "trapping offenders in their past, denying dependents an income and costing the tax payer money". Lammy (2017) also points out that half of all crimes committed in the United Kingdom are perpetrated by recidivists and cites Home Office (2015) estimations of reoffending as costing the British taxpayers between £9.5 and £13 billion per year. One unusual, yet intriguing, notion is Lammy's proposal of sealing criminal records as a means of supporting those with convictions and helping them to access the labour market post release – a process enacted elsewhere.

In the United States, a judicial procedure exists in the Massachusetts where an individual can apply to have their criminal record sealed under State Legislature MGL Chapter 276 (s.100a) if it can be demonstrated to the court that there is ample justification for doing so (Lammy, 2017). Not only those convicted of minor crimes can seek to have their records sealed, the law can also apply to some felony convictions. Being a child at the time of the offence is a criterion for sealing one's record, as well as demonstrating considerable transformation since the commission of the crime.

"Judicial rehabilitation", unfortunately, applies only to Massachusetts State law rather than enshrined throughout the country. Briefly, judicial rehabilitation declares under the law of a particular country that an individual with a criminal history has transformed and seeks to support their change (see McNeill, 2014; Herzog-Evans, 2011). However, much more palatable is to present one's case to a court of law in order to be legally acknowledged as a desister rather than completely sealing the individual's criminal record, especially in cases of serious violent/sexual offences where others have been victimised. I would never expect my own record to be sealed, nor would I even ask. However, I have no idea how other people in similar situations feel about the possibility of sealing records.

Aspects of judicial rehabilitation have been enacted into law in several European nations, undoubtedly enabling desistance and re-entry. For instance, Herzog-Evans (2011) states that "French law does not only acknowledge during a judicial court hearing that a person has actually desisted; it also helps considerably by limiting the amount of information that is available on the basis of criminal records and the number of people who can actually see those files...". Furthermore, Larrauri (2011) points out that job disqualification in Spain only applies to cases where the employment role is related to one's index offence. The process parallels Boone's (2011) discussion of a 'conduct certificate' in Holland, which sees people with convictions excluded from positions that mirror past crimes. Resocialisation is also a right embedded within the German constitution (Morgenstern, 2011). As these studies show, Europe is seemingly more progressive than the United States and Great Britain in terms of desistance and re-entry focused policy.

Weaver (2018) cites how "people with convictions [in Britain] appear to be the only group excluded from the Equality Act's 2010 anti-discrimination protections and so one implication might be that people with convictions should be legally recognised as a disadvantaged group entitled to special employment protection". While there are many obstacles to employment in the Scottish context (especially in the unprecedented Corona Virus epidemic), there has been some progress, at least in helping those convicted of less serious offences find work. Prior to my liberation in September 2019, a news article appeared that outlined plans to help people with criminal records gain entry into the labour force. The formulation of a third-sector organization called Release Scotland described how several well-known companies have pledged their willingness to employ people with convictions (BBC News, 2018). After I read the article, I sought to participate in the initiative prior to my upcoming release.

I made attempts to contact Release Scotland while still in prison and after I had been liberated. However, the website had no phone number and no mailing address. After my release, I emailed them on at least three occasions and it was almost nine months before I received a response. The reply I received seemed perfunctory and provided me with the phone number of *another* organisation (Fair Start Scotland), whose primary focus is helping people get back into the job market rather than solely focusing on those with offending histories. Furthermore, I also contacted Police Scotland's Violence Reduction Unit (VRU), another agency that helps those with criminal pasts find gainful work. The VRU was initially formed in 2005 in Glasgow in response to a wave of serious knife attacks and I had always followed their work whilst in custody.

A few of their staff even visited me in prison and expressed the desire to help me when I was eventually released. However, the staff members I became acquainted with in custody had since moved on by the time of my liberation and replaced by new ones. When I telephoned the VRU, I was informed that I was out of the age-bracket of those who qualify for intervention. The irony remains that the *raison d'être* of these organizations is to help individuals with criminal pasts find gainful employment yet there is always an impediment of sorts obstructing one's progress, like age. This will, by extension, place barriers in the way of other people in similar circumstances.

Piacentini and colleagues (2018, p. 1) cite obstacles to employment as "transport difficulties, lack of recent employment experience and limited work history, issues surrounding transitions (from prison to community, from benefits to work), a lack of skills and or qualifications, low self-esteem, confidence and/or motivation" – all realities to which I can identify. For example, I have zero work history, which translates into all of the above, and especially low self-esteem in relation to employment.

My personal situation is compounded by the fact that I do not know how to 'sell myself' in a job interview (which could be the result of a lack of self-esteem or inexperience) or write a Curriculum Vitae. The skills I have are not necessarily translatable to the labour market. For example, being able to construct a cogent essay, may not be a skill that employers value in entry level positions. Given the fact that the prison population in Scotland has steadily increased since 2017-18 to an annual average of around 8,200 in 2019-20, primarily amongst the population of adult men only (Scottish Government, 2020), there is still more work to be done in helping people resettle into society after prison.

DISCUSSION

Arguably, scholars of desistance and re-entry describe many factors that can sustain both journeys while, at the same time, seemingly undermine them. As previously stated, there are universal and cultural barriers present in the re-entry process that can, and do, impede desistance. As Maruna (2007, p. 650) points out, "Except for those individuals who die in custody [...], the prisoner also faces the challenge of resettling back into society as an 'ex prisoner'. For many, this last test – the struggle for reintegration – can be the most difficult of all". But how does society (re)integrate those leaving prison if, as Wacquant (2010, p. 612) claims, they were "never integrated in the first place and there is no viable social structure to accommodate them outside"? How does the argument resonate with my own lived experience of the Scottish re-entry/desistance context?

Upon re-entering society, I saw big changes in the general community and broader society, as well as among those living there. For instance, my son was born two weeks *after* I entered prison and was eight years old by the time I returned home. Although he came to visit me in prison throughout my sentence, we both seemed a little unsure of how to react in the moment when finally reunited. But what are the long-term costs of my prolonged incarceration vis-à-vis my relationship with my son? How has this affected our filial bond? Sadly, some scholars argue parental incarceration perpetuate "levels of disadvantage to already disadvantaged kids" (Wildeman, 2009; Arditti, 2012; Wakefield & Wildeman, 2013; Wakefield et al., 2016, cited in Haney, 2018). Others argue that young children experience developmental delays, separation anxiety, and attachment difficulties (Cho, 2009; Geller et al., 2009), and school-age children have behavioural problems, educational delays, and emotional troubles (Seymour & Hairston, 2001). I can relate to separation anxiety and certain aspects of developmental delays, but definitely do not identify with attachment difficulties in regard to my child. My love for him is beyond questioning, although I am aware that certain issues can and do materialize in the parenting role.

For example, my son is diagnosed as manifesting traits of Asperger's Syndrome. The diagnosis was made while I was still in prison, prompting me to learn as much information as I could about Autistic Spectrum Disorders so I would comprehend the challenges the disorder may present. Moreover, I was unable to be included in all aspects of my son's education, which was very troubling. Education has played not only a huge role in my life, in my transformation, and I prioritize my son's education. I missed his first day of school, his first steps, his first words, not to mention every single one of his birthdays. The first birthday we shared was when he turned nine years old, one year after my release.

I have seen first-hand that there are massive social costs to incarceration. Haney (2018, p. 4) introduces the notion of "debt of imprisonment" to describe the material costs of incarceration that impact on fathers in custody and their kids' lives. In this way, I have first-hand experience of the debt of imprisonment judging by all of the important milestones I missed in my son's life where he needed his father. That being said, we saw each other at visits in the prison and kept in touch by telephone. The area where I have lived all of my life (and returned to after prison) was classed as one of the most deprived communities in Scotland. In fact, one local councillor claimed that the poverty levels in the area were "unprecedented" (Kenealy, 2016). When I returned home, I noticed a lot of talk of food banks and other welfare services that were unheard of before I went to prison. Thankfully, although I have never had to use one, the services are finally here.

When I exited prison, my close friend and older brother were experiencing addiction issues and the years that had passed since our last meetings was evident to me in their general presentation. A few weeks after my release, my friend was admitted to the hospital's Intensive Care Unit, due to health complications catalysed by his severe substance misuse. When I saw him lying in a hospital bed, I did not think he was going to come home. In fact, the subconscious enormity of seeing him in this dire situation induced an anxiety attack of such magnitude that I almost exited the room. I faced the psychological weight of the physical manifestation that human life is finite and the choices we make can lengthen or shorten our days on this planet. Thankfully, I was able to compose myself and distract from my own overwhelming thoughts by engaging my friend in discussion.

In a surreal moment, we both spoke about our lives and I told him that desistance from crime was somewhat similar to refraining from drug abuse in the context of individuals struggling to cease a pattern of destructive behaviour. For example, I explained that we must identify the triggers that catalyse our offending behaviour/drug usage and initiate a process of self-reflection that helps us achieve a semblance of a pro-social lifestyle. My friend seemed taken aback by my own personal transformation and expressed a determination to give up drugs if he recovered. Miller (2014, p. 324) points out how "the 'addicts' [in Narcotics Anonymous] are engaged in an ongoing process of personal transformation in which they learn to manage their 'allergy of the body' and 'disease of the mind' by avoiding 'triggers' to use substances and reframe negative patterns associated with substance use 'one day at a time'. The addict is in a constant and lifelong pursuit of recovery".

The parallels between desisters/re-entrees and 'addicts' are evident: avoiding triggers, managing negative thought patterns in relation to addiction/criminal thinking in a process of seeking (and securing) some form of personal transformation. Moreover, high incidences of substance misuse amongst people entering and leaving custody (see Maruna, 2001; Giordano et al., 2002; Travis & Petersilia, 2001) also renders this topic more complex. I also know from personal experience that illicit drugs are endemic in Scottish prisons.

Although I have experimented with certain substances in the past, I have never suffered from any addiction issues. However, my friend had been in the grip of severe addiction for almost 15 years and it did not have a happy ending. Against all odds, the hospital discharged him after two months of recuperation. We spent every day together, catching up on lost time and laughing about old times. Close family and friends rallied around him, but the Hydra still lurked deep within. Two weeks before Christmas 2019, my friend passed away, leaving behind a fourteen-year-old daughter. Strangely enough, the parallels between this situation and that of my own Dad's sudden passing – also from a drug-related incident – at the age of 14 was not lost on me.

In the midst of the upheaval, my own re-entry was exacerbated by the constraints I experienced trying to 'go online' and access 'critical services' as a citizen. For example, I discovered that multiple pieces of identification are required to open a bank account, register with a doctor and other basic but nonetheless crucial necessities. Prior to my release, I was handed a piece of paper specifying numerous types of identification, as well as the daunting fact that I would be required to present at least three separate pieces of documentation just to confirm my identity. Oddly, these prerequisites consisted of photographic identification and official letters, like a tax or utility bill (documentation that I suspect most, if not all, of those leaving prison do not have in their possession). I must admit that I was completely ignorant of the massive role that such documentation plays in the day-to-day life of average citizens. I was also totally unprepared.

On the day of my release, I visited several banks accompanied by a social worker, who advised that times had moved on and bank accounts are required for social security payments and employment purposes. I volunteered for social work support, a service that was provided on the day I left prison. Given that I had served almost my entire 16-year sentence, I was not subject to any restrictions or supervisory measures. Therefore, I was offered (and accepted) voluntary social work intervention. Immediately upon liberation, my social worker and I met at a prearranged location and went on a frustrating myriad of unannounced visits to banks in a seemingly rigged quest to open an account.

To my frustration, these financial institutions explained to me that I could not open an account without photographic identification such as a driver's license or passport. Moreover, social security staff informed me that I had to present identification to the Job Centre not only to prove my identity, but also to verify that I had successfully opened a bank account to qualify for benefits. Yes, banks would not entertain me without photographic identification, while the Job Centre wanted proof of my identity and an active bank account. To quickly overcome this dilemma, I could purchase a new passport (somewhere between £70-£100) or a provisional driver's license (£40). Liberated, I had only £170 in my possession, making neither financially practical at that time. I felt like I was trying to solve an angry Rubik's Cube.

By the time I successfully opened a bank account, three months had passed since my release. In that period, I had to use my ex-partner's bank account.

Although we were estranged, her parents brought my son to visit me throughout my incarceration and I spent a lot of time at her home after my release. My primary reason for this was to spend as much time as possible with my son to nurture "precisely those relationships proven essential for reintegration after prison: familial relations of care, reciprocity, and interdependence", to borrow from Haney (2018, p. 1). Haney (2018, p. 5) describes the notion of "incarcerated fatherhood" to describe "...how the financial confinement of debt and poverty interrelates with the physical confinement of incarceration for many poor fathers". Although my son had a relatively comfortable life during my years in prison, I did not contribute financially to his upbringing. I did feel bad about this but knew it was beyond my control. There are ways to earn money during custodial spells (e.g. selling drugs) but I was not prepared to go down that road.

My next step was to register with a doctor, which took four months from my re-entry into society because, again, I had no photographic identification. Fortunately, an accommodation support worker eventually telephoned my local doctor who I have known since I was four years old and explained my situation. Exclusion from services for want of proof of identification for those leaving prison appears to enforce the notion of "collateral consequences" (Pinard, 2010). Briefly, Tyner and Fry (2020, p. 360) describe collateral consequences as "hidden sanctions that emerge automatically at the onset of a criminal conviction".

Several studies (e.g. Pager, 2007; Pager & Quillian, 2005; Prager et al., 2009) point out that many employers refuse to hire people with convictions in the Unites States (cited in Miller, 2014). In the United Kingdom, 75 per cent of surveyed employers stated that they would not hire an individual with a criminal record (BBC News, 2018). However, recent news reports claim that the government plans to hire one thousand probation officers and are open to the possibility of hiring former prisoners (ITV News, 2020). In the Scottish context, there is the conundrum of people re-entering society being required to show photographic identification to access the same services that people with convictions in the United States are completely prohibited from using. The contrast here exhibits a level of 'hard power' in the United States yet 'soft power' in Britain. Whatever the culturally or geographically unique idiosyncrasies towards people leaving custody, collateral consequences operate in a sort of opaque space where 'invisible punishment' is unhindered:

Unlike formal collateral consequences, such as loss of public housing eligibility, deportation, occupational disqualification, or electoral disenfranchisement, these consequences do not attach by express operation of law. Rather, they are informal in origin, arising independently of specific legal authority, and concern the gamut of negative social, economic, medical, and psychological consequences of conviction (Logan, 2013, p. 1104).

Encouragingly, collateral consequences have been explored in the Scottish context, specifically the disclosure of convictions (Weaver, 2018), along with the barriers to employability of people in and out of prison (Piacentini et al., 2018). While recent changes to disclosure laws in Scotland have reduced the length of time individuals are obliged to disclose certain convictions to prospective employers are encouraging, there is very little progress in relation to people with more serious convictions.

Recently, STV News (2020) revealed that the prerequisite period in which individuals with convictions must disclose prison sentences or community payback orders to potential employers is being reduced. Specifically, sentences of 12 months in prison require disclosing for three years post release rather than 10 years and Community Payback Orders disclosure is cut from five years to 12 months or the length of the order. Noticeably absent from the change is any talk of acknowledging desistance. BBC News (2019) reported that the British Government proposed to scrap disclosure of convictions to prospective employers, although a policy that would not apply to the most serious offences. Encouragingly, we may be closer to judicial rehabilitation in Britain or the recognizing the desisters.

That people with a serious criminal record must always disclose their convictions when applying for a job produces and sustains liminality (Honeywell, 2019, p. 195) – a purgatory-like space where one hovers between two worlds never belonging to either. I wonder if this liminality sustains pro-criminal behaviour and renders individuals as 'doomed to deviance' (Maruna, 2001) through lack of socio-economic opportunities. Worryingly, the notion of being 'doomed to deviance' refers to how some people involved in persistent offending behaviour believe that they have little choice but to continue offending due to issues of substance misuse, poverty, and socio-economic marginalization, as well as the stigma of a criminal record (Maruna, 2001). This resembles Maruna's (2001) "condemnation script", which describes a narrative in which 'offenders' believe they are consigned to their fate as criminals and so 'going straight' is an insurmountable obstacle.

In my experience, the majority of the aforementioned obstructions have played some part in my own desistance/re-entry journey. I have zero employment history and a lack of basic skills that many employers require. In turn, I am certain my lack of job skills has exacerbated an already fraught personal situation given the usual difficulties people with convictions experience trying to find gainful employment in the first instance (let alone those with no experience of employment). How can someone with such a checkered past ever 'sell themselves' to prospective employers? There have been discussions on the language used in penology and desistance, swapping terms like 'ex-offender' with 'convicted person' for example (Boppre & Hart-Johnson, 2019). In my personal view, it does not matter to me what terminology is used. Frankly, the focus should be on people 'going straight', recognized as desisters (as the case in some European countries) or helping former prisoners find employment.

I have received help in different ways since my return to the community, whether it be moral support, financial help or just kind words. Many people have commented on my evident attempt to stay out of trouble and they are helping me acclimatize myself to society. As Brickman and colleagues (1982) point out, "people who help others are more likely to receive help in comparison to those who do not" (cited in Maruna, 2001, p. 124). I returned home and tried to encourage my brother and friend to desist from hard drug use.

My transformation and clear desire to be a good father and finally 'go straight' perhaps demonstrates to some people that I have, indeed, transformed. This may enforce Maruna's (2001) notion of a "redemption script", which describes three facets: (1) optimism to surmount barriers; (2) enthusiasm to contribute to a cause greater than oneself; and (3) belief in one's 'good self'. Writing and publishing academic articles, while arguably reinforcing my redemption script, does not minimize my past.

On the flip side, it could be argued that academic writing does maximize my desire to desist by functioning as a way of positive reinforcement. While I have little prospects of gainful employment, I have made some use of opportunities to pursue academic advancement. For example, I hope to study for a doctorate at the University of Glasgow subject to funding requirements. While studying for and eventually earning a doctorate is my ultimate goal, education provides something purposeful to focus on in the midst of the angst and uncertainty of trying to provide for a child, gain employment, cope with transformation, and maintain desistance, especially during the general malaise and uncertainty of the Coronavirus pandemic.

In the interim, I have explored opportunities offered in my local community since my release. For example, I enrolled in a parent-child cookery class that was offered in the local community centre prior to the pandemic. These free lessons provided a new medium through which to bond with my son as well as demonstrate to people in the local area that I was serious about change and not simply paying lip service. Moreover, I also had to familiarize myself with parental responsibilities, such as taking my son to and from school every day and to Karate lessons once a week. In the same way that other academics have described marriage as a protective factor in maintaining desistance (Giordano et al., 2002), my relationship with my son functions in a similar manner.

Unlimited access to my child was my anchor in society. I now have a purpose of focus that would keep me out of trouble and an opportunity to create a new narrative where being a good role model for my son is core. Although I missed the first eight years of his life, I still have much to look forward to. "Men got upset when discussing how they had missed much of their kids upbringing; they cried when recounting how bonds that were once strong became mediated and frayed" (Haney, 2018, p. 12). Although I "missed much of [my] kid's upbringing", I did have access to my child throughout my incarceration, albeit limited. I felt blessed because there are so many incarcerated parents who do not see their kids.

Fortunately, I also had other avenues where I could nurture my own embryonic desistance journey. For instance, prior to the COVID-19 lockdown measures I attended Vox Liminis, an organization exploring experiences of prison and rehabilitation through the arts, specifically music and poetry. The eclectic group of individuals get together regularly to explore, practice and support social reintegration (Urie et al., 2019). These small social gatherings provided a space where I personally could detach myself from daily life and look at recent events objectively whilst, at the same time, experience the benefits of a pro-social milieu. These visits occurred around the time leading up to (and during) of my friend's death and provided a milieu where I could, paradoxically, switch off from events while at the same time think objectively.

Many people do go on to offend after release (Miller, 2014), socio-economic opportunities, family bonds and maintaining my own place of residence are huge protective factors, especially in my own case. Former Justice Secretary Michael Gove explained to prison newspaper *Inside Time* that the three primary factors that provided a 'firewall' (to use a cyber analogy) against the temptations of recidivism are employment, strong family connections, and a stable home (James, 2016). The social bond theory (Farrington, 1992) refers to alteration of criminal behaviour during the life course, catalysed by maturation, family bonds, and employment/education (cited in Maruna, 1999). Maruna (2011) further argues that rehabilitation must address the corollary of convictions and the stigma entailed or be 'doomed to fail' (cited in McNeill, 2014). Moreover, a high number of people released from custody go on to reoffend within a period of two to three years (Miller, 2014), which may reinforce Maruna's (2001) claim of some individuals are 'doomed to deviance'.

In my own case, I have secured a stable home since my re-entry and have started to rebuild familial bonds weakened by long spells in custody. When I returned to the community, I had been provided with supported accommodation until such times as a permanent residence could be sourced (this process took me three months). However, I spent every single day at the home of my ex-partner and my son. My ex-partner and I are no longer romantically involved (we split up not long into my incarceration), but she was supportive of my desire to build a relationship with my son – a gesture for my son's own well-being, rather than to any bond she and I shared.

Luckily, I secured a permanent residence in my local area, which is a stone's throw from my ex-partner's home. However, issues between my ex-partner mushroomed, resulting in me taking custody of my son, which was his wish as well as my own. The employment front is where my biggest challenge lies. While I have very little prospects of employment (even more so during the pandemic), I am hopeful that I can study for my doctorate soon. In fact, I am in the midst of completing my application and research proposal. If my application is successful and I can secure funding, I am almost certain that access to higher education will transform my life in so many ways (for examples of transformative potential of education in the lives of people with criminal backgrounds, see Livingston Runell, 2015; Behan, 2014).

The fact is that I embarked on my own desistance journey whilst still in custody only to continue it after release. Slowly, I refrained from committing offences and immersed myself in academic pursuits during my carceral spell, slowly shedding my criminal identity and gradually replacing it with an academic one. However, I like to think of prison as the theory part of my desistance journey as opposed to the practice in society. Although it seems I have been on this road for a long time, the truth is the current chapter is still in the embryonic stage. Nevertheless, I am confident that my refashioned narrative (pro-social as opposed to anti-social) provides me with the "redemption script" (Maruna, 2001) that I need to continue building a crime-free lifestyle. Granted there are tough times ahead, but the way I see it is they surely cannot be any tougher than what I have already came through in the past. I just have to remain optimistic.

CONCLUSION

In this paper, I examined the desistance literature in conjunction with the scholarly work on prisoner re-entry. I analyzed the similarities and differences between the United States and Great Britain in regards to desistance and re-entry, and how there appears to be a myriad of obstacles impeding a smooth return to society and the potential to refrain from criminal behaviour. Furthermore, I discussed the notion of sealing criminal records in Britain and how the stigma and marginaliation of those with convictions (especially serious offences) are discriminated against in many socio-economic areas. I outlined that several European nations have enacted some form of law where people can either be legally classified as desisters or at least are not discriminated against when seeking employment (unless, of course, the job position is directly relevant to one's past convictions).

I question whether scholars speak of desistance without also considering re-entry. Are desistance and re-entry not two sides of the same metaphoric coin? How can one expect people to desist if they are still struggling with the same issues they experienced prior to custody? Is it not the case that the custodial experience magnifies these 'risks' and 'deficits'?

ACKNOWLEDGEMENTS

Boomer, thank you for just being you. You are awesome and hope you know how much you mean to me.

REFERENCES

Aresti, Andreas, Virginia Eatough and Belinda Brooks-Gordon (2010) "Doing Time After Time: An Interpretative Phenomenological Analysis of Reformed Ex-offenders Experiences of Self-change, Identity and Career Opportunities", *Psychology, Crime and Law*, 16(3): 169-190.

BBC News (2019) "Some convicted killers could have prison records wiped", *BBC News* - August 20, retrieved from https://www.bbc.co.uk/news/amp/uk-48975391

BBC News (2018) "New body aims to get ex-prisoners back into work", *BBC News* - May 28. Retrieved from http://www.bbc.co.uk/news/uk-scotland-glasgow-west-44196724

Behan, Cormac (2014) "Learning to Escape: Prison Education, Rehabilitation and the Potential for Transformation", *Journal of Prison Education and Reentry*, 1(1): 20-31.

Boone, Miranda (2011) "Judicial Rehabilitation in the Netherlands: Balancing between safety and privacy", *European Journal of Probation*, 3(1): 63-78.

Boppre, Breanna and Avon Hart-Johnson (2019) "Using Person-Centered Language to Humanize Those Impacted by the Legal System", *International Prisoner's Family Conference.org*, retrieved from https://prisonersfamilyconference.org/advocacy-in-action-coalition

Drake, Deborah and Ben Gunn (2013) "Convict Criminology", in Eugene McLaughlin and John Muncie (eds.), *SAGE Dictionary of Criminology* (3rd edition), London: SAGE Publications, pp. 79-81.

Durnescu, Ioan (2019) "Pains of Re-entry Revisited", *International Journal of Offender Therapy and Comparative Criminology*, 63(8): 1-17.

Giordano, Peggy, Stephen Cernkovich, and Jennifer Rudolph (2002) "Gender, Crime and Desistance: Toward a Theory of Cognitive Transformation", *American Journal of Sociology*, 107(4): 990-1064.

Haney, Lynne (2018) "Incarcerated Fatherhood: The Entanglements of Child Support Debt and Mass Imprisonment", *American Journal of Sociology*, 124(1): 1-48.

Herzog-Evans, Martine (2011) "Judicial Rehabilitation in France: Helping with the Desisting Process and Acknowledging Achieved Desistance", *European Journal of Probation*, 3(1): 4-19.

Honeywell, David (2019) "Ex-Prisoners and the Transformative Power of Higher Education", in Rod Earle and James Mehigan (eds.), *Degrees of Freedom: Prison Education at The Open University*, Bristol: Policy Press, pp. 195-208.

ITV News (2020) "Plans to hire ex-offenders as pledge to recruit 1,000 new probation officers by next year", *ITV News* - July 30. Retrieved from https://www.itv.com/news/2020-07-30/plans-to-hire-ex-offenders-as-part-of-pledge-to-recruit-1000-new-probation-officers-by-next-year

James, Erwin (2016) "People with convictions need the dignity of work!", *Inside Time.org* - July 29. Retrieved from https://insidetime.org/people-with-convictions-need-the-dignity-of-work

Justice Directorate (2020) "Scottish Prison Population: Statistics 2019 to 2020", *Gov. Scot* - July 14. Retrieved from https://www.gov.scot/publications/scottish-prison-population-statistics-2019-20/

Justice Directorate (2019) "Reconviction rates in Scotland: 2016-2017 offender cohort", *Gov.Scot* – June 24. Retrieved from https://www.gov.scot/publications/reconviction-rates-scotland-2016-17-offender-cohort/pages/2/

Kazemian, Lila (2007) "Desistance from Crime: Theoretical, Empirical, Methodological and Policy Considerations", *Journal of Contemporary Criminal Justice*, 23(5): 5-27.

Kenealy, Edel (2016) "Deprivation on our doorstep: Rutherglen and Cambuslang still struggling despite job booms", *Dailyrecord.co.uk* – September 5. Retrieved from https://www.dailyrecord.co.uk/incoming/deprivation-doorstep-rutherglen-cambuslang-still-8740814

Lammy, David (2017) "The Lammy Review: An independent review into the treatment of, and outcomes for, Black, Asian, Minority Ethnic individuals in the Criminal Justice System", *Gov.UK* – September 8. Retrieved from http://www.gov.uk/government/publications/lammy-review-final-report

Larrauri, Elena (2011) "Conviction Records in Spain: Obstacles to Reintegration of Offenders?", *European Journal of Probation*, 3(1): 50-62.

Logan, Wayne A. (2013) "Informal Collateral Consequences", *Washington Law Review*, 88(3): 1103-1117.

Macedo, Donaldo (2000) "Introduction", in Paulo Freire (ed.), *Pedagogy of the Oppressed*, New York: Continuum Books, pp. 11-29.

MacPherson, Kris (2017a) "Desistance: an inside view", *Discovering Desistance* – July 26. Retrieved from http://blogs.iriss.org.uk/discoveringdesistance/2017/07/26/desistance-an-inside-view

Maruna, Shadd (2007) "After Prison, What? The Ex-prisoner's Struggle to Desist from Crime", in Yvonne Jewkes (ed.), *Handbook on Prisons*, Cullompton: Willan Publishing, pp. 650-672.

Maruna, Shadd (2001) *Making Good: How ex-convicts reform and rebuild their lives*, Washington DC: American Psychological Association.

Maruna, Shadd (1999) "Desistance and Development: The Psychosocial Processes of Going Straight", *The British Criminology Conferences: Selected Proceedings*, 2: 1-25.

Maruna, Shadd and Stephen Farrall (2004) "Desistance-Focused Criminal Justice Policy Research: Introduction to a Special Issue on Desistance from Crime and Public Policy", *The Howard Journal of Criminal Justice*, Volume 43(4): 358-367.

McNeill, Fergus (2014) "Punishment as Rehabilitation", in Gerben Bruinsma, and David Weisburd (eds.), *Encyclopedia of Criminology and Criminal Justice*, New York: Springer, pp. 4195-4206.

McNeill, Fergus and Beth Weaver (2010) *Changing Lives? Desistance Research and Offender Management*, Glasgow: Scottish Centre for Crime and Justice Research.

Miller, Reuben Jonathan (2014) "Devolving the Carceral State: Race, Prisoner Re-entry and the Micro-Politics of Urban Poverty Management", *Punishment & Society*, 16(3): 305-335.

Morgenstern, Christine (2011) "Judicial Rehabilitation in Germany: The Use of Criminal Records and the Removal of Recorded Convictions", *European Journal of Probation*, 3(1): 20-35.

Nugent, Briege and Marguerite Schinkel (2016) "The Pains of Desistance", *Criminology and Criminal Justice*, 16(5): 568-564.

Paternoster, Ray and Shawn Bushway (2009) "Desistance and the Feared Self: Toward an Identity Theory of Criminal Desistance", *Journal of Criminal Law and Criminology*, 99(4): 1103-1156.

Piacentini, Laura., Beth Weaver and Cara Jardine (2018) "Employment and Employability in Scottish Prisons: A Research Briefing Paper", *SCCJR.ac.uk* – February. Retrieved from http://www.sccjr.ac.uk/wpcontent/uploads/2018/02/Research_Briefing_Prisons_Employability.pdf

Quince, Will (2020) "Employment hotline opens for offenders in Scotland's largest prison: Press briefing", *Gov.UK* – January 23. Retrieved from https://www.gov.uk/government/news/employment-hotline-opens-for-offenders-in-scotland-s-largest-prison

Runell, Lindsey Livingston (2015) "Identifying Desistance Pathways in a Higher Education Program for Formerly Incarcerated Individuals", *International Journal of Offender Therapy and Comparative Criminology*, 61(8): 894-918.

STV News (2020) "New law on disclosing convictions 'will help people into work'", *STV News* - November 23. Retrieved from https://news.stv.tv/scotland/new-law-on-disclosing-convictions-will-help-people-into-work?top

Travis, Jeremy and Joan Petersilia (2001) "Re-entry Reconsidered: A New Look at an Old Question", *Crime & Delinquency*, 47(3): 291-313.

Tyner, Artika Rene and Darlene Fry (2020) 'Iron Shackles to Invisible Chains: Breaking the Binds of Collateral Consequences', *University of Baltimore Law Review*, 49(3): 357-382.

Urie, Alison., Fergus McNeill, Lucy Cathcart-Fröden, Jo Collinson-Scott, Phil Crockett-Thomas, Oliver Escobar, Sandy Macleod and Graeme McKerracher (2019) "Reintegration, Hospitality and Hostility: Song Writing and Song Sharing in Criminal Justice", *Journal of Extreme Anthropology*, 3(1): 2535-3241.

Wacquant, Loic (2010) "Prisoner Re-entry as Myth and Ceremony", *Dialectical Anthropology*, 34: 605-620.

Weaver, Elizabeth (2018) "Time for Policy Redemption: A Review of the Evidence on Disclosure of Criminal Records", *SCCJR and The University of Strathclyde*, pp. 1-20 - March.

ABOUT THE AUTHOR

Kris MacPherson was freed from a Scottish prison in September 2019 and currently lives in Glasgow with his son.

Co-producing Desistance Opportunities with Women in Prison: Reflections of a Sports Coach Developer
Christopher Kay, Carolynne Mason and Tom Hartley

ABSTRACT

The following paper provides a sport coach developer's reflective narrative account of his first experience of delivering a football-based development programme within a women's prison. The account highlights the notion that initial 'up-front' desistance work can be a process of co-production where all those involved engage in a journey of discovery in which the seeds of desistance are planted and begin to take root. The *interplay* between practitioners and service users involved navigating issues including vulnerability, trust and the impact of environmental factors, as well as highlights the idea that initial desistance efforts result from co-produced efforts between the person initiating change and those tasked with supporting this process. The paper calls for greater attention to the lived experience of *facilitating* early desistance transitions, as this will result in furthering our understanding of desistance processes.

INTRODUCTION

It is widely recognized within the study of criminology that those who are involved in offending will, at one time or another, cease this involvement (Laub & Sampson, 2001). Yet, interestingly, attempts to understand the processes through which individuals move away from offending (also referred to as 'desistance from crime') have only gained prominence in recent years (King, 2013a). While it is generally accepted that desistance is a process of identity transformation "that is produced through an *interplay* between individual choices, and a range of wider social forces, institutional and societal practices which are beyond the control of the individual" (Farrall & Bowling, 1999, p. 261), questions remain about how desistance from crime is *actually* undertaken and subsequently maintained.

In part, this may be because the majority of desistance research has tended to focus on the latter stages of the desistance process. Perhaps the most well-known typology of desistance was offered by Maruna & Farrall (2004, p. 4) who propose a two stage "labelling theory of desistance", where "primary desistance" concerns lulls in periods of offending, whilst "secondary desistance" concerns movement from non-offending "to the assumption of a role or identity of a non-offender or a 'changed person'". Subsequently McNeil (2016) proposed an additional tertiary stage of desistance which involves recognition by others that change has occurred, along with the development of a sense of belonging for the individual concerned (also see Nugent & Schinkel, 2016). Given the zig-zag nature of desistance processes, with regular lulls throughout a criminal career, these lulls did not warrant much theoretical interest in comparison to the latter stages of the desistance process (secondary desistance) where we can begin to understand how an individual becomes an ex-offender (Maruna et al., 2004). The concern here, however, is that such a position neglects a lot of the 'up-front' work that goes into initiating desistance transitions in the first place, along with factors which may kick start desistance efforts "in the minds and lives of individuals *on the threshold of change*" (Healy, 2012, p. 35 – original emphasis). Studying the early stages of the desistance process may be valuable. King (2013b, p. 137) suggests that "the mechanisms which underpin primary desistance may be different from those which underpin secondary desistance, [and that] experiences during primary desistance may provide an insight into how secondary desistance develops and also into the specific areas which may be more appropriate for intervention".

The early stages of desistance have recently received increased academic scrutiny (Goodwin, 2020; King, 2013b). A common theme is that maintaining desistance efforts is rarely a solo endeavour. Indeed, Weaver (2013) in her work on the relational nature of desistance argues that our actions are, in part, down to a reflection of how we see ourselves and also how we see ourselves reflected in the eyes of others (also see Maruna et al., 2004). Therefore, while it is important to remember that the desistance process is agentically driven, requiring both the will of the individual to desist as well the ways in which to do so, we must also consider the role of the supporting players in this process. Maruna (2001, p. 96) noted that while desistance "almost always came from within", there was usually a "catalyst for change" – an outside force – which "removes the brick wall, but it is up to the individual to 'take-off'". Whilst it is acknowledged that there are complex broader structures that can undermine the desistance process, the role of external forces in supporting the desistance process is increasingly documented, with some arguing that positive testimony from such forces can solidify "the initial tentative moves towards desistance" (King, 2013a, p. 159; also see Rex, 1999). Interestingly, firsthand narrative accounts from this outside force or 'catalyst for change' are largely absent from the available desistance literature apart from scholarship surrounding peer mentoring (Stacer & Roberts, 2018). It is this concern the current article addresses.

The Twinning Project involves a partnership between Her Majesty's Prison and Probation Service (HMPPS) and professional football clubs that links prisons in England and Wales with a local professional football club. Through the Twinning Project prisoners engage in football-based development programmes which aim to improve their mental and physical health and wellbeing, whilst also aiming to improve life-chances on release. This article presents a reflexive account of the lead author's first experience of delivering a Twinning Project course in a women's prison in the south of England to a cohort of women who (for the most part) were due to be released within a few months of completing the course. Access to sport and physical activity (SPA) within the prison environment is a core component of prison policy, with prison rule 29 stating that "arrangements shall be made for [...] a convicted prisoner to participate in physical education for two hours a week on average" (The Prison Rules, 1999). This rule is informed by legislation from the United Nations (2015) and the European Prison Rules (2006) regarding access to SPA. A limited, but expanding, body of literature suggests that SPA can be significant elements of daily life for some prisoners (Norman, 2017), and that these experiences may result in positive outcomes including promoting mental health inside prison and supporting successful reintegration post-release (Meek, 2014; Meek & Lewis, 2014a, 2014b; Norman, 2015).

Yet while research has demonstrated that SPA within a prison environment has been considered valuable in supporting rehabilitation efforts, it has also found that "availability of such opportunities [are] locally contingent and highly variable between institutions" (Meek and Lewis, 2014a, p. 167). Indeed, it has been argued that to be most effective "tailored sports provision should be embedded within multimodal interventions which draw on internal and external partnerships and promote opportunities for ongoing sporting participation" (Meek & Lewis, 2012, p. 117). A national initiative such as the Twinning Project allowed for another avenue for engagement with SPA within the prison environment. The Twinning Project course delivery combines classroom activities, for example learning about the qualities of an effective coach, and practical coaching sessions which provide participants with an introduction to coaching football. The course is delivered over a minimum of 36 guided learning hours. The intention here was not to develop competitive footballers, but rather the course sought to develop a range of qualities and skills in the learners such as teamwork, trust, resilience, and confidence through a range of football related activities both in the classroom and on the football pitch. The women who took part in the course were recruited by prison staff who believed that the women who were selected would be the most willing (or least unwilling) to participate in this pilot project. It was important for all stakeholders involved that this course was perceived to be successful by the women involved to ensure that the Twinning Project would continue and therefore provide opportunities for other women to be involved in the future. Minimising the risk of the project being unsuccessful for the women involved was a primary consideration and therefore the recruitment of the women for this pilot was deliberate and focused.

The account highlights the importance of agency and identity, and the relational dynamics at play in the early formation of desistance efforts by the women enrolled in the programme.[1] Tom is a sports coach developer with 20 years of experience coaching at different stages of the player development pathway, from the grass roots (recreational) through to academy level (elite). As a sport coach developer Tom's role supports the development of athletes, usually young people playing football, and the people who support the athletes, such as tutors and mentors. In this instance, Tom utilised the skills of a tutor to deliver a football-based coaching course. This, however, was his first experience of delivering within a prison setting. While this provides a valuable opportunity to explore the experiences of those who potentially facilitate and support initial desistance transitions, it also allows for an exploration of the lived experience of delivering within a criminal justice setting for the first time. While there are academic accounts reflecting on the experience of conducting prison research for the first time (Quina et al., 2007; Liebling, 1999), there are few accounts of this experience from non-academic outsiders.

Some of the ideas presented in Tom's narrative reflect the available desistance literature, with themes such as identity transformation (Maruna, 2001) and co-production (Weaver, 2013), along with more practical factors such as vulnerability and the importance of listening (King, 2013b; Rex, 1999) all evident in the account provided. Tom's account also provides an example of how tensions that arose on the pitch through their engagement in competitive sport enabled the women involved to manage confrontation and achieve a resolution. There are, however, contextual insights rooted within the discussion which bring to life the 'up-front' work which must be undertaken by each of the women attempting to change their lives. Tom draws on his experience as a sports coach developer to reflect on the experience of delivering a football-based development programme *with* a cohort of women in an unfamiliar environment. As such, the narrative provided below offers a unique insight into the ways in which early desistance transitions are relationally developed, along with an understanding of the ways in which this brick wall is removed, one brick at a time.

This paper was inspired by the work of both Weaver and Weaver (2013) and Hart and Healy (2018) who call for a greater use of complete insider narratives within criminology. Both sets of authors adopt a convict criminology approach, which aims to "aims to authentically represent offenders' lived experiences, correct misconceptions about crime and criminal justice and formulate policy and practice recommendations" (Hart & Healy, 2018, p. 104). While this paper is not within the remit of convict criminology, it does answer the call for the greater use of first-person narratives in desistance studies. This is significant because whilst "unbroken narratives reveal the messy, complex and often contradictory reality of human existence" (ibid, p. 104), they are often omitted from criminological research. Where such narratives are presented they tend to "have been fragmented, lifted out of context, trimmed to support particular criminological theories or policy initiatives in ways that make nonsense of taking offender perspectives seriously" (Weaver & Weaver, 2013, p. 260). While the paper provides a discussion of the links between academic theorizing and the lived experience of facilitating initial desistance transitions, the reflexive accounts provided below are provided in their entirety, unedited by the second and third authors. It is hoped that the discussion will contribute to the field of desistance studies by highlighting the 'up-front' work that goes into supporting initial desistance transitions and the importance of reflexivity in the process.

TOM'S STORY

Misconceptions About Prison

Before I had any connection with the prison world, I can honestly say my view of prison and the people inside it was one dimensional. I had never seen myself working in prison and, looking back, I had some fixed views on the purpose of the prison establishment. I looked at the prisoners in a narrow context and generalized my feelings to people in this environment. I was not able to think about some of the circumstances and wider context of why people may have been involved in crime. Everything changed when I started to deliver football coaching in prison. Now, my understanding of prison, and the role it plays in society, is transformed. I can appreciate that going to prison is the punishment, but life for the people in prison should be a journey to return to society the best possible version of yourself, whenever that may be. Ultimately prison is not full of prisoners. It is full of people.

Alien in Your World

As someone who had spent their whole career working in coaching and football at various levels of the game, predominantly with young people, stepping into the prison environment to lead a football coaching and coach development programme was one of the most extreme environments that I have ever been placed into. Building on this change of coaching environment, while also being a man in a women's prison, was more significant than I had anticipated it to be. Over time, I realised that a significant amount of these women's experiences with men had been complicated at best, and necessarily it took time to build trust and rapport. I believe that I was able to gain credibility and some social capital by demonstrating to them that I was stepping into something outside of my expertise by coming and coaching in prison. The simple use of a smile, handshake, and investing time to understand the women as people went a long way to building strong bonds. Before stepping through the gate and into the prison I was (understandably so) apprehensive and anxious about what might unfold in front of me when coaching in prison. I had never knowingly spent any time with people who had committed serious crimes and the thought of being placed into a space which was completely unknown to me felt unsettling to say the least. However, when the initial nervousness and apprehension fell away, the experience of supporting people in an unorthodox environment was one of the most humbling, impactful, and important moments of my coaching career. The opportunity to step into the prison estate as an alien in their world gave me a privileged opportunity to see prison life with fresh eyes, from a different point of view, and completely changed my perception of the criminal justice system. It also highlighted the potential that exists to transform lives on a human level.

From quite early on prison life felt cold, unwelcoming, and hostile. The tall walls, wire, cell doors, and regulation reinforced what you would expect from a prison in a physical sense. However, to support positive change it felt important to dig deeper than the aesthetics of the environment and to truly connect with people. This was not an environment that I had been familiar coaching in and the football content of the coaching course was not familiar to the women involved. As a result of this the prison landscape provided a context to co-create an environment where everyone was playing an active part as an architect of learning. The co-creation of the environment allowed individuals to take ownership of the skills, confidence, and self-belief they needed to reinvent themselves and reconnect with forgotten identities. Football was the vehicle for inspiring transformational change and was certainly not the most important element of the course. People regularly talk about football being an "international language" and the term "the power of football" is commonly associated with social engagement projects. On this project, football had made an introduction between club and prison, however the importance of developing strong interpersonal relationships and genuinely caring for the person in front of you enabled the bond to flourish.

Shaping an Effective Micro-environment
On the morning of day one of the coaching programme I met 16 women who sat on two benches in the prison gymnasium with their heads down, arms crossed, with no desire to connect. Their body language demonstrated that there was an apprehension about making a connection, and possibly a complicated and challenging relationship with learning or meeting new people. The environment in which these women lived their lives was heavily controlled and lacked a large degree of autonomy. Thus, it was important to develop an environment which was, on the surface, friendly, informal, and interesting, but on a deeper level was psychologically safe and co-created. At the prison I was fortunate to work with a group of progressive and other-centred prison officers who genuinely cared about the women in

their supervision. Together, we made changes to the physical environment that the women entered on a weekly basis, which played a significant part in building trust, relationships, and confidence to be themselves. The walls were covered in positive imagery with key words and phrases linking to several of the development intentions for the coaching course. Beyond the setup of the room, all learners were given a green Twinning Project kit, which figuratively and literally aided each individual stepping out of prison and into a micro-environment that was radically different to the rest of prison life. The learning environment proved vital to helping the women have positive, authentic, and memorable experiences regarding the football course. Greeting each of the women with a smile, a high five or a handshake reduced formality, and facilitated an environment that was shared and organic. This environment was not mine that the women entered, but rather it was something that was mutual between us. This approach afforded each individual the opportunity to take responsibility for the standards of the environment, but also the accountability to contribute to its maintenance. When looking back at how the room felt, it was happy and connected and a place where the women could be themselves without the traditional shackles of prison life.

The co-created learning environment was extended onto the artificial turf football pitch where the same principles of teamwork and trust applied. As an outsider to the prison world my assumptions were that the prison system makes an attempt to help people reflect on their true identity and take appropriate action to modify it so that when stepping back into the wider society they are more likely to break the cycle of offending and ideally find employment. However, when standing on the edge of a cold, wet, and windy artificial turf pitch watching women of all ages charge around with every atom of their being smiling and laughing there was a realisation that perhaps in the outside world, and especially in prison life, who these women truly are is buried under layers of status and stigma. From my experiences at this prison, facilitating and supporting an environment where these women could shake off their emotional disguise and at heart be playful, created an opportunity for them to reconnect with their true identities. They were liberated despite not having their freedom.

The Beauty of Vulnerability
Modelling pro-social behaviour such as vulnerability has been proven to be transformative in its impact on the people that you coach. Sometimes when

coaching and working with academy players being intentional with these types of behaviour is important, to make them stand out. However, when working at this prison I did not need to try too hard to bring this to life. By stepping into the prison, I put myself in a position where I felt I was making myself vulnerable and taking a calculated risk. How is this going to go? Am I at risk? How will the content land? Will I struggle to connect? What will they make of me? However, from very early on in my experiences of coaching at the prison I found that by stepping into the world these women lived in I noticed that this vulnerability went both ways. When looking back at my time working with the learners in this cohort, it became clear to me that their relationships with learning and trust are complex to say the least. Add to that the fact that I am a male coach with perceived authority in a female and hierarchical environment highlights a plethora of ecological challenges that could be perceived by some as barriers to supporting development and positive change. The outcome, however, could not have been more different. The women were clearly conscious that I was taking some risk. I was trying something new, with participants who were not the usual cohort of a coach development course and I was trying out some new ways of making a connection and impact. I was embracing vulnerability by investing time, energy, and commitment in them. It felt that a mutual respect had been fostered, and with this, an invitation for the women to take a risk themselves. For them, however, the risk of being open, sharing their thoughts, feelings, and exposing themselves to making mistakes was vulnerability in its truest sense.

One occasion, which compounded this as a 'wow' and 'ouch' moment almost simultaneously, springs to mind. We were working on the football topic of refereeing but disguised in the learning was the opportunity for the women to have, and to challenge, authority in an appropriate way. One of the learners was refereeing a game on the artificial turf pitch and awarded what can only be described as a dubious free kick and red card in a moment of hot-headedness. This did not land well with the rest of the group who quickly began to shout loudly at each other ineloquently sharing their views on why the infringement was not a free kick and absolutely not a red card offence. Very quickly, however, the women began to recognize the situation and started to manage and deal with each other in an appropriate way. The intensity of the shouting decreased and the women started to talk about the situation, and point out to the referee why their decision was not entirely correct. I did not need to do anything but acknowledge the bravery that it would have taken to approach the situation in a balanced and mindful way. The women took agency in their own learning and experience, and were bold and brave to take a risk at trying something new.

Learning in this environment feels like the wind. It is always there, sometimes we notice it and sometimes we do not, and sometimes the learning almost knocks you off your feet. For me, it was my role to help the wind blow a little stronger at poignant moments throughout the coaching course. I wanted the women to understand that there was learning in everything. Not just the PowerPoint slides and flipchart paper tasks, and not just from what I said to the group. Collectively there was a lot of life experience, knowledge, and life skill amongst everyone taking part. Everyone had areas to develop, but everyone also had a lot of the answers within themselves and needed the support in enticing these out. Learning was in the walk to the football pitch and talking about the women's children and family life. Learning was in supporting each other to get through leading a coaching practice. Learning was in recognizing when other people had done everything they could to get the best out of the day.

Together We Create
At the heart of the learning environment in this prison was taking the opportunity to build authentic and caring relationships with the women taking part in the coaching course and some of the wider prison community. As a sport coach developer, I am aware of the importance of developing meaningful relationships with learners, but again the importance and consequence of this in a prison environment is paramount. It occurred to me quite quickly that seeing these women on a weekly basis for seven weeks was possibly the most consistent contact they had with someone from outside of the prison during the whole time they had been in the establishment. I was physically and emotionally connecting with these women more often than their families and friends. This connection came with great responsibility as I found it significantly import to be consistent with my attendance – there was nothing that was going to stop me getting to the prison on the days that I had committed to. The football was completely secondary (at most) on every visit to the prison. It was simply the mechanism for creating the foundations for building positive relationships. It was important to adopt a position of caring to understand before being understood. To give the opportunity to the women to be themselves and to cultivate trust and confidence was vital.

One of the most important things to date that I have learnt from the experience of coaching in prison is that listening is crucial. The people you meet have interesting, sometimes complicated, and very personal stories and perhaps along the way have not had someone who is impartial to share these stories with. For me, listening and just being present and patient was incredibly valuable with every interaction with every person. The perception of the support I was able to offer was as impactful as the support itself. Understanding this helped me be subtle and intentional with the way I supported and interacted, tailoring the learning environment and knowing the learners as people first. I firmly believe that if you look after and care for the person in front of you the other qualities within them that you have the intention of developing will look after themselves. From listening to challenges about 'bang up', the 'crap food' or how much people miss their families and young children helped me understand the complex and challenging life that people in prison lead, inspiring me to want to play a part in making that experience a tiny bit more personal, enjoyable, and progressive.

Dialling Up Choice

Self Determination theory (Deci & Ryan, 1985) explains the three main components of motivation: autonomy, relatedness, and mastery. Without a shadow of a doubt, allowing these components to flourish when working at this prison was a significant contributor to the engagement and connectivity of the group of women taking part in the coaching course. When driving home from one of the coaching days at the prison and reflecting on how things went (and there was a huge amount of emotional luggage that came out of prison with me) it became clear that these women had very little choice in any element of their lives currently. Prison life had taken that choice away but the way in which the coaching course was delivered gave an element of choice back, and allowed the women to take some control about the direction and pace of their learning. Choice lived in every element of the coaching course. From where you sat, who you would work with, what workshop you would like to do and what type of coaching practice would you like to take part in or coach. Choice gave the women the opportunity to select their preferences on how they would like to contribute to the course in a way that was right for them. The choice gave them the opportunity to embrace vulnerability for themselves, but with handrails and support, to feel safe and supported. If someone was having a bad day or something else was happening in their wider lives the coaching course could be flexible and bend around what they needed at that point in time. This choice was energizing and allowed the women to learn, develop, and flex at a rate appropriate to them.

Without doubt one of the most impactful questions I asked the group was, "how would you like to learn today?" I assume that this approach is not consistent with other environments the women have learnt in and it was effective with the appropriate support. In essence, the activities and tasks that were created to engage and support the women took them on a journey from high structure to high support, with more prescriptive activities at the start which set the tone and helped the women understand more about coaching, football, and each other, moving to moments of learning where my role was to guide, ask questions, and offer support, rather than provide instruction. Learners were provided with tools to aid their understanding of some of the technical elements of the course such as coaching session plans and models for example. Individuals could choose the practice they wanted to coach based on their confidence and preference, and as the course developed they were supported to design their own practices based on a set of overarching principles. Nothing within the course was prescriptive and the design of activities was less like a flag planted in Everest – a definite learning outcome, but more like a treasure map with multiple possibilities and consequences. For learners, and for me as the coach, the experience of the coaching course was a journey of discovery and curiosity, rather than a highly structured framework or syllabus.

On a Journey Together

It could be considered by some that learning support offered to people in prison by third parties is a one-way process. People who hold the keys to qualifications and learning come into the prison environment and provide a service which is enriching and developmental for the men and women in jail, but then leave again and repeat this process later in the year or within another establishment. From my experiences, this could not be further from the truth. The experience of becoming a regular guest at this prison and sharing some of the 'football stuff' that I know has been as impactful, important, and inspiring for me as I hope it has been for the women I have worked with. Learning is multidimensional and is in everything. What I have been fortunate to learn about prison, and life within it, has impacted me on a professional and personal level, contributing to me becoming a better coach, as well as a more compassionate and understanding person.

Approaching and during the experience of working at the prison, nothing was certain. With no experience in this environment and no formal education in this area, everything that we (learners and coach) tried was, in essence, an experiment. And as we know, experiments can go wrong or go well, and either way they tell us things we did not already know. Some days in prison things did not go well at all. I recall one occasion when our coaching session had to dramatically change based on the disposition of the women. It was the Tuesday after Easter weekend and the women were argumentative, aggravated, and struggling to concentrate on the activities. I learned subsequently that over the long weekend the women had spent the majority of the time locked up in their cells and quite honestly, if that had been me, I would have probably responded in a very similar way. We changed course on that day and quickly abandoned any classroom-based activities switching our plans to being solely on the football pitch. Coaching or trying to step in was senseless and the most critical idea was to step back. Making no intervention was an intervention in itself. This reflection is not critical, it was about working with people in prison, and it is important because it is about working with people and being empathetic, as well as responsive, to their needs.

Final Thoughts

As a curious coach I am always interested in asking questions and searching for learning on the fringes of the sports coaching world. Coaching in prison has shone a light on what is really important about working with other people and has reinforced my opinion that if you look after, and support the person, the athletic qualities within them will look after themselves. Rather than adding barriers, working in prison has enabled me to be creative with my approach to supporting others, and challenged my thought process as a sport coach developer on the qualities of an effective and memorable learning environment. It has highlighted that the learning happens around the football activities and that if you build an appropriate learning environment with the person you are trying to impact the most you can make a difference on a very personal level. I have been a sport coach developer for over 20 years, and it has always been important to be critically reflective of myself and the programmes I have developed or coaching sessions that I have delivered. When stepping into coaching in prison, it was the first time in a long time when I have felt a novice at something and that is at times a little scary, but also really important. It is a reminder of what it is like to try something out for the first time, making mistakes, being persistent, and resilient. This brought the women and myself closer together from day one. Our stories up until that point may have been quite different, but this was new for everyone and we were *all* in that moment a novice.

CO-PRODUCING DESISTANCE OPPORTUNITIES FOR WOMEN IN PRISON

The remainder of this article presents an academic commentary provided in to consolidate Tom's reflections through the lens of the desistance research that is currently available. While there are certain points of resonance between the two, there are also points of divergence which allow for an exploration of the experience of co-producing desistance transitions in custody. But first, the authors provide a brief discussion of the power of sport within the context of the prison environment, particularly a women's prison.

Prison, Sport and Desistance

The growing body of literature surrounding the role of sport in a prison environment has demonstrated multiple advantages, in relation to both health and rehabilitation potential, for prisoners who participate in some form of sport and physical activity during their time in custody. While research has demonstrated perhaps some of the more obvious benefits of involvement in sport such as improved fitness (Meek & Lewis, 2012), it has also demonstrated improvements in prisoner mental health, particularly around anxiety and depression (Buckaloo et al., 2009). Involvement in sport within a prison environment has also been shown to support the rehabilitation process by boosting self-confidence, supporting the development of pro-social identities (Meek & Lewis, 2014a), while also improving communication skills and coping strategies (Leberman, 2007; see also Woods et al., 2017). Most of this work, however, still focuses upon experiences in male prisons. The research that does exist has highlighted that there are "gender specific gains associated with females' participation in sport, including increased confidence, assertiveness, self-worth, empowerment and improved body image", while also alleviating some of the psychological pains associated with imprisonment, thereby supporting desistance efforts (Meek & Lewis 2014b, p. 152, see also Leberman, 2007). Despite women making up only 5% of the prison population, 80% of female prisoners report mental health concerns, and nearly 20% of all self-harm incidents in prison in 2019 were by women (Prison Reform Trust, 2019). The need for investigation into the role of sport in improving outcomes for incarcerated women has never been greater.

Identity
A central idea in Tom's account relates to the notion of identity in several forms. This is consistent with the available desistance literature, where notions of identity and identity transformation are widely discussed. Throughout his reflection, Tom refers to multiple identities at play and interacting with each other, within the micro-environment of the prison classroom and football pitch (i.e. prison identities, twinning project participant, true selves, coach identities, etc.), all of which were equally important to facilitating initial desistance attempts. This aligns with literature which suggests that an individual's larger self is made up of multiple personalities that are "sometimes said to be organised in a hierarchy in service of the self" (Rocque et al., 2016, p. 47; see also Stryker & Burke, 2000). In this instance, some of the 'up-front' desistance work taking place was about facilitating a reshuffling of this hierarchy for the women on the course.

At various points, Tom mentions the women were able to express their "true identities" or "true selves" during the programme whilst wearing the green Twinning Project kit, in stark contrast to the standard grey prison PE attire. The notion of a true self being central to early desistance efforts is evident throughout the available literature. Maruna (2001, p. 88) argues that the establishment of a "true identity" or a "real me" is "essential to every desisting narrative", and that by drawing on these true identities the women were able to "deemphasize the centrality of crime in the life history" (ibid; also see Stone, 2016). Expressing this true self can be difficult however within a prison environment, which can not only be seen to centralise crime in the life history of prisoners (Rowe, 2011), suspending full engagement with one's "true self" while inside. Research has highlighted that those in prison can sometimes be seen to put their identities 'on hold' until they are released (Jewkes, 2012). Jewkes (2002) utilised a study of a maximum-security prison in the United States (Schmid & Jones, 1991) to argue that in order to make sense of, and articulate their imprisonment, prisoners tended to suspend their pre-prison identities and fashion for a less authentic identity in order to mask their 'true self' (see also Goffman's [1959] work on front-stage and back-stage identities). This is something Tom refers to in relation to the women he worked with as an 'emotional disguise'. Other research has gone so far as to suggest that periods of incarceration can result in an "organic corrosion to the self and person" (Rowe, 2011, p. 578). As such, we can see a clear distinction between that which is required to undertake the initial tentative steps towards desistance, and the impact of the prison environment on one's ability to do so, something which Tom identifies in his discussion.

Reconnecting with, and expressing, this true self can be a difficult and frightening process, particularly so in the face of high levels of stigma, exclusion, and victimization experienced by women in prison (Corston, 2007; LeBel, 2012; Singh et al., 2018). Fredriksson and Gålander (2020, p. 4) suggest that reconnecting with one's true self is a process of "re-making sense of [at times long standing] boundaries between the self and its circumstances", which can be an unfamiliar and frightening prospect. In embracing the unfamiliar and engaging with the course, the women in the prison were allowing themselves to be vulnerable, in an environment where expressing vulnerability represents a significant risk, in order to make tentative steps towards desistance.

Vulnerability was evident throughout Tom's account. While notions of prisoner vulnerability are evident in the available prison literature (Liebling, 2012), as is the role of vulnerability and taking risks in the scholarship surrounding researching prisons (Liebling, 1999; Quina et al., 2008), vulnerability and risk taking within the field of desistance studies remain underexplored. Tom's narrative provides an interesting discussion of the role of vulnerability and risk taking in the desistance process. The women demonstrated their acceptance to be vulnerable by expressing themselves freely on the football pitch and in the classroom, by embracing new skills and by openly engaging with Tom – an outsider – who expressed his own sense of vulnerability through his engagement with the women on the course. This is interesting in that it suggests that the desistance process requires an element of vulnerability from all involved. Most desistance efforts, by their very nature, demand an element of risk taking and vulnerability, as what is essentially being asked is a reformulation of oneself into something new or at least unfamiliar. Yet, while the literature may recognise that desistance efforts may require somewhat of a leap of faith on the part of the desister (Maruna, 2001), those facilitating this leap may also have to jump. The women on the course sacrificed a degree of their "frontstage" identity (or image that one wishes to present to another) (Jewkes, 2012), while Tom embraced his own sense of vulnerability in undertaking work in an unfamiliar environment with an unfamiliar cohort. The recognition of this vulnerability, and level of investment from both parties, allowed for the development of a desistance narrative that was co-produced between the women and their coach.

Co-production
Co-production broadly describes an approach which involves professionals and others working collaboratively to achieve better outcomes for those involved (Bovaird & Loeffler, 2008). Co-production has been described as a fluid and elastic concept (and practice) valuable because it is considered to be foundational to desistance whilst also being recognized as being a distant and idealised concept, reliant on respect, collaboration, equality, and empowerment (McCulloch & Members of Positive Prison? Positive Futures, 2016). Very little is known about the contribution of professionals to the relationship (Brandsen & Honingh, 2016) and this paper therefore makes an important contribution in focusing exclusively on the experiences of one of the professionals engaged in co-production with women in prison.

Slay and Stephen (2013) describe six general principles underpinning co-production namely assets-based approach, building on existing capabilities, reciprocity and mutuality, peer support, blurring distinctions between professionals and recipients, and finally facilitation instead of delivery. These principles are all evident within Tom's account. From the outset, Tom perceives his role to be one of a facilitator, enabling the participants to draw on the assets and capabilities that they possessed at the outset of the programme. In this way he is not there to create new capacity but instead he aims to support the women find their assumed, pre-existing, capacities through a structured and supported journey of discovery. Importantly, Tom is on a similar journey of discovery during the process where he constantly reflects and revises what he thought he knew about the women and about life in prison, and this helps create a relationship based on reciprocity and mutuality. As noted previously Tom recognizes that he is vulnerable due to his reliance on the women choosing to engage in the programme in meaningful ways. Football is a team endeavour providing opportunities for the women to engage in peer support, both on and off the field, and the example of the controversial refereeing decision highlights that peer support can take on numerous guises.

Tom's reflections on his experiences indicate a blurring between his role and those of the women he worked with. Whilst he was responsible for ensuring the delivery happened, the women had the greatest influence in the way in which delivery took place as evidenced by the session where the classroom learning was abandoned and by Tom's concern to ensure the women had control over how they learned. Brandsen and Honingh (2016) argue that participants engaging in co-production each bring different types of knowledge to the process and again this is very evident in Tom's experience where he identifies several gaps in his knowledge in areas on which the women were experts. As an experienced coach developer Tom is flexible in his approach and he is willing and able to adapt planned activities to work with the women participants in ways that prioritize maintenance of the relationship that he has built with them.

In creating opportunities for learning Tom has provided opportunities for the women engaged in the programme to succeed and partake in novel activities where they gain social acceptance from others in real-time. Galnander (2020) states that the idea that desistance requires desisters to re-evaluate their past may be more relevant to the men who have predominantly featured in desistance research (Stone et al., 2018), and suggests that additional shaming of women may be counterproductive due to their experiences of multidimensional stigma and shame. Galnander (2020, p. 16) further suggests that the desistance of heavily stigmatized women may be better supported when they are viewed on their current and future actions and are not dependent on changing "from something 'bad' into something better". Tom aspires to help the women reconnect with themselves, and in so doing, Tom indicates that he makes no attempt to encourage these women to distance themselves from a former self, but instead he listens to what these women wanted to tell him. Some of the women chose to speak about their lives before, and during prison, but this was organic and was not expected as part of their engagement in the football programme. Tom's relationship with the women he met existed in the present and on their engagement in the football programme where women had a chance to 'be' in the moment and not feel the strain of becoming someone else. In their experiences of learning and engaging in football the women gained personalised glimpses of normalcy associated with the freedoms of an idealized childhood – running, playing, laughing, arguing, resolving disputes – within the confines of a prison setting. It seems possible that these experiences may help these women to familiarize themselves with both personal and social acceptance without having to make a wholesale commitment to embarking on their change to something better. These opportunities may also enable them to find previously undiscovered positive elements of their identities which may assist them in re-evaluating their past when starting their desistance journeys.

The Prison Environment

Finally, it is necessary to say a few words about the prison environment and its impact upon an individual's initial steps towards desistance. As part of their context of change model, Burrowes and Needs (2009, p. 43) argue that it is important to consider the "environment of change" in the desistance process, asserting that "the prison as a building, the prison regime, the staff and other inmates [...] may affect an individual's readiness to change". Indeed, the account provided by Tom demonstrates that the prison environment played its part in the facilitation of early desistance work with the women. Yet while he notes the imposing physical presence of the prison itself, the main points of reflection come from the impact of incarceration for the women on the course. The available literature suggests that there are a range of deprivations that people experience during periods of incarceration, generally referred to as the "pains of imprisonment" (Sykes, 1958). Such deprivations relate to things like the deprivation of liberty, individual choice and security, but also factors such as loneliness (Nugent & Schinkel, 2016), shame and stigma (Rowe, 2011), along with the identity deprivations and 'erosion of the self' as discussed above. Imprisoned women are also more likely to be further removed from family networks and children owing to the smaller number of women's prisons in England and Wales, meaning attempts to maintain family ties, which are fundamental in the desistance process (Farrall, 2011), can be more difficult. These difficulties surrounding the experience of incarceration were evidenced in Tom's account of his interaction with the women. As such, Tom notes that it was important to create an environment – both physical and relational – within the prison that made the pains of imprisonment a little less painful. Firstly, the learning space was created *with* the women on the course, which was centred around ownership and autonomy. The women were involved in discussions surrounding not only how they wanted to learn each week but were also responsible for the upkeep of the learning environment, making them active participants in the process. Indeed, the link between co-produced, active, and participatory involvement in interventions and successful intervention outcomes has been well documented in the available literature (McGuire, 1995; Rex, 1999).

The learning environment evidenced by Tom in his account also included a relational aspect which has been shown to be effective in supporting the change process. For instance, Tom talks about the importance of effective communication and active listening both amongst the women and in his interactions with them. Here the account mirrors research on the components of successful supervision. King (2013b, p. 138) noted that "talking and listening are fundamental aspects of probation work, both as a method of dealing with particular problems and as a means of nurturing the relationship necessary to enable probationers to be receptive to more direct guidance". Tom also stressed the importance of consistency, whereby he made sure that he kept his side of the bargain by delivering the course on the days outlined at the start. In doing so, Tom evidenced a commitment to the women and to the course which was returned to him in kind. Research has shown that such commitment by practitioners to their clients can engender loyalty upon which change efforts can be built (Rex, 1999). The key here is that while there was little that could be physically changed about the external environment in which the course was delivered, there were a range of co-produced opportunities within the learning environment which could be seized to promote learning and change.

An important point to remember, however, is that although efforts were made to reduce the pains of imprisonment experienced, and to provide element of choice and empowerment by the women on the course, the nature of the prison environment/regime will always limit any sense of empowerment and choice that the women were able to exercise (Cruikshank, 1993; Hannah-Moffat, 1995; Moore & Hannah-Moffat, 2005). It has been argued that women in prison "lack the power and autonomy to make even the most mundane decisions and choices" and that such factors "frame women's experiences as a prisoner" (Hannah-Moffatt, 1995, p. 148). The relations that can be found between prisoners and non-prisoners are also "structured by unequal power relations", which delimit the potential for empowerment (ibid, p. 148). While Tom worked to overcome some of these issues with the women on the course, it is important to remember that the environment in which the course was being delivered will dictate the extent to which this is possible.

CONCLUSION

In recent years the early stages of desistance transitions have grown in prominence as a core component of desistance studies. Such accounts, however, tend to provide sterilized academic accounts of these processes and how they are undertaken by people on the 'threshold of change' (Healy, 2013). The growth of the discipline of convict criminology has sought to provide a greater voice to those who are experiencing these transitions firsthand, both in the form of academic research and narrative accounts, and there is a growing body of work within this field (Weaver & Weaver, 2013; Hart & Healy, 2018). This should be commended and encouraged, but it is also important to note that desistance is rarely undertaken in isolation, and the narratives from the supporting cast in desistance efforts (these 'catalysts for change') are rarely evident in the literature. We have attempted to add to the body of single narratives within desistance studies by providing the account of the lead author's first experience of delivering a rehabilitation program with women in prison. While it cannot be said that these women were necessarily desisting, what we can see is an account of the 'up-front' work that takes place with individuals who may be taking their first steps towards change and how this change is supported externally. While some of the common factors relating to the seeds of desistance were evident in Tom's account (e.g. identity and agency), there was also an identification of the struggles the women had to work through in order for these seeds to plant roots (e.g. vulnerability, trust, environmental factors). From this account, we can see the value of the *interplay* between practitioners and service users, highlighting the idea that initial desistance efforts are a result of a co-produced effort between the person initiating change and those tasked with supporting this process. Moving forward, it is recommended that more attention is given to the lived experience of *facilitating* early desistance transitions. Without this knowledge, our understanding of desistance processes can only go so far.

ENDNOTES

[1] Given the non-linear or 'zigzag' nature of initial desistance efforts (Phillips, 2016), the authors are not able to categorically state that the women in the course were desisting at the time.

REFERENCES

Bovaird, Tony and Elke Loeffler (2008) "User and Community Co-production of Public Services: Fad or Fact, Nuisance or Necessity?", Briefing Paper 12, Third Sector Research Centre.

Brandsen, Taco and Marlies Honingh (2016) "Distinguishing Different Types of Co-production: A Conceptual Analysis Based on the Classical Definition", *Public Administration Review*, 76(3): 427-435.

Buckaloo, Bobby J., Kevin S. Krug, and Koury B. Nelson (2009) "Exercise and the Low-Security Inmate: Changes in Depression, Stress, and Anxiety", *The Prison Journal*, 89(3): 328-343.

Burrows, Nina and Adrian Needs (2009) "Time to Contemplate Change? A Framework for Assessing Readiness to Change with Offenders", *Aggression and Violent Behaviour*, 14(1): 39-49.

Corston, Jean (2007) *The Corston Report* – March, London: National Information Centre for Children of Offenders.

Crewe, Ben and Jamie Bennet (eds.) (2012) *The Prisoner*, London: Routledge.

Cruikshank, Barbara (1993) "Revolutions within: Self-government and Self-esteem", *Economy and Society*, 22: 327-343.

Deci, Edward L. and Richard M. Ryan, (1985) *Intrinsic Motivation and Self-determination in Human Behavior,* New York: Plenum.

European Committee for the Prevention of Torture and Inhumane or Degrading Treatment (2006) *European Prison Rules* – June.

Farrall, Stephen (2011) "Social capital and offender reintegration: making probation desistance focussed", in Shadd Maruna and Russ Immarigeon (eds.), *After Crime and Punishment: Pathways to offender reintegration*, Abingdon: Routledge, pp. 57-85.

Galnander, Robin (2020) "'Shark in the Fish Tank': Secrets And Stigma In Relational Desistance", *British Journal of Criminology*, 60(5): 1302-1319.

Goffman, Erving (1959) *The Presentation of Self in Everyday Life*, New York: Knopf Doubleday Publishing Group.

Goodwin, Sarah (2020) "'Keeping Busy' as Agency in Early Desistance", *Criminology and Criminal Justice*, 22(1): 43-58.

Hannah-Moffat, Kelly (1995) "Feminine Fortresses: Women Centred Prisons", *The Prison Journal*, 75(2): 135-164.

Hart, Wayne and Deirdre Healy (2018) "'An Inside Job': An Autobiographical Account of Desistance", *European Journal of Probation*, 10(2): 103-119.

Healy, Deirdre (2012a) *The Dynamics of Desistance: Charting Pathways Through Change*, London: Routledge.

Jewkes, Yvonne (2012) "Identity and Adaptation in Prison", in Ben Crewe and Jamie Bennet (eds.), *The Prisoner*, London: Routledge.

Jewkes, Yvonne (2002) *Captive Audience: Media, Masculinity and Power in Prisons*, Cullompton: Willan Publishing.

Kay, Christopher (2020) "Rethinking Social Capital in the Desistance Process: The 'Artful Dodger' Complex", *European Journal of Criminology*, 1-17.

King, Sam (2013a) "Early Desistance Narratives: A Qualitative Analysis of Probationers' Transitions Towards Desistance", *Punishment and Society*, 15(2): 147–165.

King, Sam (2013b) "Assisted Desistance and Experiences of Probation Supervision", *Probation Journal*, 60(2): 136-151.

Laub, John H. and Robert J. Sampson (2001) "Understanding Desistance from Crime", *Crime and Justice*, 28: 1-69.

LeBel, Thomas (2012) "Invisible Stripes? Incarcerated Persons' Perceptions of Stigma", *Deviant Behaviour*, 33: 89-107.

Leberman, Sarah (2007) "Voices behind the Walls: Female Offenders and Experiential Learning", *Journal of Adventure Education and Outdoor Learning*, 7(3): 113–130.

Liebling, Alison (1999) "Doing Research in Prison: Breaking the Silence?", *Theoretical Criminology*, 3(2): 147-173.

Maruna, Shadd (2001) *Making Good: How Ex-convicts Reform and Rebuild their Lives*, Washington, DC: American Psychological Association.

Maruna, Shadd and Stephen Farrall (2004) "Desistance from Crime: A Theoretical Reformulation", *Kölner Zeitschrift für Soziologie und Sozialpsychologie*, 43: 171-194.

Maruna, Shadd, Thomas LeBel, Nick Mitchell and Michelle Naples (2004) "Pygmalion in the Reintegration Process: Desistance from Crime Through the Looking Glass", *Psychology, Crime and Law*, 10(3): 271-281.

McCulloch, Trish with members of Positive Prison? Positive Futures (2016) "Co-Producing Justice Sanctions? Citizen Perspectives", *Criminology and Criminal Justice*, 16(4): 431–451.

McGuire, James (1995) *What Works: Reducing Reoffending*, Chichester: John Wiley.

McNeill, Fergus (2016) "Desistance and Criminal Justice in Scotland", in Hazel Croall, Gerry Mooney and Mary Munro (eds.), *Crime, Justice and Society in Scotland*. London: Routledge.

Meek Rosie (2014) *Sport in Prison: Exploring the Role of Physical Activity in Correctional Settings*, New York: Routledge.

Meek, Rosie, and Gwen Eleanor Lewis (2014a) "Promoting Well-Being and Desistance Through Sport and Physical Activity: The Opportunities and Barriers Experienced by Women in English Prisons", *Women & Criminal Justice*, 24(2): 151-172.

Meek, Rosie and Gwen Eleanor Lewis (2014b) "The Role of Sport in Promoting Prisoner Health", *International Journal of Prisoner Health*, 8 (3/4): 117-130.

Moore, Dawn and Kelly Hannah-Moffat (2005) "The Liberal Veil: Revisiting Canadian Penalty", in John Pratt, David Brown, Mark Brown, Simon Hallsworth, and Wayne Morrison (eds.), *The New Punitiveness*, Cullompton: Willan Publishing, pp. 85-100.

Norman, Mark (2017) "Sport in the Underlife of a Total Institution: Social Control and Resistance in Canadian Prisons", *International Review for the Sociology of Sport*, 52(5): 598–614.

Nugent, Briege and Marguerite Schinkel (2016) "The Pains of Desistance", *Criminology and Criminal Justice*, 16(5): 568-584.

Phillips, Jake (2017) "Towards a Rhizomatic Understanding of the Desistance Journey", *The Howard Journal of Crime and Justice*, 56(1): 92-104.

Prison Reform Trust (2019) "Prison: The Facts (Summer 2019)" – June 14. Retrieved from http://www.prisonreformtrust.org.uk/Portals/0/Documents/Bromley%20Briefings/Prison%20the%20facts%20Summer%202019.pdf

The Prison Rules (1999) "Rule 29: Physical Education", *The Prison (Amendment) (No.2) Rules* 2005 – December 14. Retrieved from https://www.legislation.gov.uk/uksi/1999/728/article/29/made

Quina, Kathryn, Ann Varna Garis, John Stevenson, Maria Garrido, Jody Brown, Roberta Richman, Jeffrey Renzi, Judith Fox and Kimberly Mitchell (2008) "Through the Bullet-Proof Glass: Conducting Research in Prison Settings", *Journal of Trauma and Dissociation*, 8(2): 123-139.

Rex, Sue (1999) "Desistance from Offending: Experiences of Probation", *The Howard Journal*, 38(4): 366-383.

Rocque, Michael, Chad Posick, and Ray Paternoster (2016) "Identities Through Time: An Exploration of Identity Change as a Cause of Desistance", *Justice Quarterly*, 33(1): 45-72.

Rowe, Abigail (2011) "Narratives of Self and Identity in Women's Prisons: Stigma and the Struggle for Self-Definition in Penal Regimes", *Punishment and Society*, 13(5): 571-591.

Schmid, Thomas and Richard Jones (1991) "Suspended Identity: Identity Transformation in a Maximum Security Prison", *Symbolic Interaction*, 14(4): 415-32.

Singh, Sara, Jess Cale and Kat Armstrong (2018) "Breaking the Cycle: Understanding the Needs of Women Involved in the Criminal Justice System and the Role of Mentoring in Promoting Desistance", *International Journal of Offender Therapy and Comparative Criminology*, 63(8): 1330-1353.

Slay, Julia and Lucie Stephens (2013) *Co-Production in Mental Health: A Literature Review*, London: New Economics Foundation, p. 3.

Stacer, Melissa J. and Melinda R. Roberts (2018) "Reversing the Trend: The Role of Mentoring in Offender Re-entry", *Journal of Offender Rehabilitation*, 57(4): 1-21.

Stone, Rebecca (2016) "Desistance and Identity Repair: Redemption Narratives as Resistance to Stigma", *British Journal of Criminology*, 56(5): 956-975.

Stone, Rebecca, Merry Morash, Marva Goodson, Sandi Smith and Jennifer Cobbina (2018) "Women on Parole, Identity Processes, and Primary Desistance", *Feminist Criminology*, 13(4): 382–403.

Stryker, Sheldon, and Peter J. Burke (2000) "The Past, Present, and Future of an Identity Theory", *Social Psychology Quarterly*, 63(4): 284-297.

Sykes, Gresham (1958) *The Society of Captives: A Study of a Maximum Security Prison*, Princeton, (NJ): Princeton University Press.

United Nations (2015) *Standard Minimum Rules for the Treatment of Prisoners* – December.

Weaver, Beth (2013) "Co-Producing Desistance", in Ioan Durnescu and Fergus McNeill (eds.), *Understanding Penal Practice*, London: Routledge, pp. 193-205.

Weaver, Beth (2011) "Co-Producing Community Justice: The Transformative Potential of Personalisation for Penal Sanctions", *British Journal of Social Work*, 41(6): 1038–1057.

Weaver, Beth and Claire Lightowler (2012) "Shaping the Criminal Justice System: The Role of Those Supported by Criminal Justice Services", *Iriss.org.uk* – February 15. Retrieved from www.iriss.org.uk/sites/ default/files/iriss-insight-13.pdf

Weaver, Beth, Claire Lightowler and Kristina Moodie (2019) "Inclusive Justice Co-Producing change. A Practical Guide to Service User Involvement in Community Justice", University of Strathclyde - June 30, Retrieved from https://pure.strath. ac.uk/ws/portalfiles/portal/88977529/Lightowler_Weaver_CYCJ_2019_Inclusive_ justice_co_producing_change_a_practical_guide.pdf.

Woods, David, Gavin Breslin and David Hassan (2017) "A Systematic Review of the Impact of Sport-Based Interventions on the Psychological Well-Being of People in Prison", *Mental Health and Physical Activity*, 12: 50-61.

ABOUT THE AUTHORS

Tom Hartley is a Coach Programme & Pathway Manager at UK Coaching. With over 20 years of experience working across the athlete development pathway as a coach, coach developer and transformational leader, Tom has extensive experience of creating memorable and impactful learning environments, designing, and implementing athlete and coach development pathways, and leading the delivery of game-changing strategy. Tom has worked in football and sport across a variety of levels shaping the future of coaching.

Dr. Carolynne Mason is a Senior Lecturer in Sport Management at Loughborough University. Her research critically examines the role of sport and physical activity in promoting social justice and in enhancing the lives of children, young people, and adults.

Dr. Christopher Kay is a Senior Lecturer in Criminology at Loughborough University. His research aims to understand the lived experience of criminal justice, along with how sport-based interventions can be used to promote desistance and rehabilitation for people with convictions.

Desistance and Prison Culture:
A Trifurcated Prisoner Classification Theory
Ruth Utnage

ABSTRACT

Social scientists have debated "real desistance" (Maruna et al., 2004) from crime for years. Criminal activity happens before incarceration and institutions are expected to correct the offending behaviour. In the current article, I explore prison culture through the lens of a participant observer with 9.5 years of direct cultural immersion. Prisoner culture is unique and the prison environment has an impact on what a prisoner views as possible within the carceral space, but prisoner culture also impacts what information is transmitted about prison. I introduce a trifurcated classification theory of people in prison as: Active Persistors, Passive Desistors, and Dedicated Desistors.

INTRODUCTION

In this paper, I propose that to understand why or how desistance occurs, we must start with an exploration of prisoner culture. I posit that a more holistic understanding of prison cultures' impact on desistance can be better understood via cultural immersion or "participant observation"—a process through which a researcher becomes a temporary member of the group being studied (Shepard, 2013). Most prisoners' behaviour and presentation of self is altered significantly in interactions between non-prisoners and prisoners, which I attribute, at least in part, to prisoners wanting to appear socially acceptable (see "Incarcerated Offender Culture"). Prisoners seek to satisfy their non-prisoner observers and differentiate the authority/power or perceived authority/power of the staff/volunteers. I also explore in the current article the trifurcated classification of the incarcerated population. My hope is that instead of challenging current theories I can provide an intelligent and coherent exploration that will spur further and more comprehensive research.

TRIFURCATED CLASSIFICATION THEORY

In the *Encyclopedia of Criminological Theory* desistance is defined as "...a process of maintaining crime-free behavior in the face of life's obstacles and temptations" (Sundt, 2010). The definition makes clear that "rather than an event or a decision, desistance is a process", which shifts our focus from trying to understand turning points in a person's life (why did they desist?) to instead thinking about how people desist from crime" (Sundt, 2010). I believe the distinction is critical because environments can have influence on human behaviour. However, what is less known is the degree of impact of different environments have on different individuals. Prison culture distinctly differs from other cultures (see "Incarcerated Prisoner Culture"). I assert that prison culture plays a critical role in understanding how prisoners may or may not engage in the desisting process. My experience as a current incarcerated individual allows me to conduct participant observation. In my experience I have observed three types of incarcerated individuals, which I distinguish through a "Trifurcation Classification Theory".

In my admittedly limited capacity to research (I am in prison with no open library currently due to statewide COVID 19 protocols, no access to the internet, and an education confined to self-teaching), I have only found a bifurcated classification system of prisoners that is painfully polarized. I assert that new terminology is completely necessary to understand the realities I have, and still do, reside in – multiple prisons in Washington State as a prisoner in a variety of custody levels that range from maximum to long-term minimum security and a general population to protective custody. The terminology currently used to describe desistance from crime, that I am familiar with, is persistence and desistance. When applied, all prisoners become siloed into either 'persistor' or 'desistor' categories. The two categories are insufficient to accurately describe the process of "desisting". Desistance is a process and, as with all processes, there are stages, phases, or steps.

In my first iteration and attempt to theorize prisoner classification I apply simplistic operationalizations of conceptions: those who refuse to change and currently embrace criminality (active persistors), those who do nothing to change (passive desistors), and those who are going to change no matter what (dedicated desistors). I compare my concepts to that of Havens and Cerruti (2022), who informally describe prisoners as: those who refuse to change (convicts), those who do nothing to change (inmates), and those who will change no matter what (anomalies). A challenge with the Havens terminology is that the terms are informal and have been used in other ways previously that may cause confusion. To diffuse terminological discrepancies or potential confusion I provide the following terms and their operationalization below.

Active persistor – similar to Havens and Cerruti (2022) "convict" – refers to an individual who is currently embracive of criminal engagement, and resistant and adverse to change (both in theory and practice). Active persistors, perhaps unintentionally, maintain the 'us vs. them' (inmates vs staff, gang vs gang, 'solid' vs sex offender, 'me' vs the world, etc.) culture and a gang's hierarchal dominance, as well as significant cultural influence. Active persistors may participate in rehabilitative programs often for the sole purpose of claiming social capital. Perhaps most important to the categorization is that self-initiation (i.e. any change actively being pursued) and personal agency is geared toward becoming a better criminal and/or resisting pro-socialization.

Passive desistors – consistent with Havens and Cerruti (2022) "inmates" – comprise a large majority of the incarcerated population, and are easily recognized by their idleness and lack of self-initiation. They do exclusively what is required of them – no more, no less. Reasons for their stagnant position, as I have observed, range from fear to self-doubt to a core belief that they do not need to change. Passive desistors display a sense of powerlessness and a lack of agency while incarcerated, and will speak of a successful life and happiness as something to be obtained once 'something' (i.e. probation, drug addiction, gang, prison, etc.) is no longer present. While they are not actively engaging in criminal activity they are doing nothing to correct whatever underlying issue led them to commit crime in the first place.

Dedicated desistor – terminology I employ here is consistent with that of Havens and Cerruti (2022) call "anomalies" –are committed to their future desistance and focus on identifying positive and prosocial ways to pass their time. Said prisoners self-initiate a strengths-based approach. This may include:

- construction of personal "redemption scripts" (Sundt, 2010);
- creation and/or leadership, as well as full participation in cognitive change programming;
- influencing/promoting pro-social/cultural change by passively displaying or directly providing mentorship; and

•   seeking a more comprehensive understanding of self-awareness
    to both cope with incarceration and embrace restorative justice
    practices as a matter of principle.

The term "restorative justice practices" means to take the time to
understand and actively pursue practices that can legally and safely restore
a sense of safety and/or justice to the victim(s) and/or the community. They
are cognizant of this in their endeavours and seek ways to 'make amends'
for their wrongs in some meaningful way.

In my observation, prisons are not yet equipped to understand, promote
or recognize dedicated desistors. For instance, risk-based assessment tools
may under-account for the unusually high level of achievement that these
individuals present, which I evidence by outlining two unique cases. First, a
dedicated desistor in a Washington state prison published new mathematics,
much to the befuddlement of the prison system (see Havens et al., 2020).
Second, another dedicated desistor at the same prison in Washington state
has over 65 certificates, awards, and degrees accumulated over a 9-year
period (for reference, nearly 10x the normal amount of awards over a 10-
year period). How two anomalous prisoners live within the same prison
seems like an exceptional coincidence, yet I posit that anomalous prisoners
exist at the prison because of the prison's culture – not having to fear for
safety. Nonetheless, risk assessments do not acknowledge or capture that
level of achievement, which suggests that positive change is disregarded,
even ignored, in prisons. By extension, then, dedicated desistors too are
anomalies that prison systems appear to not know how to support.

Dedicated desistors exist despite not being actively cultivated or
nourished within prison, while active persistors and passive desistors are
expected. Prisoners then may miss out on experiencing the Pygmalion
Effect (Rosenthal, 1977). For example, when an educator believes their
students are of a higher caliber of intelligence they are treated differently
by the educator resulting in higher test scores. Thus, I am suggesting that
if the prison environment can provide support to prisoners (i.e. if we can
revise prison environments to at least recognize achievement and help
prisoners), these cultural adjustments will result in a greater frequency
of dedicated desistors. Prisoners move between the three different
categorizations. A prisoner may fluctuate between being a passive desistor
to active persistor many times before, if ever, truly desisting. Dedicated

desistors find their strengths through various ways, such as through the construction and pursuit of more complex goals, defining personal morals and values, seeking critical analysis of self from others and taking corrective actions, pursuing higher education, volunteering, developing extraordinarily high levels of personal drive (or 'grit') unencumbered by risk of failure and attempting to achieve goals that are perceived as unrealistic by others, actively seek ways to improve self-awareness and self-compassion, and attempt to reshape their environments into one that fosters the growth they desire and know they need. I observe such practices when prisoners shift their peer-base to account for new directions in their life course. Dedicated desistors, which I self-identify as, look for tell-tale signs that someone is actively changing from one group to another because people change often and rarely does one who proves themselves a dedicated desistor regress into a state of criminality. Signs of dedicated desistance include, but are not limited to, a shift in peer-base, refusal to associate with active persistors, denouncement of any form of segregation, and dedication toward strengths-based pursuits. Dedicated desistors also tend not to concern themselves with the crimes of other individuals and remain extraordinarily busy (i.e. playing card games is no longer appealing). Moreover, if a dedicated desistor is regressing toward persistence, observers will notice their efforts toward positive change decrease and, typically, intervene by offering peer support.

I now turn to review prisoner culture drawing from my participant observations. Specifically, I focus on prisoner culture as evidenced in the actions and perceived beliefs of prisoners across the categories defined above.

PRISONER CULTURE

Given prison culture varies by institution and by the type of institution, I use the term prison to refer to State institutions housing individuals sentenced to a year or more (i.e. not county jails, work release centers, and transitional housing). Within the prison context, I speak from my experiences of participant observation to provide some insight into what prisoners value, which may aid in understanding why desistance occurs. One must not assume that the values of prisoners mimic those of members of free society for many reasons including a significant cultural lag and the behavioural adjustments demanded by prison environments. For instance, without traditional currency, prisoners require a new economic system. Within prisons, as well, prisoners are often unable to differentiate themselves from each other in terms of clothing, which increases the value of other forms of identity expression (e.g. tattoos and jewelry). I now turn to present what I conceptualize as the nonmaterial values of prisoners, and how these values change among active persistors, passive desistors, and dedicated desistors.

Values

Prisoners value freedom and community contact. Prison enforces a feeling of isolation from the community upon prisoners that drives a higher value being placed on community contact. Communicating with other prisoners does not alleviate the feeling of isolation because prisoners are intentionally isolated from free society. Many prisoners desire being accepted in society, seeking to make community connections and are proud to demonstrate these connections. The desire for societal acceptance and the resulting social capital can, in part, explain why communication with other prisoners is not an alternative to community support. Prisoners, I argue yearn to be an accepted back into the communities in which they are separated and deemed unfit. To feel 'normal' once more, imprisoned people require community acceptance more than rehabilitation or desistance although both are key to community acceptance. Prisoners in "doing" rehabilitation and "working" towards desistance are creating their "pathway or process" (Turner et al., 2019) toward the end goal of community acceptance, which marks the cessation of the stigma of incarceration.

Impacts of Values on Non-Criminalized People

I argue that some prisoners try to 'please' the non-prisoners (e.g. staff, volunteers, a visitor or other community member) they meet in prison. The objective of pleasing is to persuade further contact and/or prolong interactions with them. Despite the difference in objective, just like how the subject of a research study may act to please the researcher,[1] prisoners try to please non-prisoners. The desire to please can influence how prisoners self-present, including opting for atypical self-presentations, especially if the non-offender has community prestige. The practice is particularly valuable because in prison social capital differentiates status from prisoner to another, not material wealth.

Only the active persistor is maliciously deceptive when pleasing. For the most part the prisoner, largely the passive and/or dedicated desistor, is unaware of their atypical presentation of self and I would go so far as to say their atypical self-presentation is normal and socially acceptable. To present one's best self is standard practice for most people, however, for prisoners opportunities to engage with those that will increase their social capital (i.e. non-prisoners) is limited; hence its 'value'. For many prisoners, these infrequent interactions are the only opportunities to differentiate themselves from other prisoners, or better yet, to feel accepted by a community member. Social interactions with virtually anyone who is a non-prisoner is a reward, both personally and within prison culture.

I argue that researchers and penal/correctional administrators either ignore or underestimate and overlook the prisoner's presentation of an atypical self. Prisoners are unique in that they live around one another and see each other's backstage self (Goffman, 1959). An atypical self-presentation includes, for instance, when a prisoner who is aggressive and derogatory or engaged in criminal or hurtful behaviour when only around other prisoners becomes the 'ideal prisoner' and sells this to non-prisoners. The ways non-prisoners appear to accept the prisoner atypical self-presentation as true is often much to the dismay of onlookers who see the discrepancy in self-presentation. Moreover, there are two additional problems with this phenomenon to which I now turn.

SOCIAL INTERACTION AS A BEHAVIOURAL AND PUBLIC REWARD FOR IMPRISONED PEOPLE

The act of an active persistor presenting an atypical self to some non-prisoner who seemingly believes the façade and engages the prisoner socially can become problematic due to the social capital gained. Administration may unknowingly place these individuals in peer leadership positions (which happens quite frequently) because of their atypical (but 'ideal') presentation of self. In other words, active persistors are well-practiced at hiding their persistent offending and are often charismatic, even charming, and are able to present themselves as agents of change because they are well-versed in what the community or prison administration desires to hear. Moreover, the active persistor also receives the more often sought after reward of social interaction for the purposes of gain in the social hierarchy because, even though it may be staff, non-prisoner social capital is still the value that holds the strongest currency.

Desistors (especially dedicated desistors) who witness the non-prisoner accept the atypical presentation of self often opt not to engage with the non-prisoner in the future. The non-prisoner earns the stigma (Goffman, 1963) of being easily manipulated or not being credible (e.g. they choose to reward the active persistors behaviour with positive social capital). Programs that are peer, group therapy, or cognitive behavioural therapy based and are sponsored by non-prisoner individuals, prison administration or otherwise, who have succumbed to this dynamic (even if only perceptually), may not see the success they would have probably experienced otherwise. Passive and dedicated desistors will perceive that program sponsor as incapable of spotting, or worse, being indifferent to, true change. This gives the impression that applying cognitive changes is not valued in that program. Essentially, it puts passive and dedicated desistors at moral odds with program sponsors leaving little perceived differentiation between persistors and the program sponsor.

When a prisoner with healthier motivations (dedicated desistors especially) engages with non-prisoners the hope is to build social capital. Social capital provides a reward. What occurs is that the prisoner constructs a self that reflects any positives suggested in the opinion of the non-prisoner. The motives behind this presentation of self differ from that of active persistors to passive and dedicated desistors, specifically active persistors seeking to 'fool' non-prisoners and gain potential social capital, while dedicated desistors seek to understand how to change and impact the community positively. This 'self' can also be influenced by media outlets which portray a culture of constant criminal persistence, malicious manipulation, disjointed mental capacities, violence and aggression, drug addiction as acceptable reasoning for victimization, and making a conscious choice to remain criminologically persistent. The media portrayal can become a default expectation to live up to in the prisoner's subconscious and, in my experience, an expectation the non-prisoner seeks to affirm, which can result in inaccurate representations of prison culture and prisoners, especially when active persistors are at the centre of providing such information.

CLARIFICATION OF A CLASS SYSTEM

Many of the non-prisoners I have spoken with hold a common belief that the social hierarchy in prisons is constructed based on crime. Many prisoners also come to believe this to be true through anticipatory socialization in county jails, prison receiving and processing centres, and televised prison documentaries. This crime-base 'hierarchy' has 'solid prisoners' such as people who have committed murders and gang members at the top of the hierarchy, which other non-sex offender prison gang members are in the middle 'rungs' and the lower 'rungs' occupied by LGBTQ2+ prisoners and those who have committed sex offenses (Ricciardleli & Moir, 2013). The hierarchy is more pronounced in maximum security or closed custody facilities. However, as prisoners enter prisons that house medium and minimum security prisoners the hierarchy becomes obscured even further if not erased entirely. From my experience, a social hierarchy based on crime is reinforced through anticipatory socialization, however, I draw on nearly a decade of participant observation, from the position of a transgendered women incarcerated in a men's facility to propose a different model of social stratification or social hierarchy among prisoners.

I observe that as prisoners leave maximum and closed custody facilities they are introduced to a world where traditional active persistor mindsets no longer dominate in social positioning and where there are more passive desistors. Here, active persistors and dedicated desistors are polarized on the hierarchy with active persistors typically having more social capital among prisoners that determines one's position in the hierarchy because of underlying fears among the passive prisoner population who worry about the potentiality for violence or predation. Put another way, higher levels of social capital equate to higher levels of popularity among prisoners and popularity equates to a 'higher' status on the prisoner social hierarchy (see *Figure 1*).

Figure 1: The Revised Prisoner Social Hierarchy

Tier 1 – Popular, supported, and visited prisoners with social capital

Tier 2 – Well supported prisoners, who receive regular visitations but are less sociable or highly sociable with other prisoners with little or no non-prisoner support

Tier 3 – Unsociable or socially inept prisoners with or without support from non-prisoners (there is an inability to popularize oneself)

As a prisoner obtains more and more non-prisoner social capital the general outcome, or proof, of such capital is an abundance of material goods being provided by the social capital via purchasing books, food, electronic devices, music, and the like, alongside higher frequencies of visitation with different non-prisoner people. In short, as it becomes visible that someone is universally accepted, the prisoner population also accepts that prisoner. I posit this status elevation stems from a belief that if society accepts this person, so should I. I believe that prisoner class systems are undergoing constant nuanced changes to step in line with society (but always with cultural lag). As the prison itself (to include emphatically the beliefs of its staff) changes its beliefs and perspectives in the form of policy changes the prisoner population reacts in adjustment by accepting new norms that they perceive are more in line with free society. Such examples can include the tolerance of certain demographics that were previously shunned, like LGBTQ2+ or disabled persons, and the adoption of political beliefs, for example.

HOW CULTURE DIFFERS IN DIFFERENT INSTITUTIONS

Just like a class system of prisoner culture differs from maximum or closed custody institutions to lower custody levels (e.g. minimum or medium security facilities), so do most other aspects of prison culture. Differences in prison culture tend to revolve around prisoner perceptions of personal safety. If a prisoner feels safe enough to explore new social dynamics, they generally will, especially if that kind of behaviour is encouraged. However, when personal safety feels at risk, prisoners find it increasingly difficult to entertain notions of future planning on how to positively change their intrinsic values and cognitive behaviour toward desistance as they are too focused on safety. In maximum security and closed custody prisons, prisoners may turn to prison gangs and/or segregation for safety. Although less common in less secure facilities, such practices (e.g. checking into segregation for safety) do remain because some prisoners believe they have more safety in said institutions comparatively, especially in prisons that house protective custody prisoners. Protective custody labelled prisons are deeply associated with safety, such that there is little violence and the institution itself bears a stigma due to the nature of offenses of those housed within said facilities (see Ricciardelli & Moir, 2013). Prisoners have long understood that if an active persistor wants to change their lives they need to exit maximum security, which typically entails permanently disavowing their gang affiliations and being transferred on good behaviour to a prison with a reputation of little to no violence. Dedicated and passive desistors can be found throughout all custody levels in all institutions, but the majority will be found in facilities where there is less of a risk for violence.

CONCLUSION

Prisoner culture needs to reflect the values of normal societies to encourage more dedicated desistors. Passive desistors comprise the overwhelming majority of the prisoner population and are prime candidates for the significant reduction of recidivism, but we need to provide an environment that nurtures positive growth.

Desistance is a process. It is not a singular event and it can be witnessed before death. One of the most powerful lessons I have learned in prison is that I have agency and autonomy. As I began to self-educate and interact with prison staff, I began to shift from a thought pattern of "I equal bad criminal and staff equal good who hate bad criminals" to one of "I am a good person and staff are limited by their understanding of me to help me". The difference has been astounding and my hope is that desistors become standard and prison becomes a system of recovery and healing. My sincerest hope is that I have provided targets for further investigation.

ENDNOTES

[1]   The Hawthorne Effect refers to "when unintentional behavior on the part of the researcher influences the results, they obtained from those they are studying" (Roethlisberger & Dickson, 1964 cited in Shepard, 2013).

REFERENCES

Goffman, Erving (2012) "The Presentation of Self in Everyday Life", in Craig Calhoun, Joseph Gerteis, James Moody, Steven Pfaff, Indermohan Virk (eds.), *Contemporary Sociological Theory*, Oxford: Wiley-Blackwell, pp. 46-62.

Goffman, Erving (1963) *Stigma: Notes on the Management of Spoiled Identity*, London: Penguin Books.

Havens, Christopher, Stefano Barbero, Umbreto Cerruti and Nadir Murru (2020) "Linear Fractional Transformations and Nonlinear Leaping Convergents of Some Continued Fractions", *Research in Number Theory*, 6(11).

Havens, Christopher and Marta Cerruti (2022) "Desistance, Anomalies and Rabbit Holes: A Transformative Experience from Inside Out", *Journal of Prisoners on Prisons*, 31(1): 10-19.

Maruna, Shadd, Thomas P. LeBel, Nick Mitchell and Michelle Naples (2004) "Pygmalion in the Reintegration Process: Desistance from Crime Through the Looking Glass", *Psychology, Crime and Law*, 10(3): 271-281.

Ricciardelli, Rosemary and Moir Mackenzie (2013) "Stigmatized among the Stigmatized: Sex Offenders in Canadian Penitentiaries", *Canadian Journal of Criminology and Criminal Justice*, 55(3): 353-385.

Roethlisberger, Fitz Jules and William Dickson (1964) *Management and the Worker*, New York: Wiley

Rosenthal, Robert (1977) "The PONS Test: Measuring Sensitivity to Non-Verbal Cues", in Paul

MacReynolds (ed.), *Advances in Psychological Assessment (Volume 4)*, San Francisco: Jossey-Bass.

Shepard, Jon (2013) *Sociology (11th edition)*, Cengage Advantage Books.

Sundt, Jody L. (2010) "Redemption Scripts and Desistance", in Francis T. Cullen and Pamela Wilcox (eds.), *The Encyclopedia of Criminological Theory (Volume 2)*, Thousand Oaks: Sage Publications, pp. 574-577.

Turner, Emily, Rose Broad, Caroline Miles and Shadd Maruna (2019) "Learning Desistance Together", *Journal of Prison Education and Re-entry*, 6(96): 353-385.

ABOUT THE AUTHOR

Ruth Utnage is the Program Manager at the Prison Mathematics Project, whose goal is to reduce recidivism through desistance by helping prisoners explore higher education through mentorship and community support. She is transgender and formerly incarcerated. She loves mathematics, sociology, networking, and public speaking. Please feel free to reach out to her by email at ruth@pmathp.org. She welcomes all.

Twenty Years of Incarceration in the Garden State: Reflecting on the Barriers and Facilitators in the Desistance Process

Stephon Whitley with a forward by Nathan W. Link

FROM STUDENT TO COLLABORATOR: INSIGHTS ON DESISTANCE FROM A FORMERLY INCARCERATED STUDENT

I teach at Rutgers University in Camden, New Jersey. A few years ago, I was fortunate to have Stephon Whitley in one of my classes. At the time, he was living in a halfway house in Camden, technically still in the custody of the New Jersey Department of Corrections. Stephon was taking advantage of a Rutgers educational program for incarcerated people called NJ-STEP. A couple times per week, he was permitted to leave the halfway house to attend classes. My course was the senior seminar – *Ethics and Policy in Criminal Justice* – which takes a critical look at problems with criminal justice processes and institutions at various stages of the system. Stephon's analytical and critical mind made him stand out immediately – he was always able to engage the material in a way that, frankly, made my job seem a bit superfluous. For every concept we discussed, he could bring the material to life by sharing a relevant story. It was no surprise to me that he ended up graduating with a 3.9 GPA and was conferred with a prestigious academic award at commencement. Through discussions inside and outside of class, he and I became friends and have maintained contact since his graduation. There is little symmetry between the lives we were born into, yet we share an interest in exposing the truth and engaging in a dialogue on how prisons and other social systems can be improved. I am excited to continue to learn from him and to see what he produces in the decades to come.

In 2019, the New Jersey legislature considered a bill that puts limits on who and for how long someone could be subjected to solitary confinement – a particularly brutal yet prevalent practice in American prisons. Because I knew about Stephon's experiences with solitary, I floated the idea that he could write an op-ed about his experiences, and that I could help him shape it and pitch it to an editor. He bravely produced a very descriptive account of the deplorable conditions of solitary confinement in New Jersey and *The Star Ledger* – New Jersey's largest newspaper – published it right around the time the reform bill passed (see Whitley, 2019). It was widely shared on social media, with nearly 7,000 shares on Facebook and Twitter alone.[1]

Fast forward to the present, I encouraged Stephon to write more about his lived experiences and to consider submitting parts of his story to this special issue. Again, Stephon was intrigued by the possibility, eager to tell the all-too-often forgotten perspective. Thus, in the following essay he reflects on his prison time and the consequential events, practices, institutions, and processes that shaped him for better or worse. A few of these experiences acted as facilitators of desistance – they helped his own personal growth – while many others were barriers that diminished opportunities and the possibility of positive change. In some cases, these barriers even increased antisocial behaviour, and he elucidates these processes with rich and compelling examples.

Stephon can identify the life factors that motivated him and helped to bring about change. He focuses on the importance of family and visitation, religion and education, and how these led to changes in personal identity and goals. Research supporting the role of these institutions in the desistance process exists (e.g. Brown & Bloom, 2018; Sampson & Laub, 1995), yet he is able to colour in some of those general research ideas with detailed personal narratives, offering fresh insights into why they matter.

Stephon takes a highly critical stance toward the police and the prison system. The criticisms of prisons can be broadly categorized into three inter-related themes: 1) dehumanization and degradation; 2) a lack of work and income opportunities; and 3) cultures of violence and abuse. With few exceptions (e.g. Christian, 2005), the desistance literature places a greater emphasis on aspects that help to facilitate positive change, while relatively less research focuses on the specific state-sanctioned practices and processes that serve to diminish or even eliminate the possibility of growth and desistance. Heavily focusing on these highly problematic aspects of the system, Stephon's ultimate goal is to accelerate the crescendo calling for a total overhaul of dehumanizing prisons and the unjust societies that overfeed them. Toward this end, one of his more immediate objectives is to illuminate the critical barriers – ones that can be addressed through advocacy and policy reform – that incarcerated people face in their process of desisting from crime. He achieves this well and should be applauded for his detailed examples and insights, as well as for the bravery to reflect in public on a lifetime of adversity.

– Nathan W. Link

BARRIERS TO MY DESISTANCE

Stresses in the Transition to Living in Prison

Before I was sentenced to prison, I spent a total of twenty months in county jails. As a result, I was tired of not being able to touch my children when they were visiting, of being forced to buy snacks and cosmetics from the jail for a premium, not being able to go outside and breathe fresh air, and sleeping on a mattress that was two inches thick when new, but had been flattened to about an inch from the numerous people who had used it before me. I was told stories about East Jersey State Prison (a.k.a. Rahway State) and how the prisoners were allowed to go outside for recreation for hours, how you could sit next to and touch your visitors, and even run around and play with your children when they came to visit. If one was to do time, I heard that, overall, this was a decent place to do it. So, I wanted to be classified to that prison to do my 24-year sentence that stipulated I serve 85% of the time, totaling 20 years and four months.

To my "pleasure", I was assigned to live in East Jersey State Prison. The perks of being able to go outside, touching my family during visits, and having a TV – which they charged four times the amount that stores do – initially cheered me up a bit. However, that joy and relief did not last. We were transported to the prison on a bus full of handcuffed men tethered together with chains around our waists and ankles. When we got on the bus, the first thing I noticed was how dark it was inside the bus. I soon realized that was because they painted the windows black so we could not look out of them. So, we sat in the dark, rows of men, shackled, in pairs of two. As we were driven to our new living quarters – a bus full of mostly black men escorted by two white officers holding shotguns – I could not help but think how similar this ride was to the slave ships that brought Africans away from their countries and to this land.

Once we all were taken inside the prison, we were lined up, side-by-side, and given directives. They made us strip naked, open our mouths, and run our fingers along our gums, lift our penises and testicles, turn around, spread our cheeks, bend down, and cough. Then, we were told to go in the showers, together, and wash with lice shampoo. All of this was done by the biggest white men I had ever seen. I would say I did not understand why they did any of it, but I understood this was about dehumanizing us and exercising their authority. It meant: "Welcome to *our* house".

The prison seemed like an island, far away from the rest of the world. Behind the tall brick walls and barbed wires was what seemed to be a massive building complex. The lights were bright, but there was a sense of gloominess that encompassed the entire place. The brick walls were noticeably old, even with the depressing grey paint on the walls. However, it did not feel so massive once I began to walk through the main building, being escorted to my cell. That was because everywhere I looked there were prisoners. Some were walking, purposefully to a destination, and some were just sitting there, languishing in cages. Then, when we entered the housing wing, I was astonished by what seemed like a mile of cells, but when I looked up, I could see there were two more floors of cells, identical to the bottom floor I was standing on. There must have been hundreds of prisoners in that wing alone, and I saw at least three more wings as we walked to this one. On each of the three floors there were about 50 five-by-ten-foot cells and each cell had two prisoners inside of them. So, there were 150 cells, with 300 men in total on that wing. I later learned there were over 1,200 prisoners in that prison. Shockingly, that prison had the lowest number of prisoners out of all the maximum-security state prisons in New Jersey.

Out of all the prisons, East Jersey was the oldest. It is considered a historical site, but it is uninhabitable as a place for humans to live. The roofs throughout the entire prison leak whenever it rains; they have for over 30 years. At one point during my sentence, I was assigned as part of a crew of prisoners who were directed to install protective scaffolding so that falling bricks would not fall directly on our heads in the hallways. The scaffolding resembled the kind that were used to hold public executions. Many of the windows are cracked or broken. As a result, the winter months were extremely cold. I shared the first cell I was assigned to with another man. With the bunk beds, two tall lockers, two footlockers, shelves, and a toilet with an attached sink, there was not enough room for the two of us to walk around the space at the same time. So, one person would stay on his bed if the other was standing on the floor. We had to share that one toilet and, even worse, if one of us had to defecate while the other was in the room, that person would put a sheet up as a visual "block". However, there was no way to block out the sound or smell of waste coming out of that other human being. Because of the smells and decrepit condition of the building, birds, rats, insects, and other living things were constantly visiting us. On some mornings I would find a bird sitting on top of my covers.

The architecture and the animals were not even the most stressful aspects of the transition to prison. The officers were. They were the dominant gang of the prison. After my first week, I started to feel the same tension and stress I felt on the streets of Newark, but worse. On the streets, as a drug dealer, I was constantly in fear that someone might rob me. However, the worst threat was the potential police abuse every Black man in America knows he is subject to, at any given moment, simply due to the colour of his skin. However, in prison it was different. I felt the threat of violence with every step I took. There was a constant threat of officers ganging up and beating and/or killing me and other prisoners. It was psychological torture. I say this because every time prisoners came in contact with officers – there were a few good officers, but they had no control of the bad ones – they would harass us and behave in a menacing manner. Their demeanour expressed: "We will hurt you and there's nothing you can do about it because we have the uniforms".

Three days after I entered the prison, while we were locked in our cells, I saw about five officers walk past my cell, and they were walking as if they had a purpose. My cellmate and I went to the door to listen – we could not see down the hall. Moments later an officer said, "Open cell 124". Then, I could hear the officer telling one prisoner to step out and go wait at the front of the tier. Moments later you could hear sounds of someone being beaten and a prisoner screaming in pain. I later learned they beat the prisoner who was still in the cell because the officer felt he had looked at him too hard (i.e. intensely). These types of incidents occurred frequently and, I think on purpose, in full view of prisoners. It worked – prisoners lived in constant fear of violence from the officers. But their violence, compared to police violence on the streets, was different because of the fact that the prison was a "total institution" with no external visibility (Goffman, 1958). We prisoners could not run away and hide. Officers could come and beat you nearly to death, and there was nothing you could do about it. It was their word over yours and they knew the recipe to get away with it: write in the incident report that the prisoner assaulted the officer and suffered injuries as a result of officers trying to restrain him. This is the context I lived in for two decades.

DEHUMANIZING AND DEGRADING TREATMENT

The Department of Corrections in New Jersey keeps its prisoners in a constant state of stress and strain. Sharing a five-by-ten-foot cell with another man is the most basic example. Whenever one would be reassigned, another would come to replace him. Often these individuals were angry about how much time they had left to serve in prison, over problems with their significant others who remained on the streets, a lack of money to feed themselves, psychological and physical abuse from the officers, and over the cramped living conditions. We had to breathe it when the other person passed gas, went to the bathroom or were smelly because of being generally unclean. This was not the only instance in which prisoners being forced to be in small spaces endangered people's safety, even put their lives in jeopardy.

A daily practice that minimized our humanity and caused a lot of conflict was how we were packed into a cage like sardines in a can to leave the mess hall. On average there were about 200 prisoners in the mess hall at a time. It was a huge space with high ceilings and surrounded by dirty white brick walls. They would give us about 30 minutes to eat, but half of the time was spent standing in line waiting to get food. If you were late returning to your housing wing, the officers could write you up with a disciplinary charge that carried serious consequences. The problem was that to get back to the wing, we had to go through a cage that was about five-by-ten feet and nine feet tall. This cage was made out of thick steel in a crisscross pattern and was painted black. Another cage was centred on top of this cage, in which an officer would sit, survey the prisoners, and operate the gate to let prisoners in and out. The gate that prisoners would use to enter the cage could open to about four feet wide, but the officers would usually only open it about two-and-a-half feet, forcing the prisoners to squeeze their way in. Once inside, the smells kicked in – the space would take on the odors of 20 or so men in the cage, many of whom had not been allowed to shower yet.

Individuals were constantly stressed about returning late to their wings. Because we were always at risk of getting in trouble for returning late, prisoners would smush up against each other waiting for the gate to open and, when it did, guys would push and shove one another and squeeze against each other to fit into the gate before it closed. The officer would then close the cage. Several minutes later, they opened the other side of the cage and let people out so they could go back to their units. As soon as they let people out, they would open the first gate and fill the cage again. Again and again, they opened it, overfilled it, and emptied it with human beings. This was one the most inhumane and degrading rituals we had to go through, and we did it every day. It was a heavy metal gate and on many occasions I witnessed officers slamming the gate, causing it to hit prisoners who were trying to fit. This process could take 10 to 15 minutes, sometimes longer, because there would be a group of officers in the hall harassing prisoners. If a fight took place or movement was stopped for any reason, those stuck in the cage could be there for 30 minutes or longer, especially if the officer was especially spiteful. The inhumane process for guys coming in from the yard was the same, except the cage was bigger so it held more prisoners. Unfortunately, the inhumanity of the whole process led to prisoners getting frustrated with one another, often leading to someone getting threatened. Guys would exchange unpleasant words with each other, which would cause lingering hostility that would at times lead to a fight or someone getting stabbed. No doubt about it, those experiences in those cages made me more aggressive.

The practice of being put in the cages was counterproductive to my transformation for the better. I was bullied and beaten up a lot as a youth, and I grew up in a neighbourhood in Newark, NJ where violence was a constant and people were killed. I suffer from PTSD as a result. I learned early on that for me to survive, I had to become comfortable with violence. The cages, the angry roommates, and violent officers only triggered my fight or flight mindset (and remember there was nowhere to run). I became very aggressive and was always ready to defend myself. I refused to allow anyone to touch me when we entered the cages. In my mind, I was refusing to be treated like an animal, rejecting the prison's attempt to dehumanize me. I hated it and so I realized quickly that if I could buy commissary food instead, I could be free of the necessity to go in the mess hall cage three times per day. The problem was I did not have an income.

Employment and Income in Prison
In New Jersey, the Department of Corrections has various jobs that prisoners can work, but there are not enough jobs that every person can have one. From the time I entered the prison, I was trying to get a job. I signed up for jobs in the kitchen, the trash and laundry details, and cleaning the yard. For

years, I simply got responses that I was placed on the waiting list. What I did not know was that the jobs were rarely filled based on the list and timing of applications. Instead, prisoners were usually hired because of connections; either an officer or current worker-inmate recommending the person. Unfortunately, I did not have the social capital to get a job in my early years. This meant I had to struggle to feed myself and would often go hungry, like many other prisoners.

Similar to welfare for the jobless in America, if you do not have a job in prison they give you $27.00 per month. However, if you owe fines or fees they take a third of that money. As a result, I was receiving $18.00 per month. However, a bar of Dove soap was $3.00 alone. Therefore, the $18.00 was not enough for us to buy basic cosmetics and toilet tissue for the month. So, being able to buy food to supplement what the jail was providing (or the lack thereof), or to have the option to skip the meals that did not resemble food was not an option for me. This put me under an enormous amount of strain. I did not feel comfortable with reaching out to my family every month for money. It was bad enough that they had to pay outrageous and exploitive phone rates just to talk to me. After a few hungry nights, I made the choice to go back to the way I knew how to generate income: selling drugs.

I will be the first to agree that human agency is real, but I was being incapacitated in a prison that gave me little opportunity to use that agency to better myself. The state invested $55,000 per year to incarcerate me, yet I was being exploited by having to pay highly marked up rates for commissary items. In addition, I was not granted the ability to work – never mind the fact that those jobs paid between $1.80 - $4.00 *per day*. This only reaffirmed what I had come to believe from my years of experience as a Black person in America: the system does not work for poor people of colour. As a result, early in my prison term I had no incentive – felt no need – to desist. Instead, I sold small amounts of drugs during my first seven years in prison to feed myself things I bought at the commissary. There were other prisoners who sold drugs while inside for this reason. Others sold to generate funds knowing they would be released back into society where there would be more employment barriers for them due to their incarceration. Unfortunately, being caught by prison authorities was not the only danger one who sold drugs inside prison faced.

Cultures of Abuse and Violence

Prison culture forces one to rely on violence. Just like I was inclined to turn back to drug dealing as a way of survival, there were many prisoners whose mode of survival in society was to commit robberies and, much like me, they found it in their best interest to continue to do so while in prison. This reality caused me to always be on the defensive. There was not a day of my 20-year sentence that I did not watch for potential attacks. I was on edge constantly. One can be judgmental and argue that a human being should never take from another, but when one has been cultured to feed himself by any means, with the understanding that not only can he not depend on the system to feed him, but the same system is preventing others from feeding him, his anger and deprivation will often push him to take from others. Like with animals in the wild, we humans become part of a social hierarchical food chain. I understood this. Thus, every day – like when I was on the streets – I was prepared to defend myself with violence.

Worse than all of this was the dehumanizing and sometimes violent way that officers treated us. I remember an ex-correctional officer, who was incarcerated with us, saying that officers were taught during their training that they should not look at prisoners as humans so that they can do their job effectively. It helped me understand how the officers behaved so much worse than the meanest prisoner. We would walk to go from one part of the prison to another, and there would be ten or more officers standing in a line harassing prisoners, with the understood implication that those officers were waiting to violate someone physically or psychologically. I remember being in my cell and watching four officers beat a prisoner they had already handcuffed, who was on the ground. One of the officers was a white woman about six feet tall and 220 pounds. She jumped up and down on his head with both feet – in boots – while holding onto a gate to keep her balance.

The psychological abuse of solitary confinement ("administrative segregation" or "ad-seg" in New Jersey) was especially devastating to prisoners' well-being. I was in solitary confinement for one year because I had a cell phone. At the time I thought it was necessary because the prison phone calls were very expensive. A local 15-minute call was about $4.00. To call my relatives long distance was $18.00 or more for 15 minutes. So, I decided to get a cell phone. I had no idea that being caught with it would cause me to receive such a long sentence in solitary because I knew that individuals usually received four to six months for possession of a knife, something that could kill someone. I also did not expect the living conditions of solitary confinement to be much different than the regular day-to-day prison experience other than prisoners were restricted to their cells. However, in my opinion, other than chattel slavery, there are very few practices more dehumanizing – and worse for the desistance process – than solitary confinement.

The cell was six-by-eight feet, made out of metal, and included a bed, sink, and two small shelves. In the back wall of the cell there was a space cut out that was about three feet tall, two feet wide, and 18 inches deep. This is where we were supposed to go to the bathroom. It was designed like a porta-potty that could not be flushed, but was cleaned out every couple days. It reeked.

It was loud all the time. It seemed as if 100 people were yelling. But talking loudly and yelling was the only way we could communicate with one another, and how we passed the time while being caged for 23 hours a day. The noise and stench of urine and feces were constants. The place was also infested with mice. They scurried into our cells day and night. One prisoner was so lonely that he caught one, put it on a string, and kept it as a pet. The administration did not do anything about the mice, and in all stories about ad-seg I heard over 20 years, the mice were always there.

There were no windows and it got so hot that the metal walls would sweat. My fan broke during the summer and it had to be nearly 100 degrees during the day. I had to wait two weeks to order another fan, but when we got commissary my fan was not in my bag of items. This went on for over a month. The only relief I was given was being allowed to buy a small bag of ice every day for 75 cents. I used it to cool my face, but it provided minimal relief as it melted within minutes.

Every time I left the cell I had to be strip-searched, which meant getting naked, opening my mouth, running my fingers through my mouth, lifting my genitals, bending over, and coughing. Sometimes, after officers would ask me to lift my genitals, they would order me to start over and open my mouth, because they wanted me to put my fingers in my mouth after having touched my genitals. I constantly grappled with whether going outside or getting a visit was worth letting a corrections officer look inside me. On most occasions when I went through the process, I felt awful. But it was either that or sit in the room alone with not much to do and risk losing my mind. I did witness several people lose their grip on reality while in solitary; it devastated their mental health. They played with their own feces. Some attempted suicide. The psychiatrist walked through the tier once a week, slowed down by each cell, and asked through the bars: "Are you okay in there? Do you feel like harming yourself?" Prisoners never answered affirmatively. This was because one's neighbours could hear this inquiry and being unable to deal with solitary was a sign of weakness, which one should not display in prison.

These different forms of degradation made me very angry and cemented the notion that the criminal justice system is unjust and illegitimate. I would find myself walking around the prison in disgust of the officers. In all my years of being surrounded by criminals, I never met a group of people more disrespectful or harsh. However, there was very little recourse for us prisoners. Reporting officers was a waste of time because the people to which we were to submit complaints were sergeants and lieutenants – their coworkers who had the same culture of "us against them", "good guys versus bad guys". Even the Internal Affairs officers were ex-corrections officers. This meant they had relationships and bonds with each other. Like most prisoners, I understood that it would be unwise to confront a disrespectful officer. So, like most prisoners, I just walked around angry all the time.

In his book *Wretched of The Earth*, Frantz Fanon (2007) wrote about how in colonization, the colonized understood they could not retaliate against the colonizers, who had weaponry, because it could mean death. As a result, those who were colonized were quick to take out their frustration on other colonized people, even for the slightest crossing of boundaries. It makes little sense, but I perceived this dynamic during my time in prison. I almost always felt that I would never tolerate disrespect from another prisoner. I found myself letting out my frustration with the officers on other prisoners. This is one of the reasons incarcerated individuals return to society so violent. They were assaulted, and/or disrespected repeatedly by officers while inside, yet could not retaliate against them. As a result, they return to society with festering, extreme anger.

I conclude the first half of this paper by stating, firmly and unequivocally, that the prison system I experienced was not designed to help those convicted of crimes desist from criminality. To the contrary, the ways in which the prisons were designed and operated produced more aggressive criminals who were now equipped with legitimate grievances against the state. In contrast to the above experiences, my connections and relationships with family, my religion, and education allowed me to grow as a human being in more positive ways, which I elaborate on below.

FACILITATORS OF MY DESISTANCE

Many people think that harsh punishment will deter a person who lived a criminal lifestyle from committing future crimes. This certainly was not the case for me. I tried crime because it was a norm in my neighbourhood. I believed that poor people were at a disadvantage and would have trouble attaining wealth. In response, I chose to rebel and innovate in search of prosperity (Merton, 1938). It was easy for me to risk my freedom because I grew up in a heavily policed, carceral space that was not much different from prison. For instance, my schools – which had bars on the windows, chains on the doors, security guards with metal detectors at the doors, and my ability to do something as human as use the bathroom was decided by teachers who were given power over me – were akin to prison. Plus, a good portion of the men in my community were either in or had been in prison. Thus, I accepted the reality that incarceration was likely. After years of criminality, I rationalized that people were going to buy their drugs from somebody and that those whom I harmed were bad people who deserved it. Besides, I did not know any other way for a poor Black man to achieve financial independence. The prison system did not provide anything to help me facilitate my desistance journey. Instead, my family and their visits, religion, and access to education helped me to grow and change. It was through these institutions and opportunities that I was able to credibly develop a new identity (Maruna, 2001).

Family

I remember the first time my daughter came to visit me in prison. At 11-years-old, she said to me, "Daddy, just because you're in jail does not mean you're supposed to stop taking care of me". It broke my heart because I was so limited in what I could do for her. I knew that I needed to do everything in my power to let my children know they were loved and I started there. I would write letters and call on the phone. But my favourite moments were when my children came to visit. Unfortunately, officers again would make it difficult to enjoy our visits.

Prisons and their staff would create additional barriers to family who were lucky enough to find transportation to prison (Christian, 2005). They would hassle and harass our visitors during the process of visitor registration, scrutinizing their clothing, and scrutinizing how much contact we had with them. Often when I entered the visiting area my family would be upset. I would learn that the officers gave them a difficult time and treated them as if they were committing crimes. I concluded from the frequency and intensity of such treatment that officers were trying to discourage visitors from returning to visit their family. Sadly enough, it worked with many visitors. I would mentally prepare my family and warn them not to allow the officers to discourage and run them away. Some of my loved ones decided they were not willing to take the officers' harassment and stopped visiting. It is said, "when you go to jail, you take your family with you". That saying should be revised to reflect that you also subject them to being degraded for having the audacity to support and love you.

I also realized that my choices to commit crimes and the consequences of those actions impacted my family a great deal. I became honest with myself that it was selfish. I hated seeing the pain they were enduring. I told myself "you do not hurt those you love", and that was just what I had done. So, the thought of leaving the drug trade and criminality as a whole started entering my mind more and more. These sentiments were strengthened as my faith in my religion and knowledge of its teachings grew.

Religion

In every religion there is a promise of everlasting peace if you do what is right in this world. It also gave me a new identity – I was a Muslim. And with that came new precepts I lived by. As I learned more about my religion, I felt ashamed that I was selling drugs and so I would hide it. This helped in the sense that I no longer felt it was okay to sell drugs; I could no longer rationalize my behaviour. At the same time, I began to feel that my attention needed to be focused on doing good in the world. Over time, the deeper I got into religion, the more I began to truly feel criminality was wrong.

Although religion helped me to believe committing crime was morally wrong, it did not happen immediately. My views on criminality, especially that among Blacks, changed in an incremental way over time as my faith developed. In the beginning, I rationalized that alcohol and guns were legal to sell, and if you had the resources and access to capitalize off those trade markets, both products were more harmful than drugs. I also would argue that some drugs were actually legal to sell as well, but that the laws in this country criminalized the drug trade among the poor. With this rationalization, undergirded by an understanding of the laws and history of this country, I was firm in my view that selling drugs, as well as the violence that came along with it, were not problems (see Sykes & Matza, 1957).

During my incarceration, the prison did not offer anything that helped me feel differently. They offered a cognitive-behavioural program called "Thinking for a Change", which is an inappropriate name for a person like me who has had to constantly think about survival my whole life. Nevertheless, the goal was to help prisoners think differently. Such programs were for two hours, twice a week, for 12 to 18 weeks. In these programs there was a facilitator and about 15 to 20 prisoners. The curriculum centred on discussions to encourage thinking differently and pointing out that we would likely return to prison if we did not. One problem with that was that every person who committed the same crimes repeatedly in the class had made the conscious decision that they were willing to go to prison for whatever was to be gained from their criminality. The programs aimed to use the idea of being free as motivation to change. However, as I mentioned earlier, for a poor Black person relegated to living in the segregated and heavily policed ghetto of Newark, the notion of being free is complicated.

Education
The last facilitator, education, was extremely crucial for my desistance. As a child I was somewhat of a nerd – I loved school. However, I never made it past the ninth grade. So when I went to prison, I earned my general equivalency diploma. However, that was the highest level of education available in New Jersey prisons. Fortunately, in 2013, a group of citizens got together and found wealthy individuals and groups who were willing to donate money if they could develop an education program specifically for those in New Jersey prisons. The group put together a program called NJ-STEP, which consisted of a consortium of professors from some of the top colleges and universities in the state, including Rutgers and Princeton. More importantly, the prisoners were able to earn degrees from accredited colleges such as Rutgers (the program is offering up to a master's degree currently). This program is completely independent of the Department of Corrections.

Initially, I was intimidated because I never even graduated high school. I also did not know of anyone in my family or community who had graduated college. I believed college was for those with a level of intelligence well above my own. However, I had great professors and a strong work ethic and desire to excel that made me a good student. I was always a thinker, so I would read all the books that were given to us. One professor, Chris Hedges – a Pulitzer Prize winning journalist and New York Times best-selling author – would give us six to eight books to read in a single semester and I read them as carefully as possible. I would question why the writer chose certain words, research the etymology of the words, notice certain patterns in the writings, pay attention to the literary devices like tone, irony, and so on. Then, I would argue in my writings what I thought the writers were saying and/or trying to convey. Through access to my professors, along with their positive feedback on my writings and oral arguments in class, I began to believe for the first time that I too could do well in college.

Two readings, in particular, had the biggest impact on my realization that I did not have to be permanently relegated to criminality or the ghetto. The first was in the book *Narrative of the Life of Frederick Douglass*. There was a part in which he wrote about his slave master reprimanding his wife for teaching Douglass how to read. Douglass said his key to freedom was when the slave master said, "By teaching him how to read, he will be unfit to be a slave", and from that point his focus was learning to read, which greatly facilitated his escape from slavery (Douglass & Jacobs, 2000). I applied that to myself and decided I would also use education as my way to freedom.

The second was another idea from Frantz Fanon's (2007) book, in which he said something along the lines of "the first thing the native learns is to stay in his place and not go beyond certain limits". He was specifically writing about the colonized, but I see many similarities between the colonized and the poor person living in the ghetto. I immediately began to think of how the police would stop us when we were trying to go to affluent neighbourhoods, telling us we do not belong there and not to return. I thought of how the schools were designed to produce low-level workers, as well as how police officers would search us almost every day, placing us in the back of their police cars for long periods of time after they had already searched us and found nothing illegal. I realized that was a form of conditioning us to be comfortable with and normalized to detention and surveillance. At that moment I decided I was going to undo the conditioning that had been done to me. At that moment I strengthened my commitment to desist and to not allow incarceration, which the 13th Amendment says is the only time it is legal to enslave a person, to be something that would enslave my future.

CONCLUSION

America's prison system is not designed to assist those who are incarcerated to desist from criminality. Instead, the culture of dehumanizing practices that defines prison systems has an adverse effect on many people, as it did with me. Fortunately, I found strength, power, and the will to change in family, religion, and education. Unfortunately, the practices and policies of those running the prisons hindered the full potential of each one of those positive institutions, which made my transition to desistance more difficult and lengthier. America prides itself as being an advanced, first-world society that values freedom and equality, but those ideals are undermined and contradicted by our prisons. Their scale, their history, their colour, their conditions, and the inhumane treatment of the human beings subjected to them suggests America has a long way to go.

REFERENCES

Brown, Marilyn and Barbara Bloom (2018) "Women's Desistance from Crime: A Review of Theory and the Role Higher Education Can Play", *Sociology Compass*, 12(5): e12580.

Christian, Johnna (2005) "Riding the Bus: Barriers to Prison Visitation and Family Management Strategies", *Journal of Contemporary Criminal Justice*, 21(1): 31-48.

Douglass, Fredrick and Harriet Jacobs (eds.) (2000) *Narrative of the Life of Frederick Douglass, an American Slave and Incidents in the Life of a Slave Girl*, New York: The Modern Library.

Goffman, Erving (1958) "Characteristics of Total Institutions", in *Symposium on Preventive and Social Psychiatry* - April, US Government Printing Office, pp. 43-84.

Fanon, Frantz (2007) *The Wretched of the Earth*, New York: Grove Press

Maruna, Shadd (2001) *Making Good: How Ex-Convicts Reform and Rebuild their Lives*, Washington DC: American Psychological Association.

Merton, Robert K. (1938) "Social Structure and Anomie", *American Sociological Review*, 3(5): 672-682.

Sampson, Robert and John Laub (1995) *Crime in the Making: Pathways and Turning Points Through Life*, Boston: Harvard University Press.

Savolainen, Jukka (2009) "Work, Family and Criminal Desistance: Adult Social Bonds in a Nordic Welfare State", *British Journal of Criminology*, 49(3): 285-304.

Sykes, Gresham and Matza David (1957) "Techniques of Neutralization: A Theory of Delinquency", *American Sociological Review*, 22(6): 664-670.

ABOUT THE AUTHORS

Stephon Whitley received a bachelor's degree from Rutgers University, where he was awarded the Masterton Award for academic achievement. He lives in North Carolina and works for Industrial Areas Foundation, a social justice and advocacy organization.

Nathan W. Link is an Assistant Professor of Criminal Justice at Rutgers University in Camden, New Jersey.

Captor Story and Captive Story
Francis X. Kroncke

INTRODUCTION

In the spring of 1972, I entered Sandstone Federal Correctional Institution (FCI) to serve a maximum five-year sentence. As one of the "Minnesota 8", I had destroyed tens of thousands of "1-A" files of men about to be drafted to fight the Vietnam war.[1] Our initial indictment charge was "sabotage of the national defense". It evoked a "terrorist" image, as evoked by the judge's pre-sentence declaration that, "You gentlemen are worse than the average criminal who attacks the taxpayer's pocketbook. You strike at the foundation of government itself!" A bit of "W*ow!* This was my first offense".[2] I had only destroyed paper files, yet I shook the foundation of government? *Five years*. My shock has to be framed in the times. This was before the release of the "Pentagon Papers"[3] and the Watergate crimes of Nixon's hooligans. I was a 25 year old idealistic pacifist whose quest for radical change was anchored in a trust that at its core the System was not totally corrupt but reformable. Yet as shocking as "five years" might have sounded, little did I know what lay ahead – what it meant to be a Captive. Nor could I then have made sense out of this confounding insight – that by becoming Captive I would discover myself as Captor.[4]

Bizarre as it may seem, I gained this seminal insight into myself as a Captor the moment I accepted being a Captive. Soon thereafter I began to realize that I was the *Captor of my Captive self*! Unexpectedly, it was this insight into my Captor self that shocked me most. I was somewhat prepared to become an "inmate" and anticipated that being one was going to fuck me up a bit. Yet, I thought that my previous monastic experiences would help me adjust to another all male, highly structured institution where the daily discipline was unquestioning obedience to all rules. However, I had never thought of myself as a Captor, needless to say not as Captor of my own Captive self. *Truly weird.*

CAPTIVE STORY

As I took my first step *Inside* (as prisoners call a federal prison) so I unknowingly took my last step in the *Outside* world – referred to by prisoners as the "Free World". What did I leave behind outside? Basically, the everyday framework of intellectual and experiential references that

I shared with you as a non-prisoner. You remained a citizen with rights (personal, social, political) who could exercise a modicum of control over your private and public surroundings. I became a 'slave of the State'. At the time, I had no idea what that exactly meant. I knew the phrase, but it did not evoke any emotions, neither the fear nor dread, which were waiting for me. Quickly I learned that I had left behind the world that values common sense, logic, moral truths, decency, and freedom as I entered a locked-down, alien, terrorizing, and intensely degrading environment. My step Inside was also the beginning of a descent – into a bottomless pit, a hellish sector of Captive human existence best described as "where everything human is soon absent". Not unexpectedly, my white-male, middle-class, highly educated skin was also shed as I stepped into A&O (the Admission and Orientation room). What I never could have anticipated nor expected was the radical change about to happen in my sense of personal identity.

Prison's goal was to have me reidentify myself through retelling my personal story as Captive *inmate 8867-147* and only in vaporish memory as "Francis X. Kroncke". This re-identification and retelling of my personal story would condemn me to forever live as a Captive: constantly living in fear and dread of violent attack, with a broken human spirit, hopeless, and with an abiding sense of myself as worthless, a piece of social offal.

To discover your Captive story is more than a bit difficult because you have to look inside, twice: both prison's Inside and your own personal inside. Should you run out, commit a crime, and get locked up? Not really. But what you must do is not easy[5] – you can enter Inside but only if you are willing to execute an escape from your everyday "Free World" and "Go over the wall!" If you go over the wall of your everyday reality, heed this warning: "Dragons lie ahead!" because you will realize that there are two dimensions to *human* existence: the "Shadow realm" and the "Sunlight realm". These realms are *physically* entered and exited through identifiable geographical, spatial localities, and brick-and-mortar institutions. The journey through the Shadow realm is told through the Captive story and the one through the Sunlight realm through the Captor's story.

Inside's Shadow Realm and Outside's Sunlight Realm
Upon entering prison, if asked, "Where are you?" or "Where do you live?" I had readily accessible tools at hand to accurately answer. I might say, "I'm serving time in Sandstone FCI" or "I live in Hastings, Minnesota".

More, my saying that "I am an American" would provide multiple answers as to my location in terms of place and time: geographical, social, and cultural locations. In stark contrast I had no such tools available to aid me in understanding what was happening to my identity as I slowly became a Captive. Just the realization that I was a Captive threw me outside of any intellectual or emotional framework I had used to explain who "Francis X. Kroncke" was up to that time. I had never been asked or ever had any reason to ask, "Who are the Captives? Where are they located?" Moreover, I certainly would not have known where to look. There were no atlases handy with maps to help locate Captives.[6]

Listen up. There is an atlas that will reveal their locations. It is the exact atlas you use to locate where you are right now. The issue is not in finding an atlas as it is in knowing how to read the legend and follow directions. Sandstone, Minnesota, for example, is off Old Highway 61, northeast of the Twin Cities, just past Hinckley on your way to Duluth. Once in town just follow the signs to the FCI. Now, let me ask you to just accept for the moment that when you get there you also arrive at a physical and geographic location on the Inside where Captives live.

Prison is called many things: the penitentiary, the Big House, the slammer, the clink, and the like, but the Inside works as a good Captive locator term. Inside and Outside are interrelated and inseparable concepts, you cannot have one without the other. However, this is not a rigid duality.

I am actually saying that there is a physical geography to the Inside world of Captives. Prison is just one location. It happens to be a location where the worlds of Outside Captors and Inside Captives visually and viscerally interact. While walking around one locale, say the Inside, you shift into the other, Outside dimension here.

The transition from Outside to Inside usually happens at unpredictable times. For example. I am walking the main Yard's Inner Circle pathway when horns blare and screeching whistles pierce the air and – *Kazaam!* – armed guards are rushing *somewhere* and the loudspeakers boom, "Lock-up and Count! Lock-up and Count!", at which point I and hundreds of other prisoners immediately head Inside to the *safety* of the dorms. It is not worth one breath for me to ask, "What's up?" Someone, somewhere just got the news that his parole was denied and he lost it. I slump onto my dorm bed knowing that he will be in Solitary for a couple of weeks or so.

Some other prisoner, I bet silently to myself, is rifling through his locker as I close my eyes. When I awake, Outside "normality" should be back-on. *I hope so.*

As hard as your Captor self might be straining right now to believe me, just know that Captives have no problem in easily navigating between the Inside and the Outside. For them the stairway up and out of the underground, so to speak, is through the Shadow realm into the Sunlight realm. This Shadow realm is an Inside site where unsettling, disturbing, often cruel and evil things happen. It is where Captives gather and locate. In prison the daily routine centres around descents into and ascents out of various Shadow sectors. How a prisoner navigates and handles Shadow events determines if he will ever truly get out of the Inside or remain an imprisoned Captive all his life, "doing time on the Inside" even if released from the institution. Captors guard the border between the Shadow and Sunlight realms. Captives live Inside and venture Outside.

Captives spend their whole lives moving in and out of the Inside's Shadow realm into the Outside's Sunlight realm, which is the Captor's only realm. While Captors never intend to enter the Shadow realm, Captives purposively enter the Sunlight realm because that is where their crimes take place. In brief, the Shadow realm, with its institutions and organizations, is a lifestyle stopover area, where they enhance their skill development, networking, and promotions.

Sunlight and Shadow Stories
The Sunlight story expresses your upbeat, positive outlook on life. It makes you feel whole, healthy and happy. For some, it is the story of the "American Dream". For others, it is one of personal rescue from their own inner darkness, "Jesus Saves" or the mindful joy of "Be here now". Hearing it makes you feel that all is right with the world. It makes you feel glad to be alive and human. It fills you with a heartfelt sense that everyone can work together, doing and being Good: "Peace, Justice and the American Way!" It makes you want to dance in the streets and shout, "And God saw that it was good!"

The Shadow story takes you into hellish depths of darkness, of evil – both of the individual and group. It makes you moan the deep down dirty blues. It engenders feelings of depression, oppression, and degradation. The Christian interpretation of the biblical tradition tells a Shadow story of Original Sin, human depravity, and murderous family strife. Other Shadow traditions regale humans with like tales (e.g. that their flawed, savage human nature is sourced in inheritable violent genes) or some make a virtue out of selfishness ("Greed is good!"), or enslave through lies (the Nazis "Arbeit Macht Frei" – "Work makes you free!"). In a Shadow story other people – the "Other" – are always threats to you, named as "The Enemy", and often reviled with racist or sexist taunts ("The only good ____ is a dead ____!" "Slap the ____!"). *Note well*: my claim is that you have both a Shadow and a Sunlight story, and that they are dynamically interrelated. This means that you hear the Shadow story as an undercurrent in the Sunlight story, and vice versa.

In his Sunlight story, the Captor's self-perceived role is to carry out justice and protect society from the Shadow prisoners. On its own terms it is an upbeat, empowering story. In it the Captor is good and the Captives are bad. Of note, and a recurring theme, is that the Captor *claims that in his Sunlight realm there is no Shadow*—or at least that there should not be any Shadow. If he could, the Captor would obliterate the Shadow realm. In this vein I heard, more than once, a guard swear that he would love to "Kill every motherfucking con in this goddam joint!" Such a primal wish was ground for this key insight about the Captor's Sunlight story, that is, that it is not so much one about control and punishment as it is about the denial of the existence of the Shadow realm and/or an effort to obliterate it, along with all Captives in the process.

Pause: I need you to realize how critically important I find this Captor denial and desired obliteration of the Shadow to be. I admit that this confused me at first because of my own Captor upbringing. Let me ask, what are you answers to: What is prison's objective? Is it to reform and/or rehabilitate – turn bad guys into good guys? Is it to horrify and punish and so potentially scare guys into going straight? Or – as I judge them – are these questions wrongheaded? Instead, should you be *asking yourself*, "Are prisons more about *me* than about them? What is prison's objective in terms of my world? Is it to isolate me from the Shadow realm and keep me Outside in my Sunlight realm? In effect, for all practical purposes, to prevent me from entering the Shadow realm?" This is what I found to be true and factual, yet I realize that such an experiential insight can only become yours after you embody your own Shadow and Sunlight stories.

CAPTIVE STORY INSIDE A CAPTOR STORY

I chose to go to prison.[7] I consciously committed a crime that I intended to admit publicly to gain legitimacy as an antiwar speaker and activist. Once other prisoners figured that out they would look at me and howl laughing. "Man, who in their right *muddafucking* mind would choose to go Inside?" It was clear that going to prison was an option for me since I was a white, middle-class, highly educated male, but not so for the 99% plus other prisoners.

In light of my choice, two stories were being written, basically simultaneously. Being Inside was forcing me to discern and own a story I never thought I had – my own Captor story. Curiously, this story became clearer to me as I was discerning my Captive story as a subhuman "slave of the State". This is a very significant point. Unlike most prisoners for whom going to prison was part of a set of social expectations (of the underclass) – and so were quite aware of the Captor and Captive stories – I had never thought of myself as a Captor.

Frank, the Captor! I am sure I am not the only one who entered prison ignorant of what "reality" truly was, that is, that I was entering Inside into the Shadow realm. When I arrived from jail, somewhat irregular, I was put directly into solitary confinement. This (I eventually discerned) was part of a ploy on the part of the orientation group called the "Adjustment Committee". Theirs was an intense interrogation since they wanted to assess if I was a radical troublemaker before releasing me into the prison population. Was I like the Mafia guys who already knew what was up and would do time like a vacation holiday or was I this Kroncke guy a dyed in the wool, committed Marxist revolutionary? Possibly they had heard repeated the outlandish claim voiced by the federal prosecutor at my arraignment (re: indictment on "sabotage of the national defense") that I was "part of an international Catholic conspiracy led by the Berrigan Fathers and funded by Castro"? Or was I a namby-pamby nonviolent pacifist coward who was scared of his own shadow? They were unsure to perplexed because, in looking back, I can see that my being there threw them for a loop. They looked at me and saw a Captor like themselves. Like other war resisters I was, in the main, racially and culturally their kin, spoke like them, and so on. One of the *Minnesota 8*'s families actually owned a summer cabin down the road a bit in Sandstone, Minnesota. Lordy! We were not just from the same social class, we were neighbours.

While I did not have a clue about the Inside, I did recognize "them" in me. That was more unsettling than anything. This evoked the seminal insight that I, as 8867-147, was also one of them! This harsh somewhat schizoid reality met me at every turn. Old timers looked at me with pity, "Kroncke, you're pulling hard time!", meaning that my Captor skin was both being shed and renewed simultaneously. Consider Mr. Benson was my case worker. We chatted. He was a former Catholic priest, white, middle-class, and a social-worker. *Fuck!* He was me. *Hey, Mr. B, it's 8867-147, can you take me home to meet the wife and kids; a homemade meal!?* Everywhere I turned, new phrases, sentences, storylines emerged as my Captor story was unfolding its entwined storyline with my Captive story.

Frank, the Captive! For several hours the Committee worked to adjust me. They gave me both the overview as to how things worked Inside and a practical guide for daily living. They even gave me a work assignment. They made clear the role I was to play – I was slave, captive, convict: a prisoner of war. I was no longer citizen, son, theologian, nonviolent activist. I had fought their government and *lost!* I was their Captive. *Accept your fate! Bow down your neck!* It was now mine to shuffle along, not wail against my shackles and chains, and if I did protest, no *buts* about it, I would be beaten into submission. Fatefully, more than just being the State's Captive I was positioned as an enemy of their God, a statement repeated later by the Catholic Chaplain. I was at war with everything they valued, that is, I was striking at the foundation of not only American government but by doing so also at that pillar of Western civilization, the Judaeo-Christian biblical tradition. Without conscious intent, the Adjusters were teaching me how the Shadow realm operated. In effect they laid the seed for my growing awareness of myself as a Shadow Captive: the Other, Public Enemy, a foreigner, and most telling, as I came to discern, as *Girly Boy*!

To gain Captor control, it was critical for the Adjusters that they reorder my vision and understanding of prison reality. In prison's Shadow realm, time, space, the air, others, "now", and feelings are no longer autobiographical. Here is what keys the transition from the Sunlight down into the Shadow realm, namely, "I" as a Captive have no personal identity, rather I exist impersonally through my Shadow group identity as 'inmate', 'convict', 'outlaw', '*dogshit*' – 8867-147. In the most black and white terms I am a Captive of the Captors. Stop and catch the tectonic shift here. "Captive" is the only label the Captor needs—as all prisoners are one and the same.

This is a metaphysical re-organization, at the level that philosophers call ontological – in the realm of Being. Get this: As I transited from Captor to Captive, as I accepted living as a Shadow being – note this well! – I began to experience myself alive on the grand mythic scale. Now, I existed like Cain, Judas, the Evil One – a hellish denizen of the Shadow realm. Here I also started to grasp fleeting insights into the truly mythic story that my trial played out as the judge affirmed me as a secular Shadow creature, a "strike(r) at the foundation of government itself", a traitor in the camp of Benedict Arnold, and the forces of darkness. The confessional truth is that I was being reformed by the Inside's dark powers. I could not afford to lollygag and intellectually look back on my pre-prison years as I had to keep my eyeballs peeled as I advanced warily forward one Inside step at a time through the Shadow realm.

The Adjusters counseled me as to how a good Captive acts: "Do your own time". I was to submissively "serve time" and mark the cycle of moons and suns with prison's "Lock-up and Count!" routine – not by clock hours or days of the week. While I doubt if any of the Adjusters were conscious of their Shadow role as Captor, they knew what had to be done to maintain order on the Inside – break me down and have me accept myself as a *subhuman 8867-147.*

As Captors I am sure that the Adjusters were highly confident that the discipline of the penitentiary – "doing time" – would, as it had done to so many, inevitably transform me, actually transubstantiate me, that is, re-embody me as a Shadow Captive. For them the weird and scary world that the Inside was would without fail crush my spirit and have me scurrying back to the Catholic Chaplain swearing that once paroled I would go straight – "Forever!" More than that, they knew that I had to re-identify and be made to accept and possess my Captive story so that I, willingly or not, eventually – inevitably and inexorably in their minds – would step down the rungs to where they wanted me to stay, eternally in the Shadow sector "where everything human is soon absent".

Baffled, immobilized, downright confused: *I am Captor of myself as Captive.* Honestly, at the time I could not handle the psychic bedlam this insight unleashed. My survival instincts kicked in and within a short period of time I "adjusted" and slipped into the Shadow realm where I walked in lockstep with all the other prisoners and survived by being "inmate 8867-147", resigned to "do my time" and hope for an early release.

8867-147'S STORY: THE MAN'S GIRLY BOY!

I broke the rules of society, now I am doing so to this essay. This is 8867-147 stepping up into your face, Francis X.! You cannot keep my voice Captive. *Motherfreaker!* I know you are up to your old Captor tricks. But if you are not going to jump your Captor walls, then I will push your sorry ass over. *Reader*: A compelling story line always makes the heart go *thump!* Kroncke's talked to you about the Inside. Take a jog with me into how it *feels* – the heart of the Captive experience.

See, once Inside it took a bit of calendar time before their Adjustment took hold; they were patient. At first, I did handle being Inside a bit like my first days in the monastery. I readily accepted my digital moniker 8867-147 much like I had my monastic investiture name, Friar Otto, O.F.M., Conv. It was only a numerical silliness, so I told myself, and it did not really make me feel much differently. Fairly nonplussed, I looked at the other prisoners with a somewhat detached, almost academic eye. For a while I enjoyed regular weekly, quite chatty visits from family and friends. However, somewhere around ninety-days in, something inexplicable happened: I became fully Adjusted. To wit, I became one of them – a *subhuman*. This was not an intellectual shift. It was not the result of some radical analysis. It was not just an emotional shift – not simply that I got depressed or bummed out. It was of an order of magnitude I did not even know existed, a shift at once cosmic, personal, even genetic. What was happening? I can only give you an unsettling answer: *My body was no longer mine!*

I was suddenly present to myself in a way only other prisoners could grasp. Simply, I was no longer alive as only human. Much as the Adjustment Committee intended, I slipped down an experiential rung and met my Shadow self. Prison effectively re-embodied me as a subhuman. I became a subordinated, subjected, dispossessed, expendable, disposable, invisible entity. As they intended, in the eyes of the wardens and guards, "Francis X. Kroncke" was no longer physically present, replaced by 8867-147. Here was my first robust subhuman sense: one of disembodiment – they looked at me and saw only 8867-147. I was solely a numbered inventory of the State. As they intended, the initiatory Admission ritual made "francisxkroncke" disappear and disembodied 8867-147 floated into the prison population. Like a streetwalker, my body was no longer mine. It belonged to my pimp: "The Man". Now I was forever twice-bodied: Francis / 8867-147, never to be cleaved. Totally fucked-up, I urged people not to visit, restricting such moments to family members. I just about stopped writing to everyone. I became a slave, doing time, serving The Man.

As I became a subhuman I went way deep Inside into the darkest recesses of the Shadow realm where I ceased to experience myself as an individual, as a person with an identity, as a creature of time. The crucial insight here is that I underwent a qualitative physical transformation as I became a subhuman, as I lost my sense of what it meant to be human. I no longer knew who I was.

Being twice-bodied and treated by others as a subhuman meant having no privacy in any aspect. In prison's Shadow realm, there is no space provided where you can experience your humanity in any normal sense of the term. There is no place to go for a nanosecond of solitude – the johns are doorless, every tick-and-tock you are watched, you live exposed like a lidless eyeball. What may be incommunicable is the devastating impact of living within an utter absence of privacy – of never being left alone, of always being part of the Population. I even slept in dorms with up to seventy others who group snore, belch, and fart. It was this absolute loss of privacy – awake and asleep – that became the tipping point of my mutation into becoming a subhuman.

Five times around the clock I robotically responded to the command, "Lock up and count!" Twice more while asleep. The duty Hacks go on inventory runs: body counts and asshole numerations. They scan my blanketed body and check my digits at 3 a.m. – X a box, "Check 8867-147". All they want is my subhuman body, and since it is not a body I have ever known before I simply – ignorant naïf! – give them this body. So I surrender my subhuman self, let them do with me whatever they want: use me, abuse me, dispose of me. Slavishly I accept being a subhuman. I exist, as all slaves do, with my former one-body self-displaced somewhere out in some cosmic security locker, or something weird like that, as I slip into my twice-bodied subhumanity.

Horrified, I could not find a way to be present to others as a human being. I looked into the mirror and only saw what others saw: 8867-147, a subhuman. One condemned to forever exist as an alien other – a twice-bodied presence. I became what prison so effectively creates: a slave of the State. My body was being slowly, but surely sensately rewired. As a slave's body, my every physical act expressed my acceptance of domination. When ordered to strip and be searched, I complied. Emotionally, I lost my middle-class sense of shame, my sense of personal honour, my dignity. Servile, I bent over and spread my buttock cheeks. My presence clearly conveyed that now I was *The Man's Girly Boy*.

Now, one-bodied Captor reader, *Awake*! Subhumans sense the world just as humans do, but always with a de-humanizing twist. Man, I do not know if I can get you to make this leap, not so much in understanding as in feeling. In prison a kiss is a betrayal, always. Only Girly Boys get kissed! A simple touch, just a fingertip or a caress of a chin, is a prelude to rape. Eyes gaze upon you searching for points of entry, signs of weakness, ever ready to watch you disappear (get whacked). Smells are not for pleasuring rather what is sniffed is the aroma of your cowardice, the scent of your trembling terror as you kneel in submission, and the allure of the fright that oozes from your sweat as you walk the Yard, hyper-vigilant like hunted prey. Taste always rides upon sexual release: the breakfast donut is nipped at and mouthed letting you know that you'll like his cock. All eating is sexualized—the mess hall but a group orgy in symbolic dance. What you hear is always a variation of the basic equation of Inside survival: "Why shouldn't I waste the punk?" The punk being you – laughter rising from the poker round – hearing yourself wagered, your life tossed in as ante. So, do not make the mistake of thinking that subhumans do not feel.

Awake! Here's a deeper step down; a subhuman voice from "where everything human is soon absent". As a subhuman, I began to grasp the horror of what it means to be a female in patriarchal society – *Girly Boy!* Most prison stories are fundamentally wrong. Prison, it is alleged, is a male stronghold where the most macho and violent males are corralled and beaten into discipline by other super-males flexing the glistening muscles of steel death, brandishing the symbols of a potent sexual power. On some days it looks like that, but the appearance is quite illusionary.

With purpose and systematically, prison was transforming me into a female – the idealized woman of the patriarchal culture: submissive Eve. Here is a mythic She, a female who derives her meaning only and fully from her Man – who accepts being a derivative of his carnal rib. Like her I too became "bone of my bone, flesh of my flesh" as created from The Man. *I am his chattel and wear the clothing of khaki anonymity – which he finds fetching. He jealously protects me, constantly watches me in the daylight and in the night darkness of my time serving him. Ever courteous, he opens doors for me his helpless and hapless mate who patiently waits, keyless, cooing for my Man to unlock the knobless doors. I wait. I wait. I wait. He has a lock on the key to my heart.*

Majestically, it is his power, the fearsome force of his authoritative Inside power that makes me bend over and part my buttock cheeks. Silently scream: C'mon, it can't be, we're both guys! I, at any moment, am his: night, morning, afternoon delight. At any place: I am walking the hall and he commands, "Open your mouth!" He probes my ears, I rake my hair, shake out each shoe. ...and bend over. Oomph! It's quickly over, the backdoor bangs shut. So simple. So routine. I am The Man's Girly Boy.

Denying the Shadow Realm

Okay. 8867-147 just had to do his 'convict' thing. My Captor middle-class self-control is still challenging him, but he does bring me to the next key insight. Why am I keeping 8867-147 in the Shadow realm, speaking here in a Sunlight space to you, using the control of linear communication, and not, if he had his way, ripping at you, dumping on your racist, sexist, classist, sanctimonious ass...not helpful right now? But to give him his due, the question I have been pondering ever since release is why I, and so you, knew so little about the Shadow realm, even that it existed? What grounded our Captor story such that our higher education never told us its history or cultural role, nor its politics or mythic character? As you can see, to tell the Captive Shadow realm story is to open discussions about a social underclass, cultural outcasts, sexual violence, subhumans, and other depressing topics. Let me ask you: What is the mythic story we tell ourselves that grounds the vision and values of the Captor story?

Back then, I had no way of knowing that getting into prison would become the easiest part of my journey. I had no way of grasping either intellectually or emotionally that it was a One-way-in-No-way-out entrance into the dark, shadowy sector of the human mind and heart. So, it took me a while to realize that I was in a *mythic zone* – a place where the primal and primary stories of origin and cultural values are acted out daily.

What could it possibly mean to be a shadowy Captive? Just consider the words "captive" and "subhuman". What do they conjure up for you? What images come to mind? What feelings are aroused? Are you open to considering that when answering these questions or examining the images and feelings that arise that you reenact deep cultural Shadow and Sunlight

stories every day? If you are, then you will benefit from considering how
the biblical story of Genesis – Western culture's dominant story of human
origin – conditions how you answer the foregoing questions and determines
how you imagine and feel when responding.

Awake! One of the communication barriers that I continually encounter
when discussing the Sunlight and Shadow realms with its Captor/Captives
with Western and biblical people is their resistance to accepting that the
culturally dominant Sunlight story of origin in Genesis is one that implicitly
denies that there is any value to Shadow stories. Moreover, that Shadow
realm experiences are worthless, should be shunned, and, if possible, the
Shadow realm obliterated. Even if you are an avowed atheist or secularist,
can you sense how the Genesis stories frame the questions that you answer
culturally, such as: Does God exist? Why are humans here? What defines
human nature? Culturally, the story of Adam and Eve's "Fall" is referenced
to defend the claim that humans are inherently depraved – constantly
violent, endlessly warring, and self-destructive.

My scholarly self was quite shocked when I found that Inside everyday
prisoner conversations frequently cited Cain and Abel, Adam and Eve, the
curse of Ham, and other biblical references when talking about the big issues
such as Good and Evil, violence and nonviolence, justice and revenge. As
a philosopher/theologian[8] I can state unequivocally that the most vigorous,
impassioned, and outrageous discussions about life's Big Questions take
place Inside on a daily basis! There is a lot of down-time when "doing
time", and so more coffee-house like conversations, arguments, debates are
taking place during any given day in prison than on a university campus.

I found this biblical language aptly translated into the nonreligious
(secular) myth where the Hero slays the Dragon – he does not seek to tame
it and make it his house pet, that is, part of his personal life. His is a conquest
and vanquishment. As I read Western culture, secular values retain Genesis'
belittlement of the Shadow realm.

As attorney pro se, I had presented a "Defense of Necessity"[9] argument
to the jury, stressing that perilous times often require allegiance to a higher
law which necessitates violating a lesser law. Here, I argued that the Roman
Catholic moral tradition had strict requirements for assessing a war as a
Just War – and in Vietnam all were violated! More that the then recent
Documents of Vatican II, issued by an historic council, condemned Total
War and urged that

It is our clear duty, therefore, to strain every muscle in working for the time when all war can be completely outlawed by international consent. This goal undoubtedly requires the establishment of some universal public authority acknowledged as such by all and endowed with the power to safeguard on the behalf of all, security, regard for justice, and respect for rights ("Gaudium et Spes", 1965).

So, when the judge, after eight days of trial, made a final ruling that I and the testimony of thirteen witnesses (theologians, historians, Vietnam Veterans, ecologists, peace activists, and others) was "irrelevant and immaterial" and was *not to be heard* by the jury, it reflected his inability to hear and value a Shadow story. His actions stated that the Sunlight story (e.g. America in Vietnam as "saving the world for Democracy") had no Shadow chapters. Again, it was not that he listened, and through the jury's deliberation and judgment, heard and judged my Shadow story of nonviolent Resistance to Illegitimate Authority. Rather, the telling point is that he could not and did not let the jurors hear it because to do so would be to admit that America has a Shadow identity and story.[10]

This is the only way I can understand why the judge acted as he did, especially after allowing me an eight-day trial and thirteen witnesses. Do you sense the underlying Shadowy disturbance that permeated my trial? Can you sense the dissonance, uneasiness, noisiness, and general air of bafflement, even sinister intentions that were possibly afoot? We went from: "You can present a Defense of Necessity" to "I approve your witness list" to "Frank, you can proceed to closing argument" to "Everything which was said here for the last eight days is irrelevant and immaterial" to, finally, "You strike at the foundation of government itself! Five years in a federal penitentiary". All in all, things simply did not add up.

Likewise, in prison the official story was solely a Sunlight story – "Do your own time" and you will be rescued, saved, and once again sent Outside – "Free!" The way for any prisoner to make this story his own and obtain an early parole was for him to completely reject his Shadow story. I heard clearly that what I thought was my Sunlight story (altar boy, monk, peace activist, theologian, etc.) was actually a Shadow story and as such I was counseled to abandon it, reject it, denounce it, and so submit to re-formation. Despite my anchoring and my Resistance in a life-time's dedication to the Catholic Church and Jesus Christ, mine was not a story that held any truths or values that the prison counselors (including the Chaplain) wanted to or knew how to work with. Prison was not a place of transformation or forgiveness or reconciliation, rather it was a place of punishment, deprivation, humiliation and condemnation. Humorously, there was no penance in the *penitent*iary, so no forgiveness!

Prison's directive seemed clearly to be that I was to experience my Shadow story *not* so that I could value it and integrate it, and so become more fully human. Just the opposite: I was to be "scared straight" so that I would get a taste of being a Captive and then – based on this Captor logic – spit out my venomous past and submit to prison's adjustments and corrections. An actual Faustian Bargain was set before me: either remain a Captive forever or submit to being rescued by pledging never again to enter the Shadow realm. I was to forever forget, regret and denounce my Shadow story (which I had thought was my Sunlight story!). For most ex-prisoners such pledges were normally linked to commitments to enter rehab, therapy or move to "somewhere where no one knows your name". For me, I would have become a Sunlight star if I had repented, pledged my allegiance once more to Church and State, Judge and Archbishop, and dedicated the rest of my life to denouncing nonviolence, pacifism, civil disobedience, and such heretical notions as the One Family of all humankind.

ENDNOTES

[1] Learn about the "Minnesota 8" by visiting www.minnesota8.net. A follow-up action to the nationally largest ever Draft Board raid of the "Beaver 55" in Minneapolis and St. Paul, Minnesota (February 1970) for which no one was ever arrested and which included both the destruction of over 45 centralized urban Draft Boards and the theft of official State Director rubber classification stamps and destruction of this office. When the "Minnesota 8" were arrested, some FBI agents chanted and gloated, "Guess we got some Beavers now!" They were right.

[2] I was completing the second year of my "Alternative Service" as a Conscientious Objector as Program Director on staff at the Catholic Newman Center at the University of Minnesota which was, back then, a hot-bed of Catholic Radical activity led by Father Harry Bury (see http://www.harryjbury.com/HarryJBury/Welcome.html).

[3] Daniel Ellsberg was a witness at the trial of two of the "Minnesota 8" – myself and Mike Therriault – before he released the "Pentagon Papers" (see https://www.britannica.com/topic/Pentagon-Papers).

[4] My "growth" into awareness of this somewhat unsettling, if not psychotic (!), set of identities can be traced through the articles in *Cross Currents* from 1971 to today (see http://www.outlaw-visions.net/articles.htm).

5   I recommend that you do this inner search under the guidance of a licensed professional.
6   The web was not available back then! For a map see: https://www.bop.gov/locations/map.jsp.
7   See www.minnesota8.net and www.outlaw-visions.net.
8   I should qualify this with "as an *academic* philosopher/theologian". Many prisoners are quite "alert" and "sensitive souls" – the latter for whom life on Earth is a sector of Hell à *la* Jean-Paul Sartre.
9   A summary of the appellate decision can be found at: http://www.minnesota8.net/Trial-Documents.htm and full text at https://law.justia.com/cases/federal/appellate-courts/F2/459/697/381817/
10   See https://en.wikipedia.org/wiki/Shadow_(psychology)

What Can the Legal Profession Do For Us?
Formerly Incarcerated Attorneys and the Practice of Law as a Strengths-Based Endeavour
James Binnall

ABSTRACT

In recent years, the concept of strengths-based reentry has gained increased attention from scholars and commentators. Proponents of the strengths-based paradigm argue that the formerly incarcerated are far more than a collection of needs and risks. Rather, we bring unique skills to the reentry process that can be utilized to engage in generative activities that serve to diminish the stigma of a criminal history and to promote post-release success. Drawing on my own journey from prison to practicing attorney, this article contemplates the legal profession as one such generative activity. By serving clients at risk of criminal justice system involvement and organizing to promote experiential diversity at law schools and in the bar, many formerly incarcerated attorneys are engaged, often subconsciously, in ongoing stigma/shame management at the micro and macro levels respectively. For these reasons, this paper contends that the legal profession ought to be considered a viable, realistic option for formerly incarcerated students, as they possess the empathy to excel as attorneys and to use the law as a means of transforming their own self concept.

INTRODUCTION

Traditionally, risk-based and need-based paradigms have dominated reentry initiatives (Monahan & Skeem, 2016; Schlager, 2013; see also Andrews et al., 2011). Such paradigms presume that the formerly incarcerated possess a host of criminogenic deficits that, without targeted intervention, pose a substantial risk of recidivism (Maruna & LeBel, 2003). Conversely, strengths-based approaches to reentry and reintegration – rooted in restorative principles (Eglash, 1977) – move away from a conception of the formerly incarcerated as "merely liabilities to be supervised" (Travis, 2000, p. 7), and instead acknowledge that those who have spent time in prison come with a unique set of skills and attributes that can be exploited and utilized to aid in the desistance process (Burnett & Maruna, 2006; Hunter et al., 2016; LeBel et al., 2015). Proponents of the strengths-based approach argue "that the traditional risk-based paradigm that pervades the criminal justice system is not effective in understanding or implementing successful offender reentry and that a new narrative – a strengths-based approach – is necessary if we hope to make forward progress in our 'what works' efforts" (Schlager, 2018, p. 70).

Along these lines, many formerly incarcerated individuals seek out higher education as a means of successfully transitioning from imprisonment to freedom (e.g. Fretwell, 2019; Copenhaver et al., 2007). Research makes clear that for those who have spent time behind bars, higher education post-release can facilitate successful reentry (Halkovic, 2014). Generally, studies demonstrate that compared with formerly incarcerated individuals who do not pursue higher education, formerly incarcerated students enjoy better life outcomes and opportunities (Sokoloff & Fontaine, 2013), better economic and social mobility (Strayhorn et al., 2013), and a more promising future post-release (Livingston & Miller, 2014).

Navigating a path from prison to a college or university is a journey replete with obstacles. One of the most significant obstacles formerly incarcerated students face are the informal, interpersonal ramifications of a criminal history (LeBel, 2012). For most of us who have spent time in and adapted to prison, the stigma of a criminal conviction can make reentry and desistance exceedingly difficult (Haney, 2018; Petersilia, 2003; Travis, 2005). In the context of education, studies demonstrate that faculty (Copenhaver et al., 2007), staff (Winnick & Bodkin, 2008), and students (Halkovic & Greene, 2015) often exhibit prejudicial and even discriminatory attitudes toward the formerly incarcerated on campus. This stigma can have lasting consequences. For the formerly incarcerated who choose higher education – an endeavour that exposes one to a considerable degree of vulnerability – denigrating stereotypes are often internalized (Maruna et al., 2004). In this way, the formerly incarcerated may have difficulty shedding the 'criminal' label and ascending to the status of 'student' (Maruna & Roy, 2007; Maruna, 2001).

Research suggests that generative activities can help formerly incarcerated individuals to overcome the stigma of a criminal conviction (Hlavka et al., 2015; LeBel et al., 2015; Maruna, 2001). Engaging the formerly incarcerated in helping roles that contribute to society in prosocial ways can alter how community members view individuals with a criminal history, tempering the stigma of criminal justice system involvement ("The Second Mile") (Eglash, 1977). Further, when 'helpers' coalesce to advocate for policy reform relating to criminal justice issues ("The Third Mile"), such efforts can blunt the stigma of a criminal conviction for the formerly incarcerated population generally (LeBel & Maruna, 2009). In this way, generative, strengths work operates to attack stigma at the micro (individual) and macro (population) levels (LeBel & Maruna, 2009).

Institutions like the legal profession too often assess the value of inclusion and diversity from the perspective of those without a history of criminal justice system involvement (Clark, 2005). Such assessments typically ask, "What can formerly incarcerated individuals add to our profession?" In this article I take a different tact, asking, "What can the legal profession do for the formerly incarcerated?" Specifically, this article argues that the practice of law is a strengths-based, generative activity that can facilitate the destigmatization of the formerly incarcerated at the micro (individual) and macro (population) levels and, as such, ought to be conceived of and promoted as a legitimate educational option for those who have criminal justice system involvement.

I am a formerly incarcerated attorney who now helps other formerly incarcerated individuals achieve their goal of becoming a practicing attorney. I am also the Co-Founder and Co-Executive Director of the California System-Involved Bar Association (CSIBA), the first state-level bar association in the United States created exclusively for formerly incarcerated and system involved law students and attorneys (CSIBA, 2020). Drawing on my experiences as a reentering person, a law student, and now an attorney serving individual clients and engaging in grassroots organizing around this issue, I explore the legal profession from a strengths-based perspective. Two sources of data drive this analysis: my own reflective narrative and participant survey data from the 1ˢᵗ Annual CSIBA Convening.

Admittedly, I am not representative of all formerly incarcerated attorneys. I am a white male who had obtained an undergraduate degree and a master's degree prior to my incarceration. Accordingly, I was undoubtedly afforded opportunities that many with dissimilar demographic and educational profiles do not enjoy. Still, I believe my journey is illustrative. I, and many of my formerly incarcerated brethren, gravitated toward the law to help others like us and we continue to promote the legal profession as a means of effecting social change (e.g. Hopwood, 2018; Reza-James, 2020; Simmons,

2019). In these ways, through the practice of law, we manage our own stigma and that of our population.

Along these lines, this paper details the process of becoming an attorney before chronicling my own path from prison to the law, paying special attention to those pinch points that can derail a formerly incarcerated individual's quest to enter the legal profession. I then turn to an analysis of the legal profession as a strengths-based endeavour, drawing on Albert Eglash's four principles of restorative reentry and weaving in salient aspects of my own reentry process. Finally, the paper concludes by highlighting the benefits of a legal career for formerly incarcerated attorneys, suggesting that the practice of law can serve to mitigate stigma at an individual level and for our population writ large.

ENTERING THE LEGAL PROFESSION

Formal Access Obstacles

Becoming an attorney is a difficult task for anyone. For the formerly incarcerated, the journey comes with significant obstacles. At two distinct phases of the process, admission to law school and admission to the state bar (Aviram, 2020), an applicant must explain their criminal history and prove that they are of 'good moral character', a vague standard that has been the topic of considerable debate (for a review see Rhode, 2018). This task, which almost always requires admitting fault and establishing a record of rehabilitation, is an exacting standard for those with criminal justice system involvement who are by default deemed 'risks' to the profession (Binnall, 2009; Rhode, 1985).

Admission to Law School

To win admission to law school, not only must one complete their undergraduate degree, but they must also score well on the Law School Admission Test (LSAT). For formerly incarcerated applicants, they must also provide an explanation of their criminal record. In response, schools may ask for an in-person interview, additional court documents, and/or reference letters attesting to an applicant's 'moral character' (Weissman et al., 2010).

In recent years, legislative efforts have eased application barriers for prospective formerly incarcerated students (Evans et al., 2019; Vuolo et al., 2017). For example, in 2020, California passed Senate Bill 118, a measure that forbids public and private institutions of higher education from "inquir[ing] about a prospective student's criminal history on an initial application form or at any time during the admissions process before the institution's final decision relative to the prospective student's application for admission" (Senate Bill No. 118, 2020). Still, S.B. 118 came with exceptions. Of note is the professional licensure exception to S.B. 118, which allows law schools to continue to inquire about criminal history as part of their admission screening process (Vest et al., 2020).

An insidious by-product of up-front criminal record application questions is what some term "application attrition" (Rosenthal et. al., 2015). One study revealed that when faced with a criminal record inquiry, nearly two-thirds of college applicants forgo applying altogether (Rosenthal et al., 2015). Though research on application attrition among formerly incarcerated law school applicants is scant, a recent report by the Stanford Center on the Legal Profession and the Stanford Criminal Justice Center suggests that application attrition also plagues legal education (Cohn et al., 2019). Their "survey of 88 individuals with criminal records suggests that concerns about satisfying moral character requirements deters interested individuals from applying to law school" (Cohn et al., 2019, p. 5). These findings are all the more troubling when one considers that the U.S. population of formerly incarcerated citizens is disproportionately comprised of racial minorities (Alexander, 2012). In 2018, while Black and Latinx citizens made up only 28% of the overall U.S. adult population, they were 56% of the U.S. prison population (33% and 26% respectively) (Gramlich, 2020). In this way, law school criminal record questions likely serve to racially homogenize an already older, whiter profession (Beaulieu, 2018; Johnson Jr., 1996).

Thus, the current reality is that the vast majority of formerly incarcerated law school applicants will encounter a criminal record question during the law school admissions process, which may deter many from applying. Those that do apply will then be forced to prove to their prospective law schools that they possess good moral character – the same task they must undertake when applying for admission to a state bar after completing law school (Aviram, 2020).

Admission to the State Bar

Once a student has completed law school and passed a bar exam, they must once again prove they possess the requisite character to practice law

(Swisher, 2008). Accordingly, all law school graduates seeking to practice law must take part in their jurisdiction's moral character and fitness process, which is designed to establish that "graduating law students... meet high standards of moral character" (Arnold, 1997, p. 63). Though very few applicants without a criminal history are denied bar admission for character issues (Rhode, 1985, p. 16), for the formerly incarcerated, "the application process can become particularly troublesome" (Arnold, 1997, p. 63). As Devito (2008, p. 158) notes, "[a]pplicants with criminal acts in their past often face a heightened burden of proof of good moral character".

The moral character and fitness process begins with the requirement that bar applicants complete a lengthy questionnaire that asks a series of significantly probing questions, including a criminal history inquiry (Stone, 1995). For an applicant with a conviction, bar examiners will almost always seek out additional information about the criminal offense. Once an applicant has provided the requested information to the relevant jurisdiction, the process for determining fitness of character depends on the favored jurisdictional approach (Binnall, 2009; Carr, 1995). In some jurisdictions, a conviction disqualifies an applicant from admission to the bar, while in others a conviction merely amounts to a presumptive disqualification, creating a "rebuttable presumption that an applicant with a record of prior unlawful conduct lacks the requisite character to practice law" (Carr, 1995, p. 380).

To rebut the presumption that one with a conviction history lacks good moral character, bar applicants are forced to, once again, produce evidence of their rehabilitation. Certain jurisdictions use "specific guidelines and requirements for judging an applicant's moral character" (Graniere & McHugh, 2008, p. 223), giving applicants direction on how to prove their fitness, termed as the "guided approach" (ibid, p. 236). Other jurisdictions, like California, take an "[u]nguided approach", basing admission on "subjective personal feelings, beliefs and attitudes of the Bar Examiners" (ibid, p. 223). For an applicant, the unguided approach offers little direction, making the entire process incredibly stress inducing. Accordingly, as one scholar notes, "[a]pplicants with incidents of unlawful conduct in their past can find the road toward bar admission confusing and unpredictable" (Anderson, 1997, p. 63).

Winning admission to law school and then to a state bar are events that clearly serve as redemption rituals (Maruna, 2001). In a formal way, becoming a law student and then a practicing attorney confers a high level of trust and respect to a formerly incarcerated person. Still, such accolades tend to fade over time, leaving a formerly incarcerated attorney to find meaning in a profession where very few of us exist. In response, most formerly incarcerated attorneys – myself included – turn to helping others, doing the strengths work necessary to garner acceptance for ourselves and our population.

MY JOURNEY FROM CELL TO COURTROOM

In May 1999, at age twenty-three, I was the driver in a fatal DUI wreck that claimed the life of my passenger, my best friend. A year later, a jury convicted me of DUI Homicide and a judge sentenced me to three and a half to seven years in prison. I went inside on 16 May 2000.

Early in my imprisonment, I realized I could never go back to the life I had built prior to my offense. Once a college wrestling coach and an elementary school teacher, I was no longer fit to do either. I lost both positions when I was convicted. I also lost any hope that I would ever again run a wrestling practice or command a classroom.

I remember little of my first year in prison. Paranoid and petrified for months on end, I moved through that initial stretch in a fog. As I emerged from the haze of getting dug in, I began to contemplate my future. Prison officials assigned me to teach GED classes at the institution's school. Being around it again – the classroom and the students – reminded me of my prior existence. There, I espoused education as the key to a better life. Doing so eventually motivated me to look inward and I started to plan my own educational journey post-release.

My first step was to identify a profession or job that would inspire my passions and afford me enough to live comfortably. My career would also need to be one that permitted formerly incarcerated individual's entrance. While I considered social work and psychology, I settled on the law. The law involves adequate compensation and offers a platform for intellectual combat – like a wrestling match only a bit different. Still, I had no idea if I would be allowed to practice.

My initial step in my pursuit of a legal career was to research the possibility. Having no computer or online access, I asked my friends and family on the outside to assist me. What they told me was encouraging. While they noted that professional standards for attorneys seemed vague

– to possess 'good moral character' – in the overwhelming majority of jurisdictions, those standards were not categorical nor insurmountable for one with a felony conviction. Nonetheless, while a possibility, a career in law was far from a certainty. I would have to take a chance. I would have to enroll in law school not knowing if I would ever be licensed. I decided to roll the dice.

After settling on the law, I petitioned my Superintendent (Warden) to take the Law School Admission Test (LSAT) while incarcerated. After an initial denial, prison authorities eventually agreed to allow me to test. On a Saturday in October 2001, I took my LSAT's on the inside. The experience was surreal. My proctors were the Vocational Guidance Director and a Corrections Officer. The former encouraged my efforts, while the latter chastised me on test day, chiding "I have no idea why you are doing this, you are an inmate, and that is all that you will ever be, in here or out there!" I never forgot his admonition and have called on it many times as motivation in the nearly two decades since he uttered those words.

I scored well on my LSATs and subsequently applied to eleven law schools while still a prisoner. I was accepted to ten, but nine explained that I could only start my studies after my period of parole had ended. One school – Thomas Jefferson School of Law in San Diego, California – not only accepted me, but also awarded me a full tuition scholarship based on my LSAT score. Initially, I calculated that this acceptance, and permission to start my studies while on supervision, would win me favour with the parole board. I was wrong. At my minimum, the parole board denied my release and delayed my review for a year (a year "hit"). I was devastated. Luckily, my new law school was willing to defer my admission. My dream was still alive.

When I was re-reviewed, I was finally granted my freedom. In June 2004, I paroled to my parents' home in Boston, where I would spend the next six months waiting for word on my interstate compact application. In December 2004, I was granted my transfer and on 1 January 2005, I moved to San Diego to begin my legal studies. In the end, I loved law school. I enjoyed the systematic, linear character of the law. I also enjoyed the power that the law conferred. Knowing how to 'think like a lawyer' is empowering. I graduated near the top of my class, went on to complete a graduate law degree (LL.M.) at the Georgetown University Law Center and passed the California Bar Exam on my first try in 2008. Still, I had no idea if the State Bar of California would admit me.

I began my application to the State Bar of California in my 2L year (second year). The application was lengthy and asked explicitly about criminal convictions. One look at the specificity of the inquiries and it became abundantly clear that I would need assistance with this process. The attorney I hired had never represented an applicant who had spent time in prison. She was unsure about how to proceed and cautious about advising me on my chances. Her strategy was to simply document my conviction, history of alcohol use, and efforts to rehabilitate my character post-release. In short, she recommended complete honesty and a detailed accounting of my life. I wrote from the heart and left nothing out. Thirty pages later, my personal statement and history of alcohol use were complete. The entire process was incredibly traumatizing. In those pages, I relived the worst experience of my life, admitting fault in the death of my close friend and begging the state bar for forgiveness.

In California, when a bar applicant has a criminal history, the State Bar will typically invite the applicant to an Informal Conference. While not officially an adversarial proceeding, this administrative hearing is nonetheless stress inducing. Along with my lawyer, I agreed to attend the Informal Conference. Not long into the meeting, I was struck by the tone of my interrogators. Much like my two prior parole hearings, questions at the Informal Conference were seemingly designed to corner an applicant. Here my incarceration experience served me well, as I had previously taken part in two rather intense parole hearings. Using the lessons I learned during those hearings, I was able to avoid any major missteps. One month later, I was given a positive Moral Character and Fitness Determination and was sworn in as a licensed California attorney in December 2008.

When I was sworn in as an attorney, I suspected that my reentry had come to a successful close. I had done what precious few do after a significant period of incarceration. Still, I wondered. I struggled with self-esteem issues, imposter syndrome, and a general fear that I was simply an outlawed 'other' masquerading as an upstanding professional (Binnall, 2007). This "status fragility" plagued me early in my legal career (Tietjen & Kavish, 2020; see also de Botton, 2004). But as I began to work with formerly incarcerated people – hundreds since my swearing in – I found an identity and a purpose. Soon enough, I was not EG1900 of the Pennsylvania Department of Corrections. Instead, I am California Attorney 260974. For me, this was the power of strengths work and a closer look through the lens of restorative or strengths-based reentry illustrates just how the practice of law can mitigate the stigma of a criminal conviction.

A STRENGTHS-BASED FRAMEWORK

Strengths-based reentry models demand that the formerly incarcerated draw on their skills and attributes to contribute meaningfully to the communities to which they return (see Hunter et al., 2016). By doing so, those with criminal justice system involvement can influence how others view them. When the formerly incarcerated give back, they demonstrate a "worthiness for forgiveness" that deserves redemption or "reputational rehabilitation" (Maruna, 2009). In this way, strengths-based approaches help those who have been incarcerated overcome the stigma of their conviction and build a pro-social self-concept (Maruna, 2001).

Still, those who espouse a strengths-based approach make clear that *how* the formerly incarcerated give back is an essential question. Discussing the work of Albert Eglash (1958, 1977) – the psychologist credited with the term "restorative justice" – Maruna and LeBel (2009, p. xx) note:

> [T]raditional forms of restitution or punishment may be enough to satisfy the needs of justice, but may not be enough to earn a person's redemption. He (Eglash) argued that redemption involved going a 'second mile'. Not just paying one's debt (justice) but also demonstrating one's worthiness for forgiveness by giving something back to the community.

Expanding on this principle of 'giving back', Eglash suggested four elements of "restorative reentry". Arguably, when these elements are met, "formerly incarcerated individuals experience redemption rituals which in turn shed perceptions of stigma and signal control over one's own life" (Smith, 2018, p. 3).

Strengths Work is Constructive Activity:
Entering the Profession to Help Our People

For those who are formerly incarcerated, work is an interesting concept. Inside, many of us were given jobs that were menial. They gave us boring, mindless, repetitive tasks that did little to inspire and certainly – at cents per hour – and did not afford us much financial comfort. Upon release, many of those same types of jobs are all that are available for those of us with criminal justice system involvement (Becker, 1968; Kling, 2006). Strengths work is different. As Eglash and others explain, strengths work must "involve constructive activity that contributes tangible benefits, especially to harmed communities" (Smith, 2018, p. 3).

Prior studies suggest that formerly incarcerated individuals gravitate toward helping professions (Halcovik & Greene, 2018). As Halkovic and Greene (2018, p. 773) note, "research findings suggest many students who have spent time in jail or prison enroll into the human services fields, as opposed to more financially lucrative fields because they have a drive to serve those society has dealt the least favorable hands". Similarly, Andrew Winn, a formerly incarcerated scholar and Director of Project Rebound at California State University, Sacramento points out, "Many of the students who have incarceration experiences are really drawn towards majors like sociology, psychology, criminal justice, and social work. Those also tend to be the majors that speak most about the experiences of previously incarcerated people and those with convictions..." (Davis, 2020).

My Choice to Study Law

When I began my legal studies, I had no intention of representing criminal defendants or formerly incarcerated law students. I sought to leave the worlds of crime and incarceration forever. But studies suggest that I am the anomaly. For many of the formerly incarcerated attorneys I have represented or have come to know, the call of helping others like us drew them to the legal profession (Aviram, 2020). As Aviram (2020, p. 78) found in her interviews with justice system involved attorneys in California, "[a]ll of them, without exception, mentioned their experiences in the criminal justice system as catalysts for their decision to become lawyers, and most specifically to help [sic] their disenfranchised population". My own ongoing research with formerly incarcerated law students and lawyers suggests strong support for Aviram's findings and ostensibly demonstrates that members of our population seek out the law as a platform for performing meaningful, constructive work.

Strengths Work is Creative and Generative:
Empathizing in Service of Others

When formerly incarcerated lawyers assist other criminal justice system involved individuals, they are engaged in creative, generative strengths work (Eglash, 1957). Acting as a wounded healer (Brown, 1991) or a profession ex- (White, 2000), a formerly incarcerated attorney who goes the 'second mile' brings to the practice of law a special expertise that makes them valuable, primarily because they can empathize with our population's struggles (Binnall, 2009; West, 2012). In line with this element of Eglash's formulation then, the most obvious strengths work a formerly incarcerated attorney can undertake is the representation of those facing criminal charges or who are formerly incarcerated (Maruna & LeBel, 2009).

Research suggests – outside of the legal context – that such helping behaviour benefits the helper (LeBel, 2007; Maruna et al., 2004). In particular, in a study of 228 formerly incarcerated individuals involved in a prison reintegration program, LeBel (2007, p. 18) found "a majority of those who counseled new reentrants, those recently released from prison or otherwise less advanced in their reintegration, were more likely to express satisfaction with life and less likely to possess a criminal attitude". Similarly, LeBel and colleagues' (2015, p. 116) research revealed "those who worked as staff members exhibited prosocial attitudes and beliefs, a sense of psychological well-being, and a general satisfaction with life" (see also Heidemann et al., 2016; Perrin et al., 2017). Though scant, burgeoning empirical research focused on the wounded helper paradigm strongly suggests that "becoming more involved in helping others appears to have a positive impact on the psychological well-being of formerly incarcerated persons and possibly acts as a sort of buffer against criminality as well" (LeBel, 2007, p. 18).

In assisting members of our population, formerly incarcerated attorneys necessarily re-work a delinquent past into a source of relevant wisdom (Maruna, 2001). This wisdom combines empathy with an intricate understanding of how criminal justice systems and processes work in practice (Halkovic & Greene, 2015). Importantly, for formerly incarcerated attorneys, empathetic representation is holistic, extending to issues of gender, race, and poverty. In a nutshell, formerly incarcerated attorneys tend to have lived lives similar, if not analogous, to those of their clients. We see ourselves in our clients and for many of us their tangible successes feed our transition from 'criminal' to 'attorney'. Thus, by bringing 'holistic experiential empathy' to the practice of law – a development endorsed by many legal scholars (see Gallacher, 2012; Westaby & Jones, 2018) – formerly incarcerated attorneys can better serve both their clients and themselves.

My Own Practice

Initially, my legal practice was limited to criminal appeals. Working with an established solo practitioner for the first year of my career, I gained invaluable experience crafting briefs and then arguing their merits. Soon though, my practice took a different turn. In 2009, I founded my own law practice, specializing in the Moral Character and Fitness Determination for applicants who are formerly incarcerated. When I began to help those like me who sought to change their lives through legal education, I soon realized that I brought a unique perspective to my profession. Not only could I empathize with the pain and stress my clients faced having to recount the details of their criminal conviction, but I could also thoughtfully counsel clients with respect to other aspects of their reentry experience. In this way, my criminal history is now a tool in my lawyering arsenal rather than a stigmatizing mill weight around my neck.

Strengths Activities as Self-Determined, but Guided: Choosing to Use Our Experiences

In his formulation of strengths-based principles, Eglash (1977) asserts that for generative strengths work to positively impact the desistance process, it must first be voluntary. In this way, strengths work respects the agency of the formerly incarcerated (Vaughan, 2007).

For formerly incarcerated attorneys, drawing on our past as a tool in the practice of law is an intensely personal, risk-laden prospect. The law is an occupation rife with snobbery and judgement. Choosing to reveal a history of incarceration – our "invisible stripes" (LeBel, 2012) – can damage an attorney's reputation among colleagues, opposing counsel, and members of the judiciary. Thus, the decision to become a wounded healer or a professional ex- is a salient one with which most formerly incarcerated attorneys struggle. As Goffman (1963) noted, while one with a history of criminal conviction is 'discreditable', one who reveals that history is often 'discredited' (see also Hogan, 2020).

Eglash (1957) also suggests that strengths work must be guided. As he notes, "Only a skillful guide can encourage a man to go a second mile. I suspect that the best guide is a man who has himself gone through it" (ibid, p. 621). In making the decision to reveal a criminal history, many of us turn to the formerly incarcerated who have come before us, seeking out advice on whether and how to employ our incarceration experience in the practice of law. What has developed in the United States is an informal network of remarkable individuals that have transcended the horrors of incarceration, become attorneys, and now offer their advice to those struggling to achieve similar success (see Directly Impacted Lawyers and Legal Professionals, 2016). In this way, most formerly incarcerated attorneys perpetuate layered, helper-oriented practices that typically include pro bono efforts to assist other prospective formerly incarcerated attorneys.

Disclosing My Status

Throughout law school, I disclosed my convicted status to only my close friends and a handful of professors. My first public acknowledgment of my criminal history came in my first published work – a law review note. The feedback I got was somewhat predictable – some offered support and others reacted with condemnation. Because of my conviction history, I was denied opportunities for summer internships, asked to leave study groups, and was summarily told, by more than one hiring committee, that academia was not a place for me. Still, once I became an attorney, after careful consideration and at the urging of other formerly incarcerated attorneys, I voluntarily chose to share my past with clients. Ironically, while I am now 'discredited' among many of my professional peers, disclosure has given me a measure of credibility among those I serve. For this reason, I have never regretted revealing my incarceration history.

Strengths Activities and Esprit de Corps:
Coming Together to Combat Stigma

The final element of Eglash's (1957) model suggests that strengths work is collective. He notes that "restitution is a creative act, and the way is open for group discussion" (ibid, p. 621). As Maruna and LeBel (2009, p. 71) explain, "[i]f Eglash's "second mile" (the helper orientation of the "wounded healer") is primarily an act of stigma management, as we have argued, then these forms of "reintegration advocacy" might be thought of as going a "third mile"". In their formulation of this 'third mile', scholars suggest that "for the formerly incarcerated who identify as having transformed their identity long ago, the importance of group networks remains integral to maintaining efforts toward larger socio-political change" (Smith, 2018, p. 4).

In the past few years, the issue of inclusive legal education has gained considerable attention (Kennedy, 2019). In response, law schools have considered altering admission criteria and method of instruction (Escajada, 2019; Garth, 2020), while state bar officials have increasingly demonstrated at least a willingness to allow formerly incarcerated individuals into the profession (see In re Bar Application of Simmons, 2017). Nonetheless, reform on this front has been glacial. Law schools still ask about criminal history, despite the likelihood of application attrition, and state bar officials repeatedly muddy the moral character analysis (Rhode, 2018). In response, formerly incarcerated attorneys have begun to coalesce to form interest groups dedicated to public education, direct service, and policy analysis (e.g. CSIBA, 2020; see also Allen, 2021).

Organizing for Change

In my own career, I am proud to have been a part of the formation of one such organization. In 2018, the Stanford Criminal Justice Center hosted a first-of-its-kind event entitled, "Roundtable on Law School and Bar Admission for People with Criminal Records". The gathering brought together academics, practitioners, State Bar of California officials, and several formerly incarcerated individuals. From this event, the California System-Involved Bar Association (CSIBA) was born. In summer 2018, I co-founded CSIBA along with Frankie Guzman, a formerly incarcerated attorney (UCLA School of Law), a former Soros Fellow, and the Director of the Youth Justice Initiative at the National Center for Youth Law. In March 2020, we hosted 150 attendees at our 1st Annual Convening at the UCLA School of Law (87% of attendees were formerly incarcerated). Formalizing the helper community that has long operated in the shadows, CSIBA offers our population a sense of hope and a workable plan for success. And thus far, CSIBA has proven impactful, demonstrable through feedback from attendees at our 1st Annual Convening.

Data collected at our convening revealed that respondents found the gathering both inspirational and useful.[1] Nearly all respondents (97%) indicated that they believed the convening was very informative, while 87% reported that the convening covered issues relevant to participants' efforts to enter the legal profession. Qualitative data also revealed the need for CSIBA and its mission. As one respondent stated, "this conference was specific to our situations, so much better than other resources". Similarly, another attendee noted, "the stories were inspiring and gave me a new perspective and hope for me and my kid's future as well as the future of those I hope to help".

The mission of CSIBA is to demystify the process of becoming an attorney. Along those lines, we offer hope and a plan to those who seek to enter the legal profession with an incarceration history. We strive to empower a new generation of formerly incarcerated attorneys who seek to give back to our population. In sum, as one respondent stated, "I really enjoyed hearing all of the testimonies (at the convening) because it gives me hope to continue pursuing my dream and hopefully one day I'll be able to advocate for the individuals who have been underrepresented".[2]

When I contemplated a career in law from my prison cell, I had no idea where to find information. Nor did anyone else. No one knew for sure whether a formerly incarcerated person could even become an attorney. Even law school admissions' personnel were taken aback when my people on the street made inquiries. Today, that has changed. There are many formerly incarcerated attorneys in the United States. And perhaps more importantly, there are now many sources of information for those of you who may be considering a career in law.[3]

CONCLUSION:
A PITCH FOR THE LAW

My work assisting formerly incarcerated individuals has helped me cope with my own insecurities and self-esteem issues. By helping others reach their goal of becoming an attorney, I have come to feel less like an outsider. I am now recognized as a leading expert in my field of practice, a classification far from that of 'criminal' or 'convict'. Over the past 12 years, I have formally represented dozens of clients with an incarceration history – all are now practicing attorneys in California and in other jurisdictions across the country. Notably, none of my former clients have been subject to any disciplinary action since their admission to the profession.

My goal here is not to promote the practice of law for the law's sake, but surely though the profession is enriched by our inclusion. No, instead my goal is to endorse the law for what it can do for the formerly incarcerated. The law can provide the formerly incarcerated an opportunity to draw on their empathy and knowledge in service of our population through individual and group efforts. What we receive in return is acknowledgement that we have transcended our 'criminal' status, given back, and organized to ensure that the formerly incarcerated attorneys who come next face but a fraction of the discrimination and prejudice many of us encountered early in our careers. In this vein, I hope you will consider a career in law – not for them, but for us.

ENDNOTES

1   61 of 150 attendees completed our exit survey (40% response rate).
2   All responses were anonymous. Data on file with author.
3   CSIBA has multiple resources on our website (www.csiba.org) and you can contact us at casysteminvolvedbar@gmail.com.

REFERENCES

Alexander, Michelle (2010) *The New Jim Crow: Mass Incarceration in the Age of Colorblindness,* New York: The New Press.

Andrews, Don, James Bont and Stephen Wormith (2006) "The Recent Past and Near Future of Risk and/or Need Assessment", *Crime & Delinquency*, 52(1): 7-27.

Arnold, Richard (1997) "Presumptive Disqualification and Prior Unlawful Conduct: The Danger of Unpredictable Character Standards for Bar Applicants", *Utah Law Review*, 1: 63-100.

Arthur, Allen (2021) "Clearing a Path from Prison to the Bar", *Reasons to be Cheerful* – June 21. Retrieved from https://reasonstobecheerful.world/formerly-incarcerated-people-pass-bar-exam/

Aviram, Hadar (2019) "Moral Character: Making Sense of the Experiences of Bar Applicants with Criminal Records", *Manitoba Law Journal,* 43(4): 1.

Beaulieu, Maria (2018) "The Underrepresentation of Racial and Ethnic Minorities in Legal Occupations", University of Maine – May. Retrieved from https://digitalcommons.library.umaine.edu/cgi/viewcontent.cgi?article=1316&context=honors

Becker, Gary S. (1968) "Crime and Punishment: An Economic Approach", *Journal of Political Economy,* 76(2): 169-217.

Binnall, James (2007) "They Released Me From My Cage…But They Still Keep Me Handcuffed: A Parolee's Reaction to *Samson v. California*", *Ohio State Journal of Criminal Law*, 4: 541-553.

Burnett, Ross and Shadd Maruna (2006) "The Kindness of Prisoners: Strengths-based Resettlement in Theory and Action", *Criminology and Criminal Justice*, 6(1): 83-106.

California System-Involved Bar Association (2020) Available at: www.csiba.org.

Clark, Michael D. (2005) "The strengths perspective in criminal justice", in Dennis Saleeby (ed.), *The Strengths Perspective in Social Work Practice (4th edition),* Boston: Allyn and Bacon, pp. 97-112.

Cohn, Caroline, Debbie Mukamal and Robert Weisberg (2019) *Unlocking the Bar: Expanding Access to the Legal Profession for People with Criminal Records in California* – July, Stanford: Stanford Law School, Stanford Center on the Legal Profession & Stanford Criminal Justice Center.

Copenhaver, Anna, Tina L. Edwards-Willey and Bryan, D. Byers (2007) "Journeys in Social Stigma: The Lives of Formerly Incarcerated Felons in Higher Education", *Journal of Correctional Education*, 58(3): 268-283.

Davis, Tamar Sarai (2020) "California 'bans the box', protecting formerly incarcerated people in the college admissions process", *Prism* – November 12. Retrieved from https://www.prismreports.org/article/2020/11/12/california-bans-the-box-protecting-former-felons-in-the-college-admissions-process

De Botton, Alan (2004) *Status Anxiety,* New York: Pantheon.

DeVito, Scott (2008) "Justice and the felonious Attorney", *Santa Clara Law Review,* 48(1): 155-158.

Eglash, Albert (1977) "Beyond Restitution: Creative Restitution", in Joe Hudson and Burt Galaway (eds.), *Restitution in Criminal Justice,* Lexington: D.C. Heath, pp. 91-129.

Eglash, Albert (1958) "Adults Anonymous: A Mutual Help Program for Inmates and Ex-inmates", *Journal of Criminal Law and Criminology*, 49(3): 237-245.

Escajeda, Hilary G. (2019) "Legal Education: A New Growth Vision Part I - The Issue: Sustainable Growth or Dead Cat Bounce? A Strategic Inflection Point Analysis", *Nebraska Law Review*, 97(3): 710-711.

Evans, Douglas N., Szkola, Jason and St. John, Victor (2019) "Going Back to College? Criminal Stigma in Higher Education Admissions in Northeastern US", *Critical Criminology*, 27(2): 291-304.

Fretwell, Michelle (2019) "Punishment Beyond Bars: Pursuing Higher Education with the Degree of Incarceration", *McNair Scholars Research Journal*, 14(1): 9.

Gallacher, Ian (2012) "Thinking Like Non-Lawyers: Why Empathy is a Core Lawyering Skill and Why Legal Education Should Change to Reflect its Importance", *Syracuse University Libraries SURFACE* – July 26. Retrieved from http://surface.syr.edu/cgi/viewcontent.cgi?article=1005&context=lawpub

Garth, Bryant G. (2020) "Having it Both Ways – The Challenge of Legal Education Innovation and Reform at UCI and Elsewhere: Against the Grain and/or Aspiring to be Elite", *U.C. Irvine Law Review*, 10: 387-388.

Goffman, Erving (1963) *Stigma: Notes on the Management of Spoiled Identity*, New York: Simon and Schuster Publishing Co.

Gramlich, John (2020) "Black imprisonment rate in the U.S. has fallen by a third since 2006", *Pew Research Center* – May 6. Retrieved from https://www.pewresearch.org/fact-tank/2020/05/06/share-of-black-white-hispanic-americans-in-prison-2018-vs-2006/

Graniere, Anthony, and Hilary McHugh (2008) "Are You In or Are You Out? The Effect of a Prior Criminal Conviction on Bar Admission and a Proposed National Uniform Standard", *Hofstra Labor and Employment Law Journal*, 26(1): 223-269.

Halkovic, Alexis (2014) "Redefining Possible: Re-visioning the Prison-to-College Pipeline", *Equity & Excellence in Education,* 494-512.

Halkovic, Alexis and Andrew Cory Greene (2015) "Bearing Stigma, Carrying Gifts: What colleges can Learn from Students with Incarceration Experience", *Urban Review*, 47: 759-782.

Haney, Craig (2002) "The Psychological Impact of Incarceration: Implications for Post-Prison Adjustment", in Jeremy Travis and Michelle Waul (eds.), *Prisoners Once Removed: The Impact of Incarceration and Reentry on Children, Families and Communities*, Washington (DC): Urban Institute, pp. 33-66.

Heidemann, Gretchen, Julie A. Cederbaum, Sidney Martinez, Thomas P. LeBel (2016) "Wounded Healers: How Formerly Incarcerated Women Help Themselves by Helping Others", *Punishment & Society*, 18(1): 3-26.

Hlavka, Heather, Darren Wheelock and Richard Jones (2015) "Ex-offender Accounts of Successful Re-entry from Prison", *Journal of Offender Rehabilitation*, 54(6): 406-428.

Hogan, Samantha (2020) "Maine hires lawyers with criminal records to represent poor residents. The governor wants reform", *ProPublica* – October 14. Retrieved from https://www.propublica.org/article/maine-hires-lawyers-with-criminal-records-to-defend-poor-residents-the-governor-wants-reform?utm_source=facebook&utm_medium=social&fbclid=IwAR3QEgWNtBTpAjMzrLFfrkUqvxSbTf09UukHZeY73SsoDiVahsPDO6xRE8#1004370

Hopwood, Shon (2018) "The Legal Profession Puts Itself on an Unsupportable Pedestal*"*, *Student Lawyer*, 47(4): 119-125.

Hunter, Bronwyn, A. Stephen Lanza, Mike Lawlor, William Dyson and Gordon Derrick (2015) "A Strengths-Based Approach to Prisoner Reentry: The Fresh Start Prisoner Reentry Program", *International Journal of Offender Therapy and Comparative Criminology*, 60(11): 1298-1314.

Johnson Jr, Alex M. (1997) "The Underrepresentation of Minorities in the Legal Profession: A Critical Race Theorist's Perspective", *Michigan Law Review*, 95(4): 1005-1062.

Kennedy, Deseriee A. (2019) "Access Law Schools & Diversifying the Profession", *Temple Law Review*, 92(4): 799-811.

Kling, Jeffrey R. (2006) "Incarceration Length, Employment, and Earnings", *American Economic Review*, 96(3): 863-876.

LeBel, Thomas P. (2012) "Invisible Stripes? Formerly Incarcerated Person's Perceptions of Stigma", *Deviant Behavior*, 33(2): 89-107.

LeBel, Thomas, Matt Richie and Shadd Maruna (2015) "Helping Others as a Response to Reconcile a Criminal Past: The Role of the Wounded Healer in Prisoner Reentry Programs", *Criminal Justice and Behavior*, 42(1): 108-120.

Livingston, Lindsey and Jody Miller (2014) "Inequalities of Race, Class, and Place and Their Impact on Post-Incarceration Higher Education", *Race and Justice*, 4(3): 212-245.

Maruna, Shadd (2001) *Making Good: How Ex-Convicts Reform and Rebuild their Lives*, Washington (DC): American Psychological Association.

Maruna, Shaad and Thomas P. LeBel (2003) "Welcome Home: Examining the "Reentry Court" Concept from a Strengths-Based Perspective", *Western Criminology Review*, 4(2): 91-107.

Maruna, Shaad and Thomas P. LeBel (2009) "Strengths Based Approaches to Reentry: Extra Mileage Toward Reintegration and De-stigmatization", *Japanese Journal of Sociological Criminology*, 34: 58-80.

Maruna, Shadd, Thomas P. LeBel, Nick Mitchell and Michelle Naples (2004) "Pygmalion in the Reintegration Process: Desistance From Crime Through the Looking Glass", *Psychology Crime and Law*, 10(3): 271-81.

Maruna, Shaad, and Kevin Roy (2007) "Amputation or Reconstruction? Notes on the Concept of "Knifing Off" and Desistance From Crime", *Journal of Contemporary Criminal Justice*, 23(1): 104-124.

Monahan, John and Jennifer Skeem (2016) "Risk Assessment in Criminal Sentencing", *Annual Review of Clinical Psychology*, 12: 489-513.

Petersilia, Joan (2003) *When Prisoners Come Home: Parole and Prisoner Reentry*, New York (NY): Oxford University Press.

Reza, Antonio (2020) "How Quarantine Makes the Case for House Arrest as an Alternative to Prison", *ABA for Law Students* – May 6. Retrieved from abaforlawstudents.com/2020/05/06/how-quarantine-makes-the-case-for-house-arrest-as-an-alternative-to-prison/?fbclid=IwAR3au7voVRm8nSpKeS0t6Hy7gjA1 BNmGj21vqqRH2QTn--qMcC2pDy4fmq4

Rhode, Deborah L. (2018) "Virtue and the Law: The Good Moral Character Requirement in Occupational Licensing, Bar Regulation, and Immigration Proceedings", *Law and Social Inquiry*, 43(3): 1027-1058.

Rhode, Deborah L. (1985) "Moral Character as a Professional Credential", *Yale Law Journal*, 94(3): 491-603.

Rosenthal, Alan, Emily NaPier, Patricia Warth and Marsha Weissman (2015) *Boxed Out: Criminal History Screening and College Application Attrition*, New York: Center for Community Alternatives.

Schlager, Melinda D. (2018) "Through the Looking Glass: Taking Stock of Offender Reentry", *Journal of Contemporary Criminal Justice*, 34(1): 69-80.

Schlager, Melinda D. (2013) *Rethinking the Reentry Paradigm: A Blueprint for Action*, Durham: Carolina Academic Press.

Simmons, Tarra (2019) "Transcending the Stigma of a Criminal Record: A Proposal to Reform State Bar Character and Fitness Requirements", *Yale Law Journal Forum*, 128: 759-771.

Smith, Justin, M. (2020) "The Formerly Incarcerated, Advocacy, Activism, and Community Reintegration", *Contemporary Justice Review*, 24(1): 43-63

Sokoloff, Natalie J. and Anika Fontaine (2013) *Systemic Barriers to Higher Education: How Colleges Respond to Applicants with Criminal Records in Maryland*, New York: John Jay College of Criminal Justice.

Swisher, Keith (2008) "The Troubling Rise of the Legal Profession's Good Moral Character", *St. John's Law Review*, 82(3): 1038-39.

Tietjen, Grant and Kavish Daniel (2020) "In the Pool Without a Life Jacket: Status Fragility and Convict Criminology in the Current Criminological Era", in Jeffrey Ian Ross and Francesca Vianello (eds.), *Convict Criminology for the Future*, London: Routledge Press, pp. 66-81

Travis, Jeremy (2005) *But They All Come Back: Facing the Challenges of Prisoner Reentry*, Washington (DC): Rowman and Littlefield Publishers.

Travis, Jeremy (2000) *But They All Come Back: Rethinking Prisoner Re-entry, Research in Brief – Sentencing and Corrections: Issues for the 21st Century*, Washington (DC): U.S. Department of Justice, National Institute of Justice.

Vaughan, Barry (2007) "The Internal Narrative of Desistance", *British Journal of Criminology*, 47(3): 390-404.

Vest, Noel, Andrew Winn, Sonja Tonnesen-Casalegno and Emily Blake (2020) "Celebrating Banning the Box in Higher Education in California", *Root and Rebound* – October 27. Retrieved from https://rootandrebound.medium.com/celebrating-banning-the-box-in-higher-education-in-california-e50bf01e0f06

Vuolo, Mike, Sarah Lageson and Christopher Uggen (2017) "Criminal Record Questions in the Era of "Ban the Box"", *Criminology & Public Policy*, 16(1): 139-165.

Weissman, Marsha, Alan Rosenthal, Patricia Warth, Elaine Wolf and Michael Messina-Yauchzy (2010) *The Use of Criminal History Records in College Admissions Reconsidered*, New York: The Center for Community Alternatives.

West, Robin (2012) "The Anti-Empathetic Turn", in James Fleming (ed.), *Passions and Emotions*, New York: New York University Press, pp. 243-288

Westaby, Chalen, and Emma Jones (2018) "Empathy: An Essential Element of Legal Practice or 'Never the Twain Shall Meet'?", *International Journal of the Legal Profession*, 25(1): 107-124.

Winnick, Terri A. and Mark Bodkin (2008) "Anticipated Stigma and Stigma Management Among Those to be Labeled "Ex-con"", *Deviant Behavior*, 29(4): 295-333.

CASES CITED

In re Bar Application of Tarra Denelle Simmons, 190 Wn.2d 374, 414 P3.d 1111. 2018 Wash. LEXIS 268.

LEGISLATION CITED

California Legislative Assembly (2020) *Public Safety (2019-2020), Senate Bill No. 118*. Retrieved from https://leginfo.legislature.ca.gov/faces/billTextClient.xhtml?bill_id=201920200SB118

ABOUT THE AUTHOR

James M. Binnall is an Associate Professor of Law, Criminology, and Criminal Justice at California State University, Long Beach, where he is also the Executive Director of Project Rebound. Dr. Binnall is a formerly incarcerated person who spent just over four years in prison. While incarcerated, he took his LSATs and was accepted to law school. Once released, Dr. Binnall earned his JD and LL.M., was admitted to the State Bar of California, and received his Ph.D. in Criminology, Law and Society from University of California, Irvine. A practicing attorney, he represents law students in the State Bar of California's Moral Character and Fitness Determination process and is the Co-Founder/Co-Executive Director of the California System-Involved Bar Association, a bar association comprised entirely of formerly incarcerated and system-involved law students and lawyers. His research explores the civic marginalization of those with criminal convictions and access to the legal profession for those with prior carceral involvement.

The Contradictions of Prisoner Life and Rehabilitation: An Auto-ethnographic Life Sentence Experience

Daniel Micklethwaite

ABSTRACT

With the current Conservative government employing, once again, punitive tough on crime, tough on sentencing rhetoric, the U.K. criminal justice system may well be embarking on another voyage into ineffective attempts at crime prevention and prisoner rehabilitation. Since 2008, I have been a life sentenced prisoner. This reflective auto-ethnographic study draws on lived experience, informal observations, and personal communications to help unpack some of the many factors that play a role in prisoner rehabilitation and its continued failure. A core part of this study is the role of masculinity within the prisoner experience. Within the prisoner experience is the continued impact of powerlessness, disenfranchisement, and social exclusion that operates to reinforce negative masculine pressures. There is a need for radical change in the way prisons are conceptualized in media and political spheres. Prisons may be part of a solution to social problems, but not in their enduring vogue.

INTRODUCTION

Despite an enduring and media focus on sensationalist crimes and extreme criminal figures, the lives and experiences of the prisoners remain largely hidden. The social construction of certain crimes leads to what Stanley Cohen (1980) historically labelled as a 'moral panic'. Examples include Cohen's (1971) original research on the Mods and Rockers at Brighton beach in the 1950s and, more recently, the public outrage and political response around the release of John Warboys, an individual who had committed a series of rapes against women. The construction and dissemination of such examples not only creates public fear, but also does very little to make visible the deleterious dimensions of the prisoner experience. This is important because prisons do not and have never satisfied the mandate of crime reduction. Indeed, prisons are spaces that produce and perpetuate significant harms. Whether as result of prisoner's subsequent future crimes or the personal damage accumulated throughout a sentence, these harms inevitably find their way into mainstream society.

Despite endless political 'tough on crime' rhetoric such as the historical war on drugs in the U.S, the introduction of indeterminate public protection sentencing and policy around meting out 25-year minimum tariffs for knife crime orientated murder in the U.K., prisons continue the trend of rehabilitative failure. This alone justifies continued research into the mechanisms of this failure. This critical focuses on specific prisoner sociological phenomena and lived experience, arguing therein are inherent contradictions that militate against successful rehabilitative outcomes. Masculinities, specifically toxic masculinities, are a pervasive theme throughout prison sociology and prisoner experience (De Viggiani, 2012; Jewkes, 2005). Research has explored the dynamics of prison phenomena and masculine prisoner identity. Michalski's (2015) theory of prison violence does this well. The qualities of toxic prison masculinities are difficult to reconcile with the ideas of prisoners going on to lead pro-social crime free lives. Nonetheless the prisons rehabilitative machine impacts significantly on the prisoners therein (Crewe, 2009). In the 1990s, the mode of prison rehabilitation underwent significant change through the establishment of prison based cognitive behavioural interventions (Maguire, 1995), along with the application of the Risk, Need and Responsibility model (RnR) (Andrews et al., 2011) to the management of prisoners. The contradiction appears, here, to be that despite research showing the RnR model impacting significantly on the prevention of crime and offending (Mcguire, 1995; Andrews et al., 2011), prison populations and recidivism continue at high levels. In this paper, the author's lived experience is operationalized through autoethnographic methodology to explore and make visible the incongruence, showing the tensions between prisoner phenomenology, prison process, and prison rehabilitation.

REVIEW OF THE LITERATURE

Sykes (1958) classic deprivation model provided an early apparatus for explaining the production and reification of prison culture and prisoner identities. The nuts and bolts of this model contends that the pains experienced as consequence of incarceration and the inflicted deprivations therein moderate over prisoner behaviour and adaptations, manifesting prison culture. An alternate but also classic approach to understanding prison life is the importation model (Irwin & Cressey, 1962). This model argues that prisoners import facets of their pre-prison identities into the prison upon incarceration. When exposed to the qualities of the prison experience these dynamics moderate to produce prisoner identity and prison culture. Both models have explanatory power and, as Michalski (2015, p. 3) states, "elements of deprivation importation and situational effects influence the behaviours of inmates generally and prison violence in particular". When considered together these models can be understood as an integration model of prison culture and prisoner identity.

Goffman (1959) considered that identity, or self, represents a dynamic akin to that of a theoretical performance. This being comprised of front stage performances of socially congruent and purposeful behaviour, and backstage performances whereby the more personal, emotional, and private parts of the self can be expressed in a safer setting. A powerful moderator of the front stage presentation of self is that of fronting or the front. This is the way in which people, in this case prisoners, select and construct appropriate available fronts as modes of self-presentation and preservation in given social dynamics. The concept of fronting in prison culture is well established in the literature (Crewe, 2009; de Viggiani, 2012, Jewkes, 2005). "Wearing a mask" is arguably the most common strategy for coping with the rigours of imprisonment, and all prison researchers will be familiar with the sentiment that prisoners feel it necessary to adopt a facade while inside" (Jewkes, 2005, p. 55). In prisons, and indeed in wider society, such performances hold a pervasive masculine quality. de Viggiani (2012, p. 3) writes that "prisons are essentially microcosms of wider society where individuals perform their gender within the "rules" of the social group". The quality of this gender prison performance is described as intermale dominance and subordination, where relationships are constructed around the performance and reproduction of multiple masculinities (ibid). Such masculine prison culture can be understood as instrumental in phenomena of cultural conformity, social hierarchies and status, emotional concealment, and institutional reinforcement (Crewe, 2009; de Viggiani, 2012; Jewkes, 2005; Bandyopadhyay, 2016; Newton, 1994). These prisoner identities, performances and culture are symbolic of what is known as the prisoner code. "While actual levels of adherence to the code appeared to differ between groups of prisoners and between prisons, there was a consistent finding among studies in men's prisons of a professed code with similar elements" (Newton, 1994, p. 195).

As Crewe (2009) demonstrates in an ethnography at HMP Winchester, this prisoner code is an enduring and pervasive dynamic in the prisoner experience. This is not a code one necessarily reserves the control to get in or out of. To a greater or lesser degree, the prisoner will be impacted by and must negotiate this masculine code. Masculine or gendered codes and norms are visible throughout society. The armed forces, the police, and the building site are all spaces that include such themes. It is important to note that it is not a sex difference but a quality of socially constructed phenomena (Messerschmidt, 1986). There is now a wide base of literature around masculinities and a full review of this field is beyond the scope of this article. Of relevance, however, are the understandings that masculinities are an entrenched part of social and psychic landscapes, which are entangled with experiences and expressions of power and control, and that many of the manifestations there-of can be considered toxic or harmful hegemonies (see Connell & Messerschmidt, 1993; Messerschmidt, 1986; Newburn & Stanko, 1994; Remy, 1990).

Within the prison it is the toxic and harmful aspects of masculine hegemony that tend to become inflated and evermore powerful. Michalski's (2015) theory of prison violence makes the mechanics of this clear. Michalski's (2015) utilizes the resource structuralism paradigm to explain how prisoners face an environment of resource poverty regarding their access to identity resources. He notes, "[v]irtually every aspect of the prisoner experience threatens inmates' masculinity and strips away the various layers of their gendered identities that might include self-sufficiency, autonomy, heterosexual relations and fatherhood" (ibid, p. 1). In an environment that has such a deleterious ontological impact, Michalski argues that prisoners place a greater emphasis on those resources that are available. These are identity resources, of a symbolic quality, such a social status, honour, and respect. Many of these concepts can be understood as examples of how hegemony and the prisoner code are enacted. "Within male prison systems almost anywhere in the world, the evidence indicates that the key symbolic resource underlying the inmate status hierarchies involves various displays or evidence of masculinity" (ibid, p. 5).

A major and effective vehicle for the acquisition of these symbolic resources is violence congruent with the prevailing toxic hegemony on the prisoner code. "In effect, inmates earn respect mainly by using violence as a form of moralism to express grievances, settle disputes and protect themselves" (ibid, p. 6). There are of course, other practices that are employed that influence the acquisition of symbolic capital. de Viggiani (2012) cites social phenomena such as banter, one-upmanship and the use of exercise and sport. Importantly, however, is the recognition that the use of these practices and resources are mechanisms for the reproduction and reinforcement of toxic hegemonic prison culture. It is well documented that the prison machine plays a significant role in the causes and continuation of these harms, in the ways in which prisoners adapt to survive prison (Newton, 1994; Jewkes, 2005). Indeed, to this end de Viggiani (2012, p. 4) writes, "Prison authorities can, moreover, reinforce a hegemonic social system through measures to control behaviour and instil order and discipline. In this regard prisons may not recognise their culpability in reinforcing exploitation and social inequality". What this brief and limited exploration of prison sociological literature lays bare is the longstanding knowledge that prisoner experience includes aspects that are both malignant and damaging.

Despite the entrenched prison hegemony, the prison institution is charged with the role of rehabilitating its residents as part of its responsibility towards reducing crime, recidivism and protecting the public. Already, then, a contradiction begins to emerge in the prison mandate of both punishing and rehabilitating. The notion of rehabilitation in prisons is not new and the role of psychology is an enduring of prisons on prisoner experience. The modes and instruments of the prison rehabilitative and psychological movement have undergone significant change and development over the past hundred or so years. Given the injuring size, breadth, and significance of the prison institution in the western world, advocates and actors within prison rehabilitative and psychological roles face a huge challenge and carry a significant responsibility. The prison is nothing if not far reaching, made clear by Bierie and Mann's (2017) citation of the world prison population figures that in 2015 the U.K. saw 86,000 people incarcerated. Bierie and Mann (2017) go on to present an encouraging account of the beneficial contributions from psychology two improvements around prison function and outcomes, stating "it would be hard to find a prison in the western world without at least one psychologist dedicated to applying their training to the operation of the prison" (ibid, p. 480). This account explores ethical prison practice, treatment over warehousing prisoners, and understanding relationship dynamics within the prison. Reference is made to the finest Stanford Prison Experiment (Zimbardo, 1972), which "revealed, powerfully, that prisoners and guards were not so very different from each other (or the rest of us)" (Bierie & Mann, 2017, p. 481).

Since the 18th century psychological thought has provided ever evolving lenses through which to understand prisoners and their criminal aetiologies.

Cesare Lombroso (1876) pioneered a movement known as Biologism. This was developed around the idea that criminals were identifiable through specific biological differences, such as beady eyes or the shape of one's head, which differentiated them from the normal civilised non-criminal. Such notions have been long dispelled but, historically, represented cutting edge scientific an anthological ideology. Subsequent paradigm shift in psycho-criminological thought include the study of body type, Somatotype's, (Sheldon, 1949), Neurological explanations (Hill & Pond, 1952), Psychodynamic models (Bowlby, 1951; Freud, 1953), conditioning and operant models (Skinner, 1938, 1965), social theories (Nietzel, 1979), and cognitive behavioural theories (Ross & Fabiano, 1985). There is not, nor is there likely to be anytime soon, a silver bullet approach toward criminal aetiology or prison rehabilitation. The cognitive-behavioural approach, however, has fast become the preferred model since its emergence in prisons in the 1990s.

The cognitive-behavioural shift can be understood as a response to the prevailing dogma that 'nothing works' in prison rehabilitation and corrections (Mcguire, 1995). This enabled advocates to attribute the political attractive label of evidence-led scientific interventions. This is the very well-known what works (Mcguire, 1995) movement in prison to rehabilitation and corrections. Cognitive behaviouralism is a synthesis of cognitive and behavioural psychologies (Mcguire, 1995; Palmer, 2009; Ross & Fabiano, 1985). Cognitive behavioural interventions can therefore include a wide range of psychosocial behavioural skills and devices. For example, social skills training (Priestley et al., 1984), emotional management skills (Mcdougall et al., 1987), and moral reasoning skills (RosenKoeter et al., 1986). Evidence led cognitive behavioural interventions have yielded consistently impressive findings in comparison to other rehabilitative and correctional interventions.

A standard evaluative research tool is that a meta-analysis, which involves the aggregation and side by side analysis of large numbers of experimental studies (Mcguire, 1995, pp. 7-8). In his early meta-analysis is of the 'what works' literature Mcguire (1995, p. 18) found that cognitive behavioural multimodal programmes "afforded one of the strongest prospects of systematic reduction of reoffending rates". Findings from Redondo and colleagues (1999) support this finding within their meta-analytic finding that cognitive behavioural interventions were the most effective tool available "causing a 23% reduction in recidivism on average" (Joy Tong & Farrington, 2006, p. 4). Pearson and colleagues (2002) also undertook meta-analysis of rehabilitative and correctional inventions, concluding favourably on the efficacy of cognitive behaviouralism. Similarly, Joy Tong and Farrington (2006) conducted a meta-analysis into the effectiveness of the Reasoning and Rehabilitation programme. The reasoning and rehabilitation programme is a cognitive behavioural intervention. They state, "[a] meta-analysis showed that, overall, there was a significant 14% decrease in recidivism for programme participants compared with controls. This programme was effective in Canada, the USA and the UK. It was effective in community and institutional settings, and for low risk and high-risk offender" (ibid, p. 3). Of particular relevance in their study is there finding that, "[i]n community settings, there was a 27% increase in recidivism for controls compared to programme participants, or conversely at 21% decrease in recidivism for programme participants compared to controls" (ibid, p. 18). They further noted that, "[i]n institutional settings, there was a 16% increase in recidivism for controls compared to programme participants, or conversely a 14% decrease in recidivism for programme participants compared to controls. Both effect sizes were statistically significant. The effect size in community settings was not significantly greater than the effect size and institutional settings" (ibid).

Joy Tong and Farrington present this positively in relation to prior research showing community intervention being more successful. I explained this as a potential moderator effect of the prison and associated restrictions placed on prisoners. The variable of 'volunteering' to participate is also used as a factor as "most evaluations conducted in institutional settings had voluntary participants, while participants in many of the community evaluations had been compulsorily assigned to the R+R programme as part of a probation or parole order" (ibid, p. 20).

There is, curiously, no reference or consideration given to the moderator of prison culture and hegemony over this finding. This is certainly an interesting idea, the empirical testing of the inverse relationship between inflated hegemony and reduced intervention efficacy within the prison setting. The significance of prisoners volunteering to participate in programmes is also potentially ambiguous. Crewe (2009) provides an excellent critique of the power imbalance prisoners face in this regard. Here, Crewe explains how programmes are inextricably linked to risk assessment devices that are instrumental in prisoner sentence progression prisoners and are therefore ensnared in a coercive process of satisfying risk based rehabilitative targets. From his perspective, then, the validity of the volunteer variable needs to be weighed against its coercive context.

McNeill (2006) attends to the issue of coercion in relation to the dynamics of probation offender oversight. He notes:

> Overconfidence in the prospects for affecting change through treatment had permitted its advocates both to coerce offenders into interventions (because the treatment provider was an expert who knew best) and to ignore offenders views of their own situations (because offenders were victims of their own lack of insight). Perhaps most insidiously of all, within this ideology coerced treatment could be justified in offenders own best interests (McNeill, 2006, p.41).

Ergo the volunteer variable that Joy Tong and Farrington (2006) operationalize in their conclusion may actually be something altogether different. McNeill (2006, p. 42) provides an interpretation as "the offenders constrained consent". This also raises critical arguments around the epistemological assumptions implicit in the meta-analytical method. As Maguire (1995, p. 9) states:

> Perhaps the most telling observation is that, like many average figures, the mean effect size conceals wide variations. This there are studies in which much larger reductions in re-offence rates were obtained, and others in which recidivism rates actually worsened. Amidst this variation some clear trends can be detected concerning the ingredients of programmes with higher or lower kinds of effectiveness in reducing re-offending.

Despite the robustness of these empirical measures there is also a lot of information that is missed. The quality or robustness of the data that is fed into the meta-analytic device is also open to criticism. As Joy Tong and Farringto (2006, p. 21) acknowledge, "[a] shortcoming of the meta-analytic technique is that studies of different methodological quality might be given equal weight (Lipsey & Wilson, 2001). Some of the older and smaller-scale studies were methodologically weak, but they had low weightings in the meta-analysis because of their low sample size. One could arguably, then, interpret this method as a looking glass but from a distance. There is thus much that is missed and the reductionism therein does little to illuminate the dynamics of the 'how' or epistemology underneath the reported trends. There are, as Joy Tong and Farrington (2006) offer, techniques for reducing such problems, but there is clearly much more to be learnt than can be gleaned from the numbers alone. Also, the numbers should not be accepted as absolute.

There is another aspect of cognitive- behaviouralism that is also embedded in positivist scientific ideologies. The application of prison rehabilitation and corrections cannot be understood without reference to risk and 'what works' ideologies and technologies. Whereas cognitive behaviouralism represents a specific mode of interventions, the 'risk' dimensions of this movement do not. "When practitioners say they are doing 'what works', they usually mean that they are drawing on Risk Need Responsivity (RNR) principles or related products" (Maruna & Mann, 2019, p. 7). Within the prison system, the allocation of cognitive-behavioural resources are directed by assessment made with RNR technologies that are "[c]entral to informing programme selection decisions is the application of assessment tools which have been underpinned by the risk, need and responsivity principles" (Ramsey et al., 2019, p. 264).

Andrews colleagues (2011, p. 735) assert that the RNR model underlies some of the most widely used risk-needs offender assessment instruments, and is the only theoretical model that has been used to interpret the 'offender' treatment literature. They adopt a General Personality and Cognitive Social Learning (GPCSL) model underpinning their defence and advocacy of the RNR model. They also make clear the epistemological strengths therein and the positive impact its focus on criminogenic need has shown on recidivism and reoffending. Indeed, the aforementioned meta-analytic studies suggest as much. Strict robust empiricism informs this model, with consistently favourable findings enabling the position of centre stage in the 'what works' camp. The scientific validity of the RNR model is well established and need not to be exhaustively repeated here. There are, however, elements of this model, and its relationship with prison functions and prisoner experience, that are significant.

The RNR model has been criticized on grounds of being reductionist (Ward & Marshall, 2007; Ward et al., 2007; Ward & Brown, 2004). Indeed Andrews and colleagues (2011) respond to these, as well as the criticism around the neglect of attention to 'offender' motivation and agency, well enough with their GPCSL model advocacy. Significantly, however, they make clear that alongside the risk, need and responsivity instruments employed by professionals there are other practices and considerations that should be present (see *Table 1*).

Andrews and colleagues (2011, p. 743) also vehemently rebut criticisms that the RNR does not adequately encompass 'offender' motivation and agency, noting that motivational issues are endemic to working with this population and is a primary aspect of specific responsivity within the model. A theme that is emphasized to be a fundamental importance in the rehabilitative or correction process is that of a healthy working alliance that engenders trust a mutuality (Andrews et al., 2011; Maruna, 2012; Mcneill, 2006). Andrews and colleagues (2011, p. 746) note:

> The importance of the therapeutic alliance in correctional supervision is highlighted by our efforts to systematically train probation officers in establishing collaborative goals and establishing quality interpersonal relationships with their clients. The Strategic Training Initiative in Community Supervision project involves training probation officers in active listening skills, developing common goals with their clients, and providing non-judgmental feedback.

Table 1: The Expanded Risk-Need-Responsivity (RNR) Model

Principles	Statement
Respect for the person	Services are provided in an ethical, legal, just, moral, humane, and decent manner
Relationship skills	Relationship skills include warmth, respect, and being collaborative.

* Adapted from Andrews and colleagues, 2011, p.738).

Although writing from a distant paradigm, Maruna (2001) advocates a strength-based approach arguably congruent with Andrews and colleagues' (2011) strategic training initiatives. In reality, however, there is an overt focus on recognizing a managing risk. The alliance a mutuality that Andrews and colleagues argue for does not manifest in the experience of many prisoners. Indeed, they state, "[w]e too, share a serious concern about the application of RNR based intervention without consideration for individual differences among offenders, even among those who may exist at the same level of risk and share the same need" (ibid, pp. 746-747). Criticism is levelled, here, not at the validity of the RNR model but the ways in which practitioners interpret and apply it.

Crewe (2009) found many prisoners to be ambivalent towards the nature of the rehabilitative correctional efforts of the prison. Courses were perceived as tick box exercises with no real-world functions. Moreover, Crewe found many prisoners were fearful or resentful towards labels derived from notions of risk, only too aware of the power such things have over their life. Maruna (2012, p. 76) also states:

> The prisoners whom I have met and worked with over the years are deeply ambivalent about expert correctional treatment and highly sceptical of expert risk assessment. They are, however, very interested in the idea over redeeming themselves (i.e signalling their distance). they ask, "What do I have to do to get a second chance?" And if that means sitting through a "What works" course or smiling while a 23-year-old trainee psychologist from the suburbs risk assess them, so be it.

As the above notes, the literature shows a robust empirically proven approach to prisoner rehabilitation. This RNR cognitive behavioural approach has received criticism, which includes concerns about the ways this approach is operationalized. There appears to be some discrepancy between the need for therapeutic alliance, mutuality, motivation, and the experiences of the prisoners therein. In light of such concerns, Maruna advocates a signalling theory approach to work with offenders, even going as far as to state, "Surely, it is time to retire this "what works" phrase once and for all and to agree that the word "works" does not "work" when talking about human lives" (ibid).

This article examines the ways in which the prisoner experiences the criticism and contradiction that are clearly present between the masculine prison culture, the idea of RNR based cognitive behavioural intervention, and the manifestations therein. Although there is a wide body of literature around prisons, masculinities, rehabilitations on prisoners, relatively few studies are autoethnographic and known have specifically addressed the mechanisms of 'contradiction'. In doing so, this article aims to make grassroots experience visible, helping to fill the research gap and further knowledge of the prisoner experience.

METHODOLOGY

This research used autoethnographic methodology to produce a first-hand life sentence account of lived experience. Ethnography, particularly autoethnography, have always been a marginalized field in prison research, always seemingly in the shadow at empiricism and claims of scientific validity despite a rich body quality of scholarship exploring the nuances of prison life and prisoner sociology (see Crewe, 2009; de Viggiani, 2012; Earle, 2014; Jewkes, 2011; Phillips & Earle, 2010). Both the continued growth of groups such as convict criminology (Tietjen, 2019) and the popularity of the desistance-based interventions and research (e.g. Burnett & Maruna, 2006; Kirkwood & McNeill, 2015; Kitson-Boyce et al., 2019; Maruna, 2012; Mcneill, 2006) represent the increasing value placed upon qualitative experience-based research. The ontological and epistemological assumptions therein are difficult to refute – experience is fundamental to being human. Experience, or the consumption of, is also fundamentally how people learn. This, then, makes autoethnography a valid method for exploring lived experience. It is very often the 'human' factor that empirical measures are criticized for missing. Jewkes (2013, p. 14) makes clear that "prison statistics can similarly 'dazzle' and 'anaesthetise'". Indeed, there is certainly a different quality to the experience of reading about things happening in a prison, then the experience of seeing such things or being on the receiving end of such things. Analyzing one's experience, however, is not without its problems. This paper does not advocate an insider-outside of dualism. As Philips and Earle (2010, p. 361) state, "Social groups borrow ideas from each other rather than them being held onto by one group, and that individuals have a number of interrelated statuses and not a singular one that solely defines their behaviour and perspectives".

No perspective holds monopoly and nor is a singular perspective always helpful when analyzing experience. Philips and Earle articulate well the benefits of a post-modern approach, acknowledging identities, perspectives, and truths as intersectional. In terms of an insider perspective, I am, arguably, as insider as an insider gets. I am a mandatory life sentence prisoner and, at the time of writing, had spent approximately 14 years of my life incarcerated. However, I have not always been a prisoner. Indeed, in recent years I have had substantial access to the community as part of my resettlement and preparation for release. For this reason, the research lens can never be an absolute either-or affair. I therefore argue my researcher position as immersive and perhaps that of 'insider-out'. Insider-outsider positions considered here on a continuum, not a singular category. My hope is that my position soon changes to that of an outsider in.

Methods such as an autoethnography have potential to overstep the analytic line, indulging bias, personal opinion or emotionalism (Jewkes, 2011). Traditional modernistic ideology considers objectification as primary, with emotion often viewed as a research contaminant. However, from the perspective that all experience is coloured in some way by emotion it seems, then, that the exercising of emotion from research is the exercising of an integral human quality.

There is of course an important distinction between unhelpful emotionalism and emotion in research, with "no place for hot headedness in academic writing, but an emotional response does not equate to a lack of reason or cognition" (ibid, p. 71). From Jewkes' perspective emotion can be an important part of the research process. Otherwise, hidden dynamics and nuances may be uncovered and so benefit the research with this intrinsic human quality. This is a view I concur with; it would be very difficult to present a realistic account of my prisoner experience without the insight of emotion. "An acknowledgement that subjective experience and emotional responses can plan a roll in the formulation of knowledge would deepen our understanding of the people and context we study" (ibid, p. 72).

Following this, a key part of autoethnography is the role of reflexivity. This involves the process of simultaneously living through and the collection of data, which then requires a subsequent process of looking back and evaluating. A variable that is particularly rare here is that I undertook this research while still incarcerated, adding to "[n]umerous first-hand accounts of prison life have been written but until recently, accredited research from former prisoners equipped with higher degrees has been rare" (Newbold et al., 2004, p. 440).

My subject position throughout the entirety of the research process means that the research is totally immersed and situated. I recognize that my researcher position has over the course of my academic development throughout my sentence become perhaps more than a future ambition or a means of passing time. It is no doubt entangled with my coping, masculinity, and identity in relation to circumstance. Data collection included personal journal entries, official prison documentation relating both to myself specifically and to prisoners generally, personal communications, along with observations on interactions with the myriad facets of the prison machine. Data collection was, always is, unstructured and sporadic. It is upon the process of research formulation that certain data may take on new meaning or offer new understanding. The reflexive analysis was thematic, but with recognition of what Buetow (2010) conceptualizes as a saliency analysis. This method of analysis aims to refine with the thematic process by also interpreting importance, rather than just recurrence. This is arguably a more approachable method giving that I am considering my own lived experience. Throughout the research ethical guidelines set out by the British Psychological Society were adhered to. Although formal consent was not sought, both prison senior management and probation services well aware of my research activity around my life sentence and experience.

Data was gathered in the form of a personal journal, something that any prisoner is permitted to do and official prison documents, which all prisoners receive in relation to their journey through the prison system. All data was stored in my prison cell. My cell remained locked at all times, either by prison personnel or by myself with the use of a privacy key. Data was therefore secure. Any identifying features in the data have been changed so as to protect the anonymity of those people that I have come into contact with throughout the course of my sentence. I am of the view that the undertaking of my research did not place myself or others at any increased risk outside of that which is faced everyday by those within the prison walls. This includes both physical and emotional harm. Throughout I had support from my key work (prison officer) within the prison on a research supervisor who I had regular contact with via telephone.

The informed consent of research participants is fundamental in most research studies. However, Gelinas et al. (2016, p. 35) argue that, "Socially valuable research is justified without the consent of the participants if the research stands to intrigue no right of the participants and it is impracticable to obtain consent". I invoke both of the above justifications. The continued harms resultant from a political paralysed prison system and the public that receives skewed information from the media gives this kind of research significant social value. There is the moral argument to say that prisons should be transparent, that the public should get to see the lived realities of the prisoner they pay to house.

Given that anonymity is protected I argue that my research does infringe on the rights of those people included. To this end Gelinas and colleagues (2016, p. 36) argue:

> The main point, then, is this. The most basic function of consent is to waive rights of control, allowing others to interact with us in ways that would otherwise be wrong. Consent is needed when, and only when, interactions stand to wrong one of the parties involved, by violating their personal sovereignty all rights of control. So, it will be relatively easy to justify research without consent when such research does not violate the rights of subjects.

I argue this research does not violate the rights of those that are recorded in my journal. I also argue that if this were to represent a violation, such a violation would be minor and outweighed by the social value of the research.

Personal journals, correspondence and official discourse produced in relation to myself and my life sentence were analyzed. Recurrent and salient themes were identified and in relation to the underlying meaning regards my life sentence experience. Three superordinate themes each with three subordinate themes emerged (see *Table 2*).

Table 2: Superordinate and Subordinate Themes Arising from Data Analysis

	1 The lifer identity	2 The psychological battle	3 Masculinity and identity
1	Frankenstein's monster	Powerlessness	The training
2	Numbers factors and confusion	Hopelessness	Masculine fertiliser
3	Actual, life does mean life	The courses	Masculine compliance

THE LIFER IDENTITY

Upon receiving a life sentence, one's life will never completely belong to oneself again. The life sentence identity is permanent, represented by myriad factors many of which are outside of the prisoner's control.

> The sentence is fixed by law and am bound to impose a sentence of imprisonment for life and that is the sentence which I pass (Sentencing Remarks, 30 May 2008, p. 5).

> As and when you are released then you will be subject to licence. As I have already indicated that license will last forever and should you break the terms of it, you would be liable to serve the rest of this sentence in custody (Sentencing Remarks, 30 May 2008, p. 8).

Listening to the words above was perhaps the most disempowering experience of my life. Despite my fear and horror at the situation I had created, I was at that point in my life unable to fully understand what it meant to be a life sentence prisoner.

Frankenstein's Monster

The life sentence prisoner becomes an identity in and of itself, constructed and prescribed by professionals with a monopoly of technologies.

> The HCR-20 (version 3) is a structured violence risk assessment told and was developed by Douglas, Hart, Webster and Belfrage in 2013. It consists of 20 items, 2 of which assess historical (past) factors, 5 clinical (current/ recent) factors and 5 risk management (future) factors. (Psychological risk assessment, 19 March 2020, p. 9)

> The personality assessment inventory (PAI) is a best administrated objective inventory of adult personality, designed to provide information and critical, clinical variables also. There are 344 items that make up 22 non overlapping full scales. These comprise 4 validity scales, 11 clinical scales, 5 treatment scales and 2 interpersonal scales (Psychological report, 1 May 2008, p. 28).

Assessment technologies such as these play a significant role in the directions a life sentence experience may take. They hold significant power and have major influence over considerations of sentence progression, release, and other life events. They can often be given the recognition of truth, which outweighs anything voiced by the prisoner.

Numbers, Factors and Confusion
Prisoner assessment technologies are predominantly qualitative, prescribing risk categories that reduce human beings to percentages.

> He has 14 convictions for a total of 25 offences committed between August 1992 and June 2004. All the offences were committed as an adult. There are five of the convictions for violent offending. There is a pattern of anti-social behaviour associated with alcohol misuse. This case is being managed at level 1 category 2 (Offender Assessment System, 2020, p. 554).

Table 3: Predictor Scores for Reoffending
(Offending Assessment System, 2020, p. 560)

Predictor Scores % and Risk Category			
	Year 1	**Year 2**	**Category**
OGRS3	35	53	Medium
OGP	17	27	Low
OVP	11	19	Low

For the life sentence prisoner such representations can become symbolic of not just the powerlessness of one's predicament, but also of the fact that there is ultimately no escape from one's past. Having such labels forcibly attributed can be both confusing and frustrating as the method of calculation remains, at best, difficult to grasp.

Actually, Life Does Mean Life!

Every life sentence prisoner lives with reality that their future is and will always be subject to terms and conditions. Others will forever have responsibility over what the life sentence prisoner may or may not be permitted to do.

> Both the RMP (risk management plan) and SP (sentence plan) have been redeveloped to reflect the changing situation since Mr Micklethwaite's return to closed conditions a significant number of new controls including AP (approved premises) placement have been added to the RMP. I do not assess that this has been an escalation in risk, but the new measure served to add extra levels of control and monitoring (Offender Assessment System, 2020, p. 566).

> I continue to support Mr Micklethwaite's release into the community with a robust risk management plan including a boost of substance misuse intervention (via a substance misuse support service or his OM on an individual basis); consideration given to a stipulation regarding random phone checks, if considered warranted and a potential referral to Building Better Relationships (BBR) in the community, if recommended by those managing him. My impression is that BBR is not necessarily for his risk management. Mr Micklethwaite has completed extensive intervention to date would be at risk of 'overtreatment' (Independent Psychological Assessment, 2020, p. 38).

In order for the life sentence prisoner to achieve release, any future liberty must entail an acceptance that one will live with reduced autonomy, reduced opportunity, and the knowledge that being returned to prison depends upon decisions made by others.

THE PSYCHOLOGICAL BATTLE

In relation to notions of rehabilitation there are many facets of a life sentence that can be seen as anti-rehabilitative. There is an unavoidable and often enduring psychological battle that accompanies the survival of a life sentence.

> He was suffering from anxiety and advised that he is likely to be highly traumatised. He was suffering from symptoms of post-traumatic stress

and there was a possibility that he has a traumatic reaction to this current offence (Psychological Report, 2008).

This assessment marks the beginning of my life sentence. Whilst my position has ameliorated as adaptations set in there is a psychological quality to a life sentence that is ever threatening.

Powerlessness
This is a well-documented and pervasive theme within a life sentence. From the experience of being sentenced to the experience of sitting in front of a parole board the life sentence carries an undercurrent of powerlessness.

> I can only begin to imagine how you must be feeling, but I am not going to encourage you to wallow in any 'poor me' or system based whinging (Email to a Prisoner Service, 28 August 2019)

> I woke feeling rather negative this morning, I was also knowing I'm trapped here until others see fit to decide otherwise. There is certainly a different psychological quality to being post tariff. I realise it being returned to closed conditions has had a big impact on my wellbeing and I continue to struggle (Personal Journal, 29 February 2020).

The reality of having autonomy and freedom within the boundaries demarcated by others is fundamentally disempowering. The negative impact this can have cannot be overstated.

Hopelessness
A life sentence is not necessarily a linear journey and given that the stakes, for the prisoner, are often very high, there are at times a sense of hopelessness. There is a feeling of being trapped and with little capital to affect change.

> I have just returned from 2 weeks leave and I'm absolutely gutted for you after reading the outcome of your parole review although it wasn't entirely unexpected. It was a very difficult hearing and I feel that they focused on your decision making rather than on your risks (Memo from Offender Supervisor, July 2020).

The past ten months have been filled with uncertainty, false hope and desperation. I do not have much hope left – I can see that under the 2 or 3 years could easily be my parole outcome (Personal Journal, 6 May 2020).

The above extracts demonstrate well enough the difficult position life sentence prisoners can find themselves in. Decisions made about a prisoner's life are often absolute and any resource or opportunity for amelioration can feel hopeless.

The Courses
The life sentence is a continual process of being assessed, the outcomes of which can dictate the need for specific intervention. Courses are the means through which sentence progression is achieved. Unfortunately, there is often a gulf between the prisoner's opinion of a given course and the positive self-report they may give up on completion.

CALM is an anger and an emotional management programme run over 24 2-hour sessions for groups of 6 to 8 participants. The premise of this programme is the anger is natural but can be problematic when experienced too often, too intensely and for too long, and when it is expressed in aggressive or anti-social ways. The course looks at participants own experiences of anger aims to improve emotional self-management and communication skills through exercises designed to impact on the following areas (CALM Post Programme Report, 8 June 2012).

Progress in meeting targets set at the last meeting:
Mr Micklethwaite has completed all his targets as noted earlier. Mr Micklethwaite Have completed numerous courses including Social and Life Skills and Family Relationships in 2011, Drug Awareness for the individual, Alcohol Awareness for the individual. Level 1 award for progression – Understanding Aspects of Citizenship He has also completed the CALM programme, and this was a positive report and Mr Micklethwaite noted that he has gained a lot from the programme. In addition, he has participated in a T.C. (Therapeutic Community) well he has completed a lot of work on victim awareness. (Sentence Planning and Review Meeting Notes, 19 February 2015).

It would not be correct to say that I did not benefit from participation in some of the behaviour interventions in the past 13 years. It is also fair to say that they served their purpose in that my risk scores have reduced as a result. However, there are facets of this process that are fundamentally not rehabilitative and are not congruent with typical prison life, or indeed with the lives of many prisoners returned to upon release.

MASCULINITY AND IDENTITY

Masculinity is a pervasive part of social fabric that has an influence over social interaction, the self-concept in the complex dynamics of identity. The influence of prison experience only works to complicate these dynamics further.

> A conversation yesterday made me aware of the hooch brewing that has become more preferable – due to lockdown drugs are harder to get. But, locked out means no cell spins, so brewing is much easier (Personal Journal, 16 June 2020).

In years gone by lack of self-awareness and a skewed view of my own masculinity would have influenced my involvement in such an endeavour. The pervasive force of masculinity will often manifest in toxic practices. Binge drinking alcohol in prison is but one example.

The Training
Prior to receiving a life sentence much of my life was preoccupied with the pursuit of hegemonic status, and thus the reproduction and amplification of toxic masculine values, often resulting in harmful and offending behaviour.

> Furthermore, he was able to identify that he is engaged in similar behaviours that were demonstrated by his parents, such as drinking and being aggressive from an early age. He also discussed having the belief that aggression is good and it is "what a man it does" (CALM Post Programme Report, 8 June 2012).

> Mr Micklethwaite's experiences as a child led to the development of beliefs around violence being an acceptable way to solve problems and to show off

his masculinity. This was a result of him trying to be like his father as this is who he thought his father wanted him to be. He would then use violence to mask his insecurities and fears about himself and situations he found himself in (Psychological Risk Assessment, 19 March 2020).

Much of my pre-prison life can be understood through a masculine lens. Implicitly and explicitly, the role of toxic masculinity in my offending behaviour cannot be overstated. In prison toxic masculine identities often become more entrenched and more powerful, rather than finding amelioration.

Masculine Fertiliser

Life sentence prisoners and those serving long sentences can often experience a distancing emotionally and psychologically from many of the things that make them who they are.

At earlier stages in my sentence Christmas was always a very difficult time of year. But as the years have gone by it has simply become more and more like any other day. There is a small Christmas tree on the wing, but I hardly notice it. I have made a small effort and displayed the Christmas cards from family on my windowsill. But as yet I do not feel especially festive. I am not depressed or anxious and I do not feel negative, but nor am I particularly interested in Santa Claus. When I ring home my mother explained her stress and hectic running around trying to prepare (for Christmas) whilst my stepfather complains of the expense (of Christmas). For the most part this is fairly meaningless to me, I understand what they mean but my feelings towards it are both near and far. I had a visit on Sunday at which my nine year old son was overtly hyperactive and tangibly excited. His Christmas will be a good one, for which I'm thankful to my parents. But I'm not really part of my son's excitement, I do not really connect with it and I am unable to share it. My emotional distance is probably how I've learned to cope over the years. This is not to say that I do not feel, because I can feel greatly. But the notion of missing out, special occasions and of nostalgia just feels less real to me. My experience of Christmas is fairly empty (Personal Journal, 20 December 2016).

Mr Micklethwaite spoke about having an identity before coming into prison, a partner and a family and a fairly good life. When he arrived at prison for the first time the realisation of what he might lose has slowly dragged him down and last year the break up with his partner and the fear that he might be losing contact with his son had dragged him into new depths. He was using prescribed drugs to take him to another place but had realised he was not in control (End of Therapy Report, 18 January 2013, p. 12).

The impact of a life sentence can often equate to deprivation of identity or of the self. The prisoner has limited means and resources to maintain a coherent sense of self. The masculine identity resources available are often toxic and harmful.

Masculine Compliance

Toxic prison masculinity is pervasive. The power of the social phenomenon may fluctuate from prison to prison or wing to wing, but it is a permanent unavoidable factor in the prison experience.

> Trying to argue the case for the guy being labelled as a sex offender proved and welcome this morning. the fact that Google size is much makes my attempts close to impossible. probation assure me that he does not have any sexual convictions, which means he is being targeted for something he has never done. People were talking about wanting to 'fill him in' and 'slice him up'. I'll have to be careful to appear impartial when telling people, he's actually not a sex offender – trying to oppose prison culture is potentially dangerous. Yet it would be wrong for me to sit by and say nothing. I cannot abide bullying to begin with. The idea that he is being wrongfully labelled makes it seem even worse. For my part, I am tired of prison and the politics (Personal Journal, 2 March 2020).

> Since the episode where people were checking up on other's crimes on Google there has been a clear divide – groups of prisoners and groups have so called 'wrong uns' etc. There are also those that try to ignore the politics, such as myself, but there is no getting away from this age-old prison norm. In terms of violence is prison is really quite mild. I have been in places where this would have certainly led to violence – in one such example I witnessed a prisoner being hit on the head with a dumbbell, another whereby a prisoner had his throat slashed. With this in mind I can

live with the atmosphere here. Hopefully it won't be for too much longer (Personal Journal, 19 August 2020).

All prisoners are in some way impacted by these toxic masculine prison codes. It is a constant and can have a powerful influence over prisoner experience. Toxic masculine practices can often become a means of navigating the complex prisoner environment.

DISCUSSION

The aim of this article centres around unpacking the ways in which prisoner experience can militate against prisoner rehabilitation. These processes are unpacked in relation to masculinities and prisoner identities. Whilst the themes identified may not be entirely novel, I am unaware of other research that explores them either through an autoethnographic lens by a person serving a life sentence or in relation to the emergent contradictions regarding prisoner rehabilitation. In so doing, I add to the literature and knowledge around prison effects and situated life sentence experience.

The lifer identity is a powerful and far-reaching contraption that will, with or without the owner's compliance, dictate the course of the individual's future. The reality of what it meant to be a lifer took years for me to come to terms with. The trauma involved in this process was unlike anything I would have otherwise ever experienced. A fellow life sentence prisoner once described his experience of becoming a life sentence prisoner as akin to falling through a "trap door into another world" (Personal Communication, 2016). The experience of one's life suddenly and irrevocably changing in such an extreme way is, in itself, something that requires significant time and effort to recover from – the absolute infantilizing and emasculating effect of this constituent significant ontological attack on the self.

Such an attack often continues through the construction of the 'Frankenstein's Monster' as the prisoner's existence, the past present and future, is reconstructed by criminal justice professionals and the application of risk technologies. Within the ongoing process the prisoner has little autonomy or control, and little agency for resource if there is a disagreement regard the quality of this assessment and identity construction. The prisoner is reduced throughout this process, with much of their self being obscured. As Crewe (2009, p. 123) notes, "A significant problem is that actuarial tools are predictive of groups rather than individuals. Based on prisoners record, a psychologist can be confident that there is, say, an 80% likelihood that s/he will reoffend but cannot tell whether s/he is one of the individuals who falls into the 80% who will or the 20% who will not".

As a life sentence prisoner, I am overwhelmed by the power of these tools and the associated professional opinions. This represents a fundamental eradication of my agency, autonomy, and control regarding how my identity is construed. The removal or destruction of these fundamental ontological resources is anti-rehabilitative. Thirteen years into my life sentence there are still factors within this prescribed identity that I do not relate to and do not agree with. In this way, my autonomy will never return.

The numbers, factors, and confusion that is symbolic of much of this prescribed identity can be understood as another dimension of not only the reduction of the individual, but also another way in which agency and autonomy are taken away. The prescription of my risk category as low or medium feels arbitrary in my everyday life, despite it being the perspective from which criminal justice professionals view me. Such categories and percentages are only as reliable as the information they are calculated from. For example, my first conviction was in 1992 and at twelve years of age. My risk calculation via the Offender Assessment System states that all my offences were committed as an adult. This shows a clear incongruence. Although this may, in my example, seem a minor issue it is for many a serious cause for concern. It is perhaps little wonder that Crewe (2009) found frustration and resentment among prisoners' opinion of probation and psychology services. This also completely undermines the notion of a working therapeutic alliance, which is argued to be a fundamental important to the rehabilitative process (Andrews et al., 2011). Such errors can add up, are taken as fact, and become truth against which the prisoner is defenceless. When such errors are a more serious quality it is not difficult to understand why prisoners may be unwilling to place their trust in a system that misrepresents them. My Offender Risk Assessment presents me with a barrage a facts and figures that embody my prescribed identity, yet there is no explanation and nor do I understand exactly how these conclusions are reached and assumptions are made, or the equations used. I am, however, obliged to accept the validity of these RNR tools. For a system that purports its scientific basis (Mcguire, 1995; Andrews et al., 2011), the fact that it relied on the faith and trust of its subjects in the forging of any therapeutic alliance is another example of the power imbalance resulted from a reduction of prisoner agency and autonomy. The removal or suppression of agency and autonomy is fundamentally anti-rehabilitative.

As a life sentence prisoner progresses toward release, there can be an amelioration in this ontological attack. My experience includes accessing the community via release on temporary licence (ROTL). This enabled me to pursue an academic career and begin to gradually adjust to the pace of life in the free world. However, as the research findings make clear, life actually does mean life. Upon entering the community, it quickly became clear to me that I did not have sovereignty over my future. This goes far beyond having to abide by generic sets of licence conditions. The large sentence prisoner need not commit further crime or even increased levels of prescribed risk to have any potential future removed and placed in prison again for an undisclosed number of years. I do not enjoy the luxury of having a private life. Relationships, accommodation, finances, hobbies, and interests are all things that become transformed into a construct subject to the approval and management of others. This continued process of infantilization is only enhanced by the knowledge that it will effectively continue for the rest of one's life. Indeed, I was informed by legal representative that I do not have automatic entitlement to the same level of human rights as those in the free world (Personal Communication, 2019). A probation officer also informed me, during a supervision session, that as I was a life sentence prisoner my life was effectively not my own (Personal Communication, 2019). This continued to logical attack militates against any successful enactment of a 'new me' (Maruna, 2001). The argued empowerment offered by the assimilation of prison rehabilitative dogma stands in contrast to many of the factors at play in the dynamics of "offender management". The loss of autonomy and the masculinization described in the literature (de Viggiani, 2012; Jewkes, 2005; Michalski, 2015; Newton, 1994; Sykes, 1958) may change substance and quality, but nonetheless remains a persistent part of the life sentence prisoner's future. In this way, rather than the eradication of identity, induction into a life sentence can represent and be understood as the refusal to allow the individual to move on from a damaging past and the prescribed identity by the Criminal Justice System.

For many the preceding offence, receipt of a negotiation of a life sentence can be highly traumatic. Psychological assessments from the earliest stages of my sentence demonstrate this clearly enough. If a prisoner is to be rehabilitated, then the impact of receiving a life sentence can be understood as initially pushing the prisoner further away from the desired rehabilitative position. The powerlessness of the life sentence position is a constant theme. It is a delirious phenomenon that makes any amelioration more difficult to realize. In my experience there was little support for my trauma, aside from being monitored and having a monthly 20-minute psychiatrist appointment. In this regard, the prison's duty of care (Crewe, 2009) to my wellbeing seemed overly concerned with preventing suicide, rather than being encouraging and seeking to enhance the quality of my wellbeing. The theme of powerlessness can, naturally, changes dynamic throughout the various stages of a sentence. The process of parole is a succinct example of powerlessness that characterizes the progressive stages of a life sentence. Once one's future is effectively placed in the hands of strangers, they take influence from criminal justice professionals around assignments of risk. But to add another dimension of uncertainty the parole board reserve the right to make a decision independent of other opinions. It is in this process that the extracts for superordinate theme 2, as well as superordinate theme 1 illuminate. In this example, I was waiting for a parole hearing that was deferred on three separate occasions. The endemic powerlessness of the prisoner situation well, as Michalski (2015) makes clear, influence the prisoner to engage in attempts at empowerment and regaining a degree of control. It is no surprise then, as Murana (2012) acknowledges, to find disingenuous and ambivalent engagement by prisoners with the professionals concerned. Indeed, therein lies a potential explanation as to why some life sentence prisoners seemingly self-sabotage during the latter stages of prison progression.

Hopelessness can arguably be understood as a progression of powerlessness. In my experience it bears all the same hallmarks but with the added emotional pain that comes with the reality of being trapped indefinitely. If a situation fails hopelessly then it is difficult to see how this can be congruent with said prisoner drawing optimal benefit from what should be a rehabilitative journey. To this end Grey (2018, p. 4) right about the barriers to progression for life sentence prisoners, stating: "The maintenance of hopelessness and the "feared self" was identified as being a barrier and their ability to desist from offending in general". The rehabilitative contradiction here is clear. Martin and Stermac (2009, p. 1) situate hope as a "[p]sychological construct that has aided in the survival and wellbeing of humans for hundreds of years".

In my experience hopelessness is a large part of continuation of the way in which the processes the criminal justice system impact upon the prisoner. Hopelessness is not a novel theme in prison research and so need not be exhaustively repeated here. The point to make is that it is not simply a prisoner response to a passive or ambivalent system, it is a phenomenon that is cultivated and inflicted by a system that declared the abilities of ideals and a duty of care to its captives. The powerlessness and hopelessness of the life sentence experience can potentially be exacerbated by the prescribed need to undertake specific interventions and courses. Rehabilitation should, logically, be a process of self-improvement, empowerment preparation for the future, and based on therapeutic alliances is characterized by empathy, guidance, and mutual respect. This, then, should not be a process that many consider a tick-box exercise designed to reduce risk and satisfy criminal justice professionals. Unfortunately, my experience has often been more toward the latter. The RNR assessment criteria presents contradiction at the outset. The prisoner is disempowered and disenfranchised by the knowledge that despite the need to give consent, refusal to participate will likely make it much more difficult to progress or realize eventual release. The voluntary aspect of prison intervention is therefore often coercive, as acknowledged by McNeill (2006). The notion that cognitive behavioural interventions are contingent on powerlessness and coercion to ensure participation renders them inherently contradictory. This inherent contradiction often leads to prisoner resentment (Crewe, 2009), which can also be understood as an anti-rehabilitative influence. Moreover, in my experience, prisons do not have the cognitive behavioural resources to meet the demands of a risk-based prison economy. The outcome here is that sentence progression may stagnate whilst the prisoner awaits allocation on a course or transfer to an establishment for specific intervention. It is easy to see how a prisoner could feel tormented by this process. This scenario is no doubt made worse when the prisoner see little meaningful benefit to the prescribed intervention. As Crewe (2009, p. 134) observes:

> Programme content was demanding and ideologically rigid as some facilitators acknowledge. Role plays assumed a rational choice agent, unconstrained by, or resistant to, the kinds of pressures that dominated the cultures and communities to which prisoners would return precious to maintain "face and reputation", not to back down in the face of provocation,

and never to appear passive. In the classroom then, many prisoners functioned with a kind of dual consciousness. They often recognise that the behaviours advanced by the course had merit in principle, yet saw them as bearing little relevance to their lives.

As a life sentence prisoner having served over a decade and satisfying a raft of rehabilitative targets, I struggled to recall any prisoner, outside of the classroom, express the views that an offending behaviour course had helped them develop on a personal or internal level. I can, however, recall a conversation with a close friend and fellow life sentence prisoner in which he referred to such interventions as a waste of time. This same prisoner, currently more than halfway through a lengthy tariff, is a model prisoner who having satisfied all rehabilitative targets is now simply waiting for the time whereby a transfer to the open prisoner status is possible. To add to this are conversations I have had with prison probation officers where they have expressed the view that prison courses do not really work, but they are what parole board expects to see.

To return to the literature, this is congruent with Goffman's (1959) theory that people present fronts that serve to successfully negotiate specific social situations. Here, prisoners present criminal justice professionals with their cleanest most rehabilitated front. This front can be viewed as an attempt to empower oneself, regain a semblance of control over one's life and instil some certainty in one's future. The fundamental problem with this is that the nature of this rehabilitative maze can influence duplicity and disingenuous engagement. No life sentence prisoner in their right mind will report that they have not benefited from participation in an intervention unless they are content to stay put. This demonstrates a glaring rehabilitative incongruent and a pervasive contradictory dimension within prison based cognitive behavioural interventions. Reduced risk scores are not necessarily synonymous with prisoners rehabilitating. The interactions prisoners must negotiate in this way are often not conducive to prisoner wellbeing. So far, much of the prisoner experience framed in this discussion can be understood to be symbolic of prisoner emasculation. The process of imprisonment, in relation to sentence progression on rehabilitation, can actually manifest a process of debilitation.

As the literature states, masculinities are a pervasive psychological and sociological force, which has been my experience much of my life prior to and while being a prisoner. My offending behaviour was precipitated by maladaptive childhood experiences that influenced my development into an emotionally labile and aggressive young man. I was exposed to violence and substance abuse at an early age, and so to some degree these were normative practices for me. Toxic practices of hegemonic masculinity permeated my childhood, my adolescence, and adulthood. My offending behaviour, which typically involved binge drinking and violence, can be understood as an expression of toxic masculine identity and a pursuit of hegemonic status. Upon reflection, it is apparent that prison was always a likely outcome for me. I had been, in Goffmanian terms, fronting for most of my toxic masculine life, which may well have prepared me for prison culture. Jewkes (2005, p. 51) notes:

> The desire to prove one's manhood, which frequently leads to criminal behaviour, conviction, and imprisonment may itself, then, be a prerequisite to a successful adaptation to life inside. this might be particularly true of those who have committed very serious offences, who might be said to import with them into prison the ideology of aggressive masculine values that precipitate their crimes in the first place.

For me, Jewkes could not be more accurate. My offending was not a result of social or cognitive skills deficits. It was a result of my identity and life, which had been construed and reproduced time and again through a lens of toxic masculinity. Prison rehabilitation may be missing the masculine point. Although aspects of my cognitive behavioural experience can be viewed through a masculine lens, there is no explicit reference to masculinity. In my experience this felt like an attempt to change what people do, rather than enabling people to understand and come to terms with who they are and who they have been. For context, yes cognitive behavioural skills could have prevented my offending behaviour, but at that stage in my life I seriously doubt I would have used them.

There is also a huge contradiction in that the culture of prison works to reinforce the emasculation that, Michaliski (2015) argues, drives these toxic masculine practises. Prison culture is, then, part of the problem in that it becomes part of an ongoing aetiological explanation for toxic behaviour and, arguably, manifested offending. Goffman (1959, p. 37) asserts:

> In addition to the fact that different routines may employ the same front, it is to be noted that a given social front tends to become institutionalised

in terms of the abstract stereotyped expectation to which it gives rise,
and tends to take on a meaning and stability apart from the specific tasks
which happen at the time to be performed in its name. The front becomes
a "collective representation" and an act in its own right.

This explains both the fertilisation and pressure towards compliance of
prison masculine culture. Again, this contradicts rehabilitative efforts, "[s]
ince fronts tend to be selected, not created" and so "we may expect trouble
to arise when those who perform a given task are forced to select a suitable
front for themselves from among several quite dissimilar ones" (ibid, p. 38).

In relation to the themes in this research, a cognitive behavioural front
would not fit within the prevailing social norms or approved fronts – the
prisoner brewing hooch or those bullying a suspected perpetrator of sexual
crimes. Prisoners might not feel able or might not even desire to use
cognitive behavioural skills, regardless of demonstrations within the sterile
classroom environment. Unfortunately, the adaptations to living within
the toxic grasp of the prisoner code, while also negotiating the ontological
attacks inflicted by the prison, do not simply go away once released. It is
only logical that if prisoner imports toxic practices into the prison, they then
may well export these back out again, perhaps with the added quality of
prison experience to boot. Indeed, Hulley and (2015, p. 1) posit that: "While
earlier scholars concluded the effects of long term imprisonment were not
"cumulative" and "deleterious", adaptation to long term imprisonment
has a deep and profound impact on the prisoner, so that the process of
coping leads to fundamental changes in the self, which go far beyond the
attitudinal". This can in no way be understood as rehabilitative, as "the very
coping mechanisms that are to alleviate some of the pains and problems of
imprisonment might, as a secondary effect, be deeply transformational and
in some sense debilitating" (ibid, p. 22). It is difficult to see how this, and
the evidence presented in my research can be reconciled with notions of
rehabilitation, a duty of care or public protection.

RECOMMENDATIONS

The prison as it stands is in need of major reform. An active, progressive
prison regime that influences real prisoner empowerment is required. This
will be a complex commitment towards removing the structural catalysts
that drive toxic prison culture. Then, perhaps, there will be realistic scope

for prisons to assist in real and beneficial rehabilitation. This necessarily needs to be a reform that is guided by academic knowledge and prisoner life experience. Political engines should not be commodifying crime if this moves prison away from progressive reform – how many times will "tough on crime" rhetoric need to fail before it is commonly realized that it does not work? The media have an important role to play, which needs to be that of informing not sensationalizing. In rehabilitation, a personal approach that includes the impact masculinities have could be beneficially integrated. As the literature states, such an approach to rehabilitation can impact recidivism. It could perhaps be so much more if it was not hamstrung by so many other factors.

CONCLUSION

This paper has presented an autoethnographic life sentence account of prison rehabilitation and the contradictory mechanisms of the prisoner experience. My experience was framed here, through a lens that considered the interactions between cognitive behavioural risk-based prison rehabilitation and the toxic influence of prison culture and masculinity. It has been shown that the labelling, reducing, and management of prisoners not only contradicts but drives toxic masculine culture. Thus, prison was shown to reinforce rather than reduce offending related behaviours. The highlighted themes and the exploration of their rehabilitative incongruence adds first person lift experienced account to reinforce the well-established knowledge around ontologically deleterious prison effects. Recommendations centre around promoting prisoner empowerment and detachment of political interest in prison function, which recognizes masculine influence on prisoner rehabilitation.

ACKNOWLEDGEMENTS

Grateful thanks to Lauren Leigh for typing up this entire article.

REFERENCES

Andrews, Donald A., James Bonta, and Stephen Wormith (2011) "The Risk Need Responsivity (RNR) Model Does Adding the Good Lives Model Contribute to Effective Crime Prevention", *Criminal Justice and Behaviour*, 38(7): 735-755.

Bandyopadhyay, Mahuya (2016) "Asian Prisons", in Yvonne Jewkes, Ben Crewe and Jamie Bennett (eds.), *Handbook on Prisons*, Oxon: Routledge, pp. 441-459.

Bierie, David M. and Ruth E. Mann (2017) "The History and Future of Prison Psychology", *Psychology, Public Policy, and Law*, 23(4): 478–489.

Bowlby, John (1951) "Maternal Care and Mental Health", *Public Health*, 65: 128.

Buetow, Stephen (2010) "Thematic Analysis and Its Reconceptualization as 'Saliency Analysis'", *Journal of Health Service Research and Policy*, 15(2): 123-125.

Burnett, Ross and Shadd Maruna (2006) "The Kindness of Prisoners: Strengths-Based Resettlement in Theory and in Action", *Criminology & Criminal Justice*, 6(1): 83-106.

Cohen, Stanley (1980) *Folk Devils and Moral Panics (2nd edition)*, Oxford: Martin Robertson.

Cohen, Stanley (1971) "Mods, Rockers and the Rest: Community Reactions to Juvenile Delinquency", in Wesley George Carson and Paul Wiles (eds.), *Crime and Delinquency in Britain: Sociological Readings (Volume 1)*, Oxford: Martin Robertson, pp. 226-236.

Connell, Raewyn W. and James W. Messerschmidt (2005) "Hegemonic Masculinity: Rethinking the Concept", *Gender and Society*, 19(6): 829-859.

Crewe, Ben (2009) *The Prisoner Society Power, Adaptation, and Social Life in an English Prison*, Oxford: Oxford University Press.

De Viggiani, Nick (2012) "Trying to be Something You Are Not: Masculine Performances within a Prison Setting", *Men and Masculinities*, 15(3): 1-21.

Earle, Rod (2014) "Insider and Out: Making Sense of a Prison Experience and a Research Experience", *Qualitative Inquiry*, 20(4): 429-438.

Freud, Sigmond (1953) *Three Essays on the Theory of Sexuality*, London: Imago Publishing Co.

Gelinas, Luke, Alan Wertheimer and Franklin G. Miller (2016) "When and Why is Research Without Consent Permissible?", *Hastings Centre Report*, 46(2): 35-43.

Goffman, Erving (1959) *The Presentation of Self in Everyday Life*, New York: Vintage Books, Random House.

Gray, Lorna A. (2018) "Lifers Over Tariff: Exploring Psychological Barriers to Progression", *The Journal of Forensic Practise*, 20(2): 81-90.

Hill, Denis and D.A. Pond (1952) "Reflections on One Hundred Capital Cases Submitted to Electroencephalography", *Journal of Mental Science*, 98(410): 23-43.

Hulley, Susie, Ben Crewe and Serena Wright (2015) "Re-Examining the Problems of Long-Term Imprisonment", *British Journal of Criminology*, 56: 769-792.

Irwin, John and Donald Cressey (1962) "Thieves, Convicts and Inmate Subculture", *Social Problems*, 10(2): 142-155.

Jewkes, Yvonne (2013) "What has Prison Ethnography to Offer in an Age of Mass Incarceration?", *Criminal Justice Matters*, 91(1): 14-15.

Jewkes, Yvonne (2011) "Autoethnography and Emotion as Intellectual Resources: Doing Prison Research Differently", *Qualitative Inquiry*, 18 (1): 33-75.

Jewkes, Yvonne (2005) "Men Behind Bars: 'Doing' Masculinity as an Adaptation to Imprisonment", *Men and Masculinities*, 8(1): 44-63.

Joy Tong, L., and David Farrington (2006) "How Effective is the "Reasoning and Rehabilitation" Programme in Reducing Reoffending? A Meta-Analysis of Evaluations in Four Countries", *Psychology, Crime & Law*, 12(1): 3-24.

Kirkwood, Steve and Fergus McNeill (2015) "Integration and Reintegration: Comparing Pathways to Citizenship Through Asylum and Criminal Justice", *Criminology & Criminal Justice*, 15(5): 511-526.

Kitson-Boyce, Rosie, Nicholas Blagden, Belinda Winder and Gayle Dillon (2019) "'This Time It's Different' Preparing for Release Through a Prison-Model of CoSA: A Phenomenological and Repertory Grid Analysis", *Sexual Abuse*, 31(8): 886-907.

Lipsey, Mark W. and David B. Wilson (2001) *Practical Meta-Analysis*, London: SAGE Publications.

Lombroso, Cesare (1896) *L'Uomo Delinquente*, Turin: Fratelli Bocca Editori.

Martin, Krystle and Lana Stermac (2009) "Measuring Hope", *International Journal of Offender Therapy And Comparative Criminology*, 54(5): 693-705.

Maruna, Shadd (2012) "Elements of Successful Desistance Signaling", *Criminology & Public Policy*, 11(1): 73-86.

Maruna, Shadd (2001) *Making Good: How Ex-convicts Reform and Rebuild their Lives*, Washington (DC): American Psychological Association.

Maruna, Shadd and Ruth Mann (2019) *Reconciling 'Desistance' and 'What Works'* – February, Manchester: HM Inspectorate of Probation Academic Insights.

McDougall, C., R.M. Barnett, B. Ashurt, B. and B. Willis (1987) "Cognitive Control of Anger", in Barry J. Mcgurk, David M. Thornton and Mark Williams (eds.), *Applying Psychology to Imprisonment: Theory and Practice*, London: HMSO.

McGuire, James (ed.) (1995) *What Works: Reducing Reoffending: Guidelines from Research and Practice*, Chichester: John Wiley.

McNeill, Fergus (2006) "A Desistance Paradigm for Offender Management", *Criminology and Criminal Justice*, 6(1): 39-62.

Messerschmidt, James W. (1986) *Capitalism, Patriarchy and Crime: Toward a Socialist Feminist Criminology*, Totowa (NJ): Rowman and Littlefield.

Michalski, Joseph H. (2015) "Status Hierarchies and Hegemonic Masculinity: A General Theory of Prison Violence", *British Journal of Criminology*, 57(1): 40-60.

Newbold, Greg, Jeffrey Ian Ross, Richard S. Jones, Stephen C. Richards and Michael Lenza (2014) "Prison Research from the Inside: The Role of Convict Auto-ethnography", *Qualitative Inquiry*, 20(4): 439-448.

Newburn, Tim and Elizabeth A. Stanko (1994) *Just Boys Doing Business? Men, Masculinities and Crime (1ˢᵗ edition)*, London: Routledge.

Newton, Carolyn (1994) "Gender Theory and Prison Sociology: Using Theories of Masculinities to Interpret the Sociology of Prisons for Men", *The Howard Journal of Criminal Justice*, 33(3): 193-202.

Nietzel, Michael T. (1979) *Crime and its Modification: A Social Learning Perspective*, New York: Pergamon Press.

Palmer, David (2009) "Cognitive behaviourism", in Eugene McLaughlin and John Muncie (eds.). *The SAGE Dictionary of Criminology (Second Edition)*, London: SAGE Publications, pp. 42-43.

Pearson, Frank S., Douglas S. Lipton, Charles M. Cleland and Dorline S. Yee (2002) "The Effects of Behavioral/Cognitive-Behavioral Programs on Recidivism", *Crime & Delinquency*, 48(3): 476-496.

Phillips, Coretta and Rod Earle (2010) "Reading Difference Differently? Identity, Epistemology and Prison Ethnography", *British Journal of Criminology*, 50(2): 360-378.

Ramsey, Laura, Jamie Walton, Gavin Frost, Chloe Reway, Gemma Westley, H. Tucker, Sarah Millington, A. Dhar, Gemma Martin and Caitriona Gill (2019) "Evaluation of Offending Behaviour Programme Selection: the PNA", *Journal a Forensic Practice*, 21(4): 264-277.

Redondo, Santiago, Julio Sanchez-Meca, and Vicente Garrido (1999) "The Influence of Treatment Programmes on the Recidivism of Juvenile and Adult Offenders: A European Meta-Analytic Review", *Psychology, Crime & Law*, 5(3): 251-278.

Remy, John (1990) "Patriarchy and Fratriarchy as Forms of Androcracy", in Jeff Hearn and David H. Morgan (eds.), *Men, Masculinities and Social Theory*, London: Routledge, pp. 43-55.

Rosenkoeter, Lawrence, Stephen Landman and Stephen Marcak (1986) "The Use of Moral Discussion as an Intervention with Delinquents", *Psychological Reports*, 16: 91-94.

Ross, Robert R. and Elizabeth Fabiano (1985) *Time to Think: A Cognitive Model of Offender Rehabilitation*, Johnson City (TN): Institute of Science and Arts.

Sheldon, William (1949) "Somatotypes", *The Lancet*, 253(6549): 403-404.

Skinner, Burrhus Frederic (1965) *Science and Human Behavior*, New York: Simon and Schuster Publishing Co.

Skinner, Burrhus Frederic (1938) *The Behavior of Organisms*, London: Appleton-Century-Crofts.

Sykes, Gresham M. (1958) *The Society of Captives: A Study of Maximum Security Prison*, Princeton: Princeton University Press.

Tietjen, Grant (2019) "Convict Criminology: Learning from the Past, Confronting the Present, Expanding for the Future", *Critical Criminology*, 27(1): 101-114.

Ward, Tony and Mark Brown (2004) "The Good Lives Model and Conceptual Issues in Offender Rehabilitation", *Psychology, Crime and Law*, 10(3): 243-257.

Ward, Tony and Bill Marshall (2007) "Narrative Identity and Offender Rehabilitation", *International Journal of Offender Therapy and Comparative Criminology*, 51(3): 279-297.

Ward, Tony, Joseph Melser and Pamela Yates (2007) "Reconstructing the Risk Need Responsivity: A Theoretical Elaboration and Evaluation", *Aggression and Violent Behaviour*, 12(2): 208-228.

Zimbardo, Philip (1972) "Comment: Pathology of Imprisonment", *Society*, 9(6): 4-8.

RESPONSE

On Desistance and Resistance
Justin Piché

It has long been established that the retributive approach to criminalized acts often fails to meet the needs of those impacted (Zehr, 1990) and that imprisonment, in particular, causes great harm to human beings who endure it (Sykes, 1958). There is also considerable evidence that the collateral consequences of criminalization experienced by criminalized people (e.g. barriers in obtaining basic necessities like housing and employment), their loved ones (e.g. material and psychological impacts of forced separation from imprisoned family members), and communities (e.g. diversion of community resources towards policing and prisons) extend well beyond the punishments prescribed by the courts (see, for example, Kirk and Wakefield, 2018). It is no wonder that so many caught up in the punitive injustice system are unable to escape its clutches.

The above is certainly evident in this special issue of the *Journal of Prisoners on Prisons* (JPP) on desistance, social justice, and lived experience. The articles contained therein may prompt the reader, like it prompted me, to ask – as desistance scholars and the editors of this collection do – "*how*" do "people manage to forge and sustain a path away from criminal[*ized*] engagement" (Maier et al., 2022, p. 2 – my emphasis)? Indeed, how does one desist after having been dehumanized and degraded through practices such as solitary confinement, with little to no access to meaningful work behind bars, while living an existence where the threat of violence from staff and other imprisoned people is real as vividly described by Stephon Whitley (2022)? How does one desist after repeated assaults on their psyche, and exposure to a prison environment that promotes and rewards toxic behaviour as recounted by Daniel Micklethwaite (2022), while failing to recognize efforts to change as documented by Ruth Utnage (2022)? How does one desist when their efforts to 'do good' are met with consistent doubt, scrutiny, and barriers of the kind encountered by James Binnall (2022)?

When criminalized and imprisoned people endure so much structural violence and organized abandonment yet make changes in their lives within the narrowed field of possibilities available to them and desist from harmful behaviour, as the contributors to this special issue of the *JPP* have, it is indeed remarkable. As the pieces by Christopher Havens and Marta Cerruti (2022) on the power of access to education, Kris MacPherson on the importance of family, Christopher Kay, along with Carolynne Mason and Tom Hartley (2022) on the transformative potential of sport, also make clear, having links to the outside world during and following one's imprisonment is also critical in fostering de-carceral futures for people.

As I read this collection, I also saw parallels between the commitment of contributors to desist from harmful behaviour and abolitionist visions of accountability, which encourage perpetrators to make amends to those they have harmed and make changes in their lives with community support, yet there is a need to also push further through collective transformative justice organizing that aims to abolish structures of power that give rise to social conflict and harm (Kaba, 2020). Considering Francis Kroncke's (2022) stunning account of the pernicious and mundane violence of imprisonment he endured as a Vietnam war resister and prisoner of conscious, it is also incumbent that calls for desistance of behaviours *when* they impinge upon the safety of people include demands for the state to desist from harm, including the damage done through criminalization and punishment (Piché, forthcoming) as well. Such calls need to be bolstered by collective resistance. In the context racial capitalism and the pervasive insecurity it engenders, it is clear that we need to "change everything" (Gilmore, 2022) if we are to achieve broader desistance from harm and social justice in our time.

REFERENCES

Binnall, James (2022) "What Can the Legal Profession Do For Us? Formerly Incarcerated Attorneys and the Practice of Law as a Strengths-Based Endeavour", *Journal of Prisoners on Prisons*, 31(1): 110-131.

Gilmore, Ruth Wilson (2022) *Change Everything: Racial Capitalism and the Case for Abolition*, Chicago: Haymarket Books.

Havens, Christopher and Marta Cerruti (2022) "Desistance, Anomalies and Rabbit Holes: A Transformative Experience from Inside Out", *Journal of Prisoners on Prisons*, 31(1): 10-19.

Kaba, Miriame (2020) *We Do This 'Til We Free Us: Abolitionist Organizing and Transformative Justice*, Chicago: Haymarket Books.

Kay, Christopher, Carolynne Mason and Tom Hartley (2022) "Co-producing Desistance Opportunities with Women in Prison: Reflections of a Sports Coach Developer", *Journal of Prisoners on Prisons*, 31(1): 40-64.

Kirk, David S. and Sara Wakefield (2018) "Collateral Consequences of Punishment: A Critical Review and Path Forward", *Annual Review of Criminology*, 1: 171-194.

Kroncke, Francis X. (2022) "Captor Story and Captive Story", *Journal of Prisoners on Prisons*, 31(1): 94-109.

MacPherson, Kris (2022) "Desistance and Prisoner Re-entry: A Real-time Perspective", *Journal of Prisoners on Prisons*, 31(1): 20-39.

Maier, Katharina, Rosemary Ricciardelli and Shadd Maruna (2022) "Desistance, Social Justice and Lived Experience", *Journal of Prisoners on Prisons*, 31(1): 1-9.

Micklethwaite, Daniel (2022) "The Contradictions of Prisoner Life and Rehabilitation: An Auto-ethnographic Life Sentence Experience", *Journal of Prisoners on Prisons*, 31(1): 132-166.

Piché, Justin (ed.) (forthcoming) *Pain in Vain: Challenging the Penal System, Towards the Abolition of Punishment – On the Legacy of Louk Hulsman*, Ottawa: Red Quill Books.

Sykes, Gresham M. (2007[1958]) *The Society of Captives: A Study of a Maximum Security Prison*, New Brunswick (NJ): Princeton University Press.

Utnage, Ruth (2022) "Desistance and Prison Culture: A Trifurcated Prisoner Classification Theory", *Journal of Prisoners on Prisons*, 31(1): 65-76.

Whitley, Stephon (2022) "Twenty Years of Incarceration in the Garden State: Reflecting on the Barriers and Facilitators in the Desistance Process ", *Journal of Prisoners on Prisons*, 31(1): 77-93.

Zehr, Howard (1990) *Changing Lenses: A New Focus for Crime and Justice*, Intercourse (PA): Herald Press.

ABOUT THE AUTHOR

Justin Piché, PhD is an Associate Professor in the Department of Criminology and Director of the Carceral Studies Research Collective at the University of Ottawa. He is also an editor of the *Journal of Prisoners on Prisons* (www.jpp.org) and member of the Criminalization and Punishment Education Project (www.cp-ep.org). He can be reached by email at justin.piche@uottawa.ca or by mail at the following address:

Justin Piché, PhD
Associate Professor
Department of Criminology
University of Ottawa
120 University Private
Ottawa, Ottawa, Canada
K1N 6N5

PRISONERS' STRUGGLES

A Call for Memorials, Writing and Artwork by Imprisoned People and their Loved Ones
Mourning Our Losses

Mourning Our Losses (MOL) was launched by a volunteer group of educators, artists and organizers committed to the release of those incarcerated nationwide. In April 2020, we began hosting individual memorials to dignify and honour the lives of our brothers and sisters who were dying from COVID-19 in jails, prisons, and detention centers across the United States. Today, we continue to grow this platform for grief, healing, community, and reflection for *all* those affected by the death of a loved one due to poor conditions, medical negligence, violence, and mental health crises inside – the natural by-products of mass incarceration.

We are a team driven by our own prison experiences. Our crowd-sourced memorial site and all that we do depends upon our ties to you, our siblings still inside. Our goal is to inform public, national conversations about the dangers of mass incarceration by sharing the stories of those lost. In doing this, we let the public know that we are *all* people – not numbers, criminals or "inmates". We do not use that type of dehumanizing language in the memorials we post. We do not speak negatively about anyone or talk about the crime for which they were convicted (at all!). No one deserves to suffer at the hands of the prison industry and *no one* deserves to die inside.

YOU CAN HELP US

You may send us a memorial for a loved one who died, related creative writing, photos and/or artwork (which we may not be able to return safely). When you send your submissions in, be sure to include the name the person went by and your name as you would like it to appear on the memorial or let us know if you would like to remain anonymous. Also let us know whether you give us permission to edit spelling errors and whether we can contact you via electronic mail (JPay, Securus, GTL, etc.) to follow-up. Write to us at:

Mourning Our Losses
c/o Texas After Violence Project
P.O. Box 15005
Austin, Texas 78761
USA

We encourage you to share our website – mourningourlosses.org – with your friends and family on the outside. Memorials can be submitted on the site using the "Submit" button. We can also be reached via email at mourningourlosses@gmail.com.

COVID-19 Pandemic Struggles of Prisoners' Families
Joanne Fry

E ven though it has been some fifteen years since my son was incarcerated and I made my first visits to a Canadian federal penitentiary, I can still well remember the anxiety, fear and intimidation of those first many prison visits. My life had been devastated, my young son taken from his family and home, and I was still in disbelief. I was now living in the Twilight Zone. There is not a lot of sympathy or kindness for the family of the perpetrator of crime.

At the first visits the staff were being reasonable and speaking politely, but I noticed immediately that the other visitors – 90% or more of whom were female, like me – did not make eye contact with each other. They sat quietly, shoulders slumped, no chatting or friendly discourse between them. They all shared some things in common: they looked tired, nervous, possibly close to tears. And they did not offer to help or offer a smile of support or understanding. Those first visits were full of confusion and anxiety, making an already horrific situation feel much more daunting. I had never felt so alone or hopeless in my life.

Whether consciously or not, once I became more accustomed to the process, I would immediately reach out to the 'newbies' who stood out so vividly. I would smile, encourage them to follow me, explain the layouts of the visiting rooms, and the like. And as a life-long activist myself, I was shocked that there was little in the way of support groups or 'committees' for the loved ones of imprisoned people. CSC discourages any contact between visitors. I soon came to understand the fear and paranoia of the visitors themselves, and why there would be no personal connections.

As COVID-19 started to spread within the outside community, it was clear to anyone knowledgeable of our penitentiary system that we would very soon be in a serious state. While still attending visits I would complain about the most basic safety being absent, such as hand sanitizer. It was painfully obvious that COVID would devastate the prison community. After watching how the prison functions – or not – for many years, it was bound to develop into the worst-case scenario. And I decided that I must start some sort of committee or group as a response to COVID *before* things became dire.

One of my personal character flaws is I am technology-challenged and I do not engage in any social media. None of the visitors knew other family members names or phone numbers. So it was a very difficult and time-consuming process to get Mission Prison Family Association started, and even so, many of my goals were not easily realized. For example, I contacted the prison administration to see if we could liaise in some way, rather than the families and loved ones desperately trying to get information on their own, phoning the institution over and over with no response. Instead, I proposed that we could perhaps organize a simple plan to communicate with CSC by email or telephone, and I could inform and update the families. While simpler and more efficient for all involved, it might mitigate the terror and desperation felt by many prisoners' families during the early stages of the pandemic. CSC would not agree to co-operate – as was expected. This challenge was further compounded by many of the families being nervous about joining and having their names attached to a group. Several suggested that our list might 'get out' and they worried about retaliation.

In any case, there were many, many times that a distraught family member who had not had contact with their loved one would reach out, begging for help. We also sought legal help and eventually filed the second class-action lawsuit in the country, assisting with the development of the case and the documentation of CSC incompetence and negligence putting our loved ones at risk. This was no small feat. None of us had much experience with the legal system outside of the terrifying experience with our loved ones and none of us understood what a 'class-action' would entail. Fortunately, we managed to eventually connect with Jeff Hartman in Toronto, a prison lawyer who would patiently guide us through the process. Jeff has great interest in 'power discrepancies' within the system and has written exceptional articles that I would later incorporate into my work and lectures. His compassion and knowledge in works such as "The Crisis in Corrections is Social Distancing (but it's not what you think)" have been invaluable. I now understand that class-action cases take many years to come to any resolution, and that in Canada there is little monetary award making it extremely difficult to secure legal assistance on contingency.

A small number of us were interviewed by media or wrote articles for local news outlets. For many, though, their fear of retaliation or 'outing' held them back, as outside scrutiny and the possible re-opening of old wounds and histories was too frightening to consider. In addition, retaliation by CSC is a legitimate concern at all times. My son has been targeted by the prison management in various instances, and his security rating has risen because of his so-called dislike of CSC. It has been used to justify his 'deteriorating attitude', a label that has broad toxicity for anyone who desires to one day be free of incarceration or be successful with their future parole.

In the face of these challenges, our group nonetheless persists. The empathy and support that we have offered each other – particularly during the outbreaks and the long periods of lockdowns and isolation – have been invaluable. It saddens me greatly to know that few penitentiaries have a group that can offer that comfort and understanding.

Since the early days of the pandemic, I have become a full-time advocate and activist fighting for prison and justice reform, and some accountability within the massive bureaucracy that is CSC. I lecture about the realities of the Canadian penitentiary system to anyone who wants to listen or interview me. My son and I have partaken in issues both large and small, and we were proud to be part of a case being heard by the Canadian Human Rights Tribunal, among others. Our passion and commitment to fight the deeply entrenched, corrupted, ineffectual 'correctional' system has now become our life's work, and while it certainly feels like an uphill battle, we have had some successes and we fully expect more to come. We have managed to assist prisoners with file corrections, helped them in their search for mental health care, managed to hold some staff to account and, perhaps most importantly, each lecture provides us with the opportunity to change minds and hearts.

While there are many wonderful advocacy groups here and across the country, working hard to humanize and modernize our prison system, I have seen how that same fear and anxiety that I first witnessed during those early visiting days continues to divide us. It often imitates the David and Goliath story: CSC with the expansive and never-ending budget, both in terms of funds and manpower, and the rest of us, fighting with all we have, but often splintered, small and separated. In addition to access to funding to enable the many legitimate grievances to move forward to the courts, creating invaluable case law in my view perhaps the most important and necessary aspect required is a better co-ordination of the various organizations so that we can all identify each other and build on the wisdom and experience already gained, rather than constantly trying to re-create the wheel. CSC always presents as a unified front-backing each other regardless of the circumstance. The administration does this and the guards do it. The rest of us need to learn from that show of strength and solidarity, and replicate lessons learned in our battle for human decency, as well as prison and justice reform.

ABOUT THE AUTHOR

Joanne Fry is a parent of an incarcerated adult, an activist and advocate, and is the founder of Mission Prison Family Association. She lectures on the reality of prison life and our failing 'justice' system.

BOOK REVIEWS

Available Titles and
Call for Book Reviews
Journal of Prisoners on Prisons

The *Journal of Prisoners on Prisons* (*JPP*) welcomes book review submissions. Book reviews range from 800 to 1,200 words. Interested reviewers should contact the *JPP* with a request for one of the available titles (listed below). Should the book still be available, it will be mailed immediately.

For publishers: If you would like to have your new titles reviewed in the *JPP*, please send to the address below for consideration.

Book Reviews – Journal of Prisoners on Prisons
c/o Melissa Munn
Department of Sociology
Okanagan College
7000 College Way
Vernon, British Columbia, Canada
V1B 2N5

AVAILABLE TITLES

Berger, Dan (2015) *Captive Nation: Black Prison Organizing in the Civil Rights Era*, Chapel Hill: University of North Carolina Press, 424 pages.

Chase, Robert T. (ed.) (2019). *Caging Borders and Carceral States: Incarcerations, Immigration Detentions, and Resistance*, Chapel Hill: University of North Carolina Press, 440 pages.

Crane, Paul (ed.) (2019) *Life Beyond Crime: What Do Those at Risk of Offending, Prisoners and Ex-Offenders Need to Learn?* London: Lemos & Crane, 320 pages.

Fassin, Didier (2016) *Prison Worlds: An Ethnography of the Carceral Condition*, Maiden: Polity Press, 416 pages.

Gernain, Sheryl and Sarah Shotland (2015) *Words Without Walls: Writers on Addictions, Violence, and Incarceration*, San Antonio: Trinity University Press, 288 pages.

Graves, Anthony (2018) *Infinite Hope: The Story of One Man's Wrongful Conviction, Solitary Confinement, and Survival on Death Row*, Boston: Beacon Press, 224 pages.

Hansen, Anne (2018) *Taking the Rap: Women Doing Time for Society's Crimes*, Toronto: Between the Lines, 368 pages.

Hatch, Anthony (2019) *Silent Cells: The Secret Drugging of Captive America*, Minneapolis: University of Minnesota Press, 184 pages.

Hernández, Kelly (2017) *City of Prisoners: Conquest, Rebellion, and the Rise of Human Caging in Los Angeles*, Chapel Hill: University of North Carolina Press, 312 pages.

Huey Dye, Meredith and Ronald H. Aday (2019) *Women Lifers: Lives Before, Behind, and Beyond Bars*, Lanham: Rowman & Littlefield, 225 pages.

Jiminez Murguía, Salvador (2018) *Food as a Mechanism of Control and Resistance in Jails and Prisons: Diets of Disrepute,* Lanham: Lexington Books, 128 pages.

Kim, Alice, Erica Meiners and Jill Petty (eds.) (2018) *The Long Term: Resisting Life Sentences Working Toward Freedom*, Chicago: Haymarket Books, 250 pages.

Kotch, Seth (2019) *Lethal State: A History of the Death Penalty in North Carolina*, Chapel Hill: University of North Carolina Press, 320 pages.

Laboucane-Benson, Patti and Kelly Mellings (2015) *The Outside Circle: A Graphic Novel*, Toronto: Anansi Press, 128 pages.

Looman, Mary and John D. Carl (2015) *A Country Called Prison: Mass Incarceration and the Making of a New Nation*, New York: Oxford University Press, 264 pages.

Maratea, R.J. (2019) *Killing with Prejudice: Institutionalized Racism in American Capital Punishment*, New York: NYU Press, 224 pages.

Maynard, Robyn (2017) *Policing Black Lives: State Violence in Canada from Slavery to the Present*, Halifax: Fernwood, 244 pages.

Meiners, Erica (2016) *For the Children? Protecting Innocence in a Carceral State*, Minneapolis: University of Minnesota Press, 280 pages.

Middlemass, Keesha (2017) *Convicted and Condemned: The Politics and Policies of Prisoner Reentry*, New York: NYU Press, 288 pages.

Minaker, Joanne and Bryan Hogeveen (eds.) (2015) *Criminalized Mothers, Criminalized Mothering*, Bradford: Demeter Press, 422 pages.

Norris, Robert (2017) *Exonerated: A History of the Innocence Movement*, New York: NYU Press, 304 pages.

Parsons, Anne (2018) *From Asylum to Prison: Deinstitutionalization and the Rise of Mass Incarceration After 1945*, Chapel Hill: University of North Carolina Press, 240 pages.

Price, Joshua (2015) *Prison and Social Death*, New Brunswick (NJ): Rutgers University Press, 212 pages.

Richards, Stephen C. (ed.) (2015) *The Marion Experiment: Long-term Solitary Confinement and the Supermax Movement*, Carbondale: South Illinois University Press, 336 pages.

Rolston, Simon (2021) *Prison Life Writing: Conversion and the Literary Roots of the U.S. Prison System*. Waterloo (ON): Wilfred Laurier University Press. 301 pages.

Save the Kids (2018) *Why? America Why? Colorado Youth Prisoners and Other Incarcerated Voices*, Binghamton: Arissa Media Group, 327 pages.

Zoukis, Christopher (2017) *Prison Education Guide*, Lake Worth Beach (FL): Prison Legal News, 269 pages.

UPCOMING SPECIAL ISSUES – CALLS FOR PAPERS

Homelessness and Incarceration
Erin Dej and Dale Spencer

"We may say that the prisons are ghettos with walls,
while ghettos are prisons without walls"

– Zygmunt Bauman, 2001, p. 121

SPECIAL ISSUE EDITORS

Erin Dej, PhD – Assistant Professor, Criminology, Wilfrid Laurier University – Brantford
Dale Spencer, PhD – Associate Professor, Law and Legal Studies, Carleton University

FOCUS OF THE SPECIAL ISSUE

Whereas there is a considerable writing on incarceration and homelessness, there is very little contributions on the relationship between the two, especially from current and formerly incarcerated persons and homeless folks. In this special issue, we invite contributions that explore the connection between experiences of incarceration and homelessness. The issue takes a broad understanding of what constitutes homelessness (unsheltered, emergency sheltered, provisionally accommodated, at risk of homelessness) and what constitutes incarceration (recognizing how various systems and institutions are implicated in widening the carceral net). Different forms of contributions are encouraged, including journal articles, poems, or artistic representations. Submissions can address, but are not restricted, to the following topics:

The homelessness - incarceration pipeline
- Incarceration causes homelessness
- Homelessness causes incarceration
- The criminalization of homelessness

Experiences of homelessness and incarceration
- The lived experiences of being without a home
- Incarceration as a form of homelessness

Structural and systems drivers of homelessness and incarceration
- Discharge from corrections into homelessness
- Those without a fixed address held on denied bail/held in remand
- Unfair/unrealistic bail conditions for those without a home to maintain
- Barriers to accessing services geared towards people experiencing homelessness due to criminal record

Intersectional experiences of homelessness and incarceration
- Homelessness and incarceration as tools of settler colonialism
- Newcomers experiences of incarceration (including immigration detention centres)
- Women-identifying people's experiences of homelessness and incarceration
- Youth experiences with the criminal justice system and homelessness (including how discrimination facing LGBTQ2S+ youth impacts homelessness and/or incarceration)

PAPER FORMATS AND SUBMISSION GUIDELINES

Prisoners and former prisoners, along with other co-authors (where applicable) are encouraged to submit papers, collaborative essays, discussions transcribed from tape, book reviews, and photo or graphic essays. All contributions must follow the journal's submission guidelines below.
- The Journal will not publish any subject matter that advocates hatred, sexism, racism, violence or that supports the death penalty.
- The Journal does not publish material that usually focuses on the writer's own legal case, although the use of the writer's personal experiences as an illustration of a broader topic is encouraged.
- Articles should be no longer than 20 pages typed and double-spaced or legibly handwritten. Electronic submissions are gratefully received.
- Writers may elect to write anonymously or under a pseudonym.
- For references cited in an article, writers should attempt to provide the necessary bibliographic information. Refer to the references cited in past issues for examples.

- Editors look for developed pieces that address topics substantially. Manuscripts go through a preliminary reading and then are sent to review by the Editorial Board. Those that are of suitable interest are returned to the author with comments or suggestions. Editors work with writers on composition and form, and where necessary may help the author with referencing and bibliographic information, not readily available in prisons. Selected articles are returned to authors for their approval before publication. Papers not selected are returned with comments from the editor. Revised papers may be resubmitted.
- Please submit biographical and contact information, to be published alongside articles unless otherwise indicated.

IMPORTANT DATES

Submissions by authors:	1 May 2023
Editorial decision and reviewer comments to authors:	1 July 2023
Revised manuscripts:	1 September 2023
Final editorial decision to authors:	1 November 2023
Publication date:	2024

SUBMISSIONS

Via email to edej@wlu.ca or by mail to the address below:

Erin Dej, PhD
Department of Criminology
Wilfrid Laurier University
171 Colborne Street
Brantford, Ontario, Canada
N3T 6C9

Emotions and Carceral Spaces
Jennifer Kilty, Rachel Fayter and Justin Piché

SPECIAL ISSUE EDITORS

Jennifer M. Kilty, PhD – Professor and Chair, Department of Criminology, University of Ottawa
Rachel Fayter – PhD Candidate, Department of Criminology, University of Ottawa
Justin Piché, PhD – Associate Professor, Department of Criminology, University of Ottawa

SPECIAL ISSUE THEME

The *Journal of Prisoners on Prisons* (JPP) invites submissions for a special issue on the theme of "Emotions and Carceral Spaces". Experiences of imprisonment or living and working in various carceral settings are isolating, punitive, and at times traumatic, all of which influence the emotional experiences of both prisoners and staff. Carceral spaces are neither uniform nor orderly, and the way emotions are felt and expressed differs significantly depending on the specific setting, lived experiences, and interpersonal interactions. Different carceral environments can produce multiple emotional experiences, which can also differ based on gender, race, sexuality and other markers of difference. Individuals' age, past experiences, length of sentence, and security level can also impact one's emotions.

We encourage authors to share and critically reflect on their emotional experiences within carceral environments or how different physical spaces in jails, prisons, treatment centres, detention centres, psychiatric facilities, halfway houses or other sites of confinement affect prisoners' moods and behaviours. Submissions that reflect how emotions are organized and expressed in prison, along with where and how it is appropriate to express oneself emotionally in the culture of prison and the policy context are especially welcomed. We hope to better understand how carceral spaces can shape people's emotional experiences, while also impacting or being impacted by interpersonal relations among prisoners, as well as between prisoners and staff.

Additionally, we invite submissions concerning how emotions contribute to prison spaces being perceived as a heightened 'HIV risk environment'.

As the history of HIV/AIDS is structured by emotions such as fear, disgust, shame and pride, we seek to foreground the lived experience of HIV-positive people to explore how they manage their emotional selves in/outside the prison and how everyday decisions in these settings are affected by an 'emotion culture' that reflects the thoughts, feelings and perceptions of the emotional capacities of others. Thinking about carceral space as an 'HIV risk environment' can help with understanding the interplay of the physical, social, economic, and policy environments, and to consider how they affect the transmission of HIV. For example, considerations of the availability or unavailability of harm reduction measures and how the debate around these options (e.g., condoms, needle exchanges) are shaped by emotions are welcome. Through this process we invite contributors to explore how emotions can structure harm reduction policy debates, and to better understand how emotions challenge and/or contribute to HIV risk behaviours in prison.

We welcome submissions from current and former prisoners, criminalized people, or pieces co-authored with people who have a lived experience of incarceration and allies, advocates, practitioners, and scholars from a multidisciplinary perspective. We invite submissions drawing on lived experience and/or a wide range of fields and perspectives, including but not limited to socio-legal studies, sociology, criminology, psychology, Indigenous studies, feminist and gender studies, critical race studies, queer studies, social work, philosophy, and artistic/creative interpretations of emotions and carceral spaces. Submissions from current and former prisoners who are willing to draw on their personal narratives and lived experiences to expand understanding of emotions in prison are particularly encouraged.

PAPER FORMATS

This special issue welcomes contributions from a wide range of scholarly work including:

- Auto-ethnographic accounts that examine experiences of imprisonment to illuminate broader issues faced by incarcerated people;

- Theoretical, critical and analytical essays;
- Scholarly research articles based on quantitative, qualitative, arts-based and/or mixed- methods research;
- Book reviews;
- Artistic content – photo or graphic essays, digital art, poetry, etc.;
- Interviews or discussions transcribed from recordings; or
- Commentaries.

SUBMISSION GUIDELINES

At the *JPP*, we support incarcerated people's right to exercise freedom of expression pursuant to section 2 of the *Canadian Charter of Rights and Freedoms* and embedded in national constitutions elsewhere across the world. We believe that publishing the writing of incarcerated people is a necessary tool to facilitate transparency in carceral settings. We welcome submissions from all current and former prisoners, and are eager to hear your input on the above-mentioned issues. Please share this notice with anyone who may be interested in contributing to our journal. We ask that those who choose to submit include a short biographical statement and let us know if you would like to be published anonymously. We look forward to reviewing your submissions that follow the journal's guidelines below and hope to hear from you soon.

- The Journal will not publish any subject matter that advocates hatred, sexism, racism, violence or that supports the death penalty.
- The Journal does not publish material that usually focuses on the writer's own legal case, although the use of the writer's personal experiences as an illustration of a broader topic is encouraged.
- The Journal does not usually publish fiction and does not generally publish poetry. Illustrations, drawings and paintings may be submitted as potential cover art.
- Articles should be no longer than 20 pages typed and double-spaced or legibly handwritten. Electronic submissions are gratefully received.
- Writers may elect to write anonymously or under a pseudonym.
- For references cited in an article, writers should attempt to provide the necessary bibliographic information. Refer to the references cited in past issues for examples.

- Editors look for developed pieces that address topics substantially. Manuscripts go through a preliminary reading and then are sent to review by the Editorial Board. Those that are of suitable interest are returned to the author with comments or suggestions. Editors work with writers on composition and form, and where necessary may help the author with referencing and bibliographic information, not readily available in prisons. Selected articles are returned to authors for their approval before publication. Papers not selected are returned with comments from the editor. Revised papers may be resubmitted.
- Please submit biographical and contact information, to be published alongside articles unless otherwise indicated.

IMPORTANT DATES

Submissions by authors:	1 May 2023
Editorial decision and reviewer comments to authors:	1 July 2023
Revised manuscripts:	1 October 2023
Final editorial decision to authors:	1 December 2023
Publication date:	2024

SUBMISSIONS

Via email to jpp@uottawa.ca or by mail to the address below:

Journal of Prisoners on Prisons
c/o Department of Criminology
University of Ottawa
120 University Private – Room 14049
Ottawa, Ontario, Canada
K1N 6N5

COVER ART

Having spent a lot of time in isolation armed with little more than a pencil, a good eye for detail and the imagination born of bare stone walls, I have had to think outside the box (quite literally). I have always tried to approach my work from a position of individuality and my attitude towards art is a fearless one of trial and error. If I do not or cannot achieve what I am after, I absorb the learning curve and move onto something new. The 'something new' always fills me with a sense of excitement and nothing ever gets truly left behind. During these long years of confinement, art has been my one constant companion. Without its loyalty I would experience more of the pain and fear that shaped my life from a young age. I am no longer the product of my crime, but of my creativity. I survived the past, I am thankful for the present, and I now have a future. Fortunately, with the permission of the Governor, I have been afforded the opportunity to build a website (see https://steeldoorstudios.com) and it is our desire that this project becomes a beneficial platform for myself and other imprisoned people to find their creative voices, be able to share, connect and maybe one day return to the outside world, not as a tainted outcast but as a useful and valued member of society with something to offer.

"Transition" (front cover)
Steel Door Studios
2022

"Turbulent Tenacity" (back cover)
Steel Door Studios
2022

www.ingramcontent.com/pod-product-compliance
Lightning Source LLC
Chambersburg PA
CBHW070804280326
41934CB00012B/3055